PHYSICIANS OF THE SOUL

THE MACMILLAN COMPANY
NEW YORK · BOSTON · CHICAGO
DALLAS · ATLANTA · SAN FRANCISCO

MACMILLAN AND CO., LIMITED
LONDON · BOMBAY · CALCUTTA
MADRAS · MELBOURNE

THE MACMILLAN COMPANY
OF CANADA, LIMITED
TORONTO

Physicians of the Soul

A HISTORY OF PASTORAL COUNSELING

by Charles F. Kemp

THE MACMILLAN COMPANY · New York

1947

PRINTED IN THE UNITED STATES OF AMERICA
BY THE VAIL-BALLOU PRESS, INC., BINGHAMTON, N. Y.

To My

MOTHER and FATHER

PREFACE

We have long needed this book.

The popularity of the subject of pastoral care has been growing steadily during the past fifteen years and particularly during the war years. Those of us who have been attracted to the field of pastoral work were conscious of the fact that we stood in a great tradition, for the care and cure of souls is as old as religion, but the literature gave us little understanding of just how really great is the tradition. Our fathers in the faith were accustomed to speak of being "called to preach"; they said little about being called to care for sick and troubled persons; they spoke of proclaiming the Christian message to a confused world; they said little about personalizing for suffering persons the spirit of confidence our Lord portrayed or the spirit of love that Saint Paul wrote about in the Thirteenth Chapter to the Corinthians.

It awaited for Charles Kemp to search out and describe for us the fact that the great preachers of our tradition were first of all great pastors. The writers of our generation have done them and us a considerable disservice by failing to point out this fact. Jesus was a teacher and a pastor; Paul, one would would hardly think it of Paul, was concerned about individuals; Luther and Wesley and Baxter and Brooks and Bushnell and Drummond and Moody and Gladden: pastors first, preachers second.

One of the striking things about these pastors of the past, as well as some of those of more recent date, is that they were also evangelists. Their practice of the cure of souls lay in their belief that they knew the answer for the needs of each. How successful they always were we do not know, for they, like our contemporary brethren, kept no individual records. But this fact they recognized: to help a person we must love him. We understand this fact better today than they did, but, understanding as we do, we still cannot match their hearts of affection; their love for their suffering fellows sprang from their love of Christ. So must it always.

We are deeply grateful to Mr. Kemp for giving us this excellent study of the great "Physicians of the Soul." Over a period of seven years he has painstakingly and patiently collected his material. We are certain that he will be rewarded by a wide reception of his book for it merits the attention of all who stand in the tradition of that One Who was first of all a Shepherd.

RUSSELL L. DICKS

INTRODUCTION

This book is written in the firm conviction that there is no greater need in the Christian ministry than the ability to understand and deal effectively with the personal needs and problems of individuals. It is also felt that there is much value to be derived to enable us to do this work better if we have some knowledge of the experiences of others and some perspective as to how this function of the ministry has developed. An essential quality in the ability to perform any specialized task is some familiarity with its history and backgrounds. There is a statement credited to Disraeli to the effect that, "The more extensive a man's knowledge of what has been done, the greater will be his power of knowing what to do." So, this study of the past was made in order that it might be of some practical help to those who work in the present. There are various reasons why we should be familiar with this background. First of all, it gives us a knowledge of what others have done, their methods, their purposes, their successes and their failures. Such knowledge is essential to anyone who would carry on an effective and helpful ministry. Out of this knowledge should come a sense of perspective. It should enable us to evaluate our own day and our own efforts and help us to appraise new movements and new methods. Not the least of the values is the inspiration one receives from an awareness of what others have done, the obstacles they have overcome, the sincerity and persistence of their efforts, the spirit and faithfulness with which they carried on their tasks. The knowledge of their experience gives us the assurance that we too can follow in their footsteps and meet the needs of our people and of our generation as they met the needs of theirs. Therefore, because of the feeling that much is to be gained by understanding how others have fulfilled this responsibility and by tracing the factors that have contributed to the development of what has now become a movement, this study has been made.

Some years ago I became aware of the fact that the story of this movement had never been made available. There were histories of the church, histories of preaching, histories of doctrine and Christian thought, histories of religious education and of other specialized areas, but none had been written that attempted to trace the developments and present the backgrounds in this particular field. It seemed there might be a real value if this could be done. I consequently began to collect material. The work has been done in the midst of an active pastorate with the time and library facilities that were available. I have tried to survey the field as completely as possible. I have tried to cover (1) the movements, (2) the personalities, and (3) the literature that have had an important bearing and influence. As much as possible I have tried to deal with those related programs, both in the church and in the world of science, that have also made a contribution, either directly or indirectly. Thus, the sources have been many and varied. Histories were utilized, but histories, as a rule, have emphasized other things and only chance references were found that alluded to pastoral care. Biographies and autobiographies were especially valuable, but here also the work done in the pastoral conference was of such an intimate and confidential nature that one knew there was much more which took place, the story of which could never be recovered. The literature of such fields as pastoral theology and the psychology of religion, the Catholic confessional, Christian science and the cults was all investigated, as were the fields of psychology, psychiatry, psycho-analysis, social case work, psychosomatic medicine and mental hygiene. Of course, the whole growing field of literature on pastoral counseling and pastoral psychology was examined thoroughly. Obviously, everything in such a volume came from some source—an attempt has been made to give full credit to all sources. If there have been any omissions, I hereby state my regret and full apologies.

The story of "man's inhumanity to man" is an old story and one that has often been told. This is the opposite: it is the story of man's humanity to man; it is the story of those who have tried to relieve suffering, to minister to mankind; it is the story of those who have served as shepherds, pastors, ministers—physicians of the soul. It is not a history for history's sake. It is an historical study which was made in the hope that it might be helpful in a practical way, that the telling of the story of what others have done might provide a new awareness of the sacredness of the historic tradition in which the pastor works, a renewed sense of the tremendous value and importance of pastoral care, a broadened and deepened understanding of the function of the "cure of souls" for those who would serve in this capacity in these trying days and in the most significant days which lie ahead.

I would like to express my sincere appreciation to the many people who have helped me in this project. Several have read portions of the manuscript and have offered very helpful suggestions. I wish especially to thank Rev. Russell Dicks, Chaplain of the Wesley Memorial Hospital, Chicago, Dr. Roy Burkhart, pastor of the First Community Church, Columbus, Ohio, and my former professor, Dr. Oren H. Baker, Dean of the Colgate-Rochester Divinity School. Each of these men, although working under a tremendously crowded schedule, was kind enough to read the manuscript in its entirety and to offer much wise counsel and encouragement. Much of the value and accuracy of these pages I owe to their kindness; for any errors or points of view I am solely responsible. I wish also to thank my wife for her assistance in preparing this manuscript but, more than this, for her patience and encouragement while these pages were in preparation.

—CHARLES F. KEMP

CONTENTS

PART IV

FROM WORLD WAR I TO WORLD WAR II

Part I

FROM JESUS TO THE TWENTIETH CENTURY

Chapter 1

THE NEW TESTAMENT PERIOD

There apparently has never been a time or a place where men did not seek out their religious leaders for personal help— advice, guidance, counsel, assurance, forgiveness, comfort or health. Every primitive tribe had its medicine man or shaman. In ancient Babylon there were officials who conducted both public and private penance, using manuals similar to those later used as Christian manuals of confession. Brahman codes of early Indo-European society show the presence of directors of conscience, or spiritual guides, whose function was to instruct and also "minister to their pupils' souls." Among the Celts, the druids and priests performed a similar function; in Ireland this person was often attached to the king whom he served as adviser and guide. In the Graeco-Roman world the philosopher was the one to whom the people brought their personal troubles and religious questions.[1]

Among the early Israelites of the age of the Patriarchs, disputes were settled and problems were solved by the heads of the families or tribes. During the exodus and the wanderings, the period of the beginnings of Israel as a people, the one predominant figure was Moses. Family disputes were still settled by the heads of the families, but final appeals were made to Moses who acted as the supreme judge. This was no small task. On one occasion, at least, he was hearing cases all day long. "And it came to pass on the morrow, that Moses sat to judge the people: and the people stood about Moses from the morning until the evening." [2] In fact it was too much for one man, so, on the advice of his father-in-law, Moses selected a number of heads of families, who had already had experience in dealing with their own families; he gave them responsibility for different sized groups. They were to judge the people at all seasons. The more difficult questions were still brought to Moses but the easier ones they were to handle themselves.[3]

During the time of the settling of the land of Canaan and the period of the rule of the judges, when there was no centralized authority, the elders and the judges of the tribes fulfilled this function. This was especially true of those who had a strong personality. In the case of Deborah, it was a woman whose judgment was respected, and the people sought her out to have their controversies settled and for advice as to procedure as a nation. Samuel, the greatest of this period, traveled about the country, hearing controversies, giving judgments, preaching, teaching, giving counsel, as the case might require.

These periods were not without superstition and magic, as might well be expected. Among the injunctions in the law was one that a "witch" should not be permitted to live, a passage that was to cause untold tragedy in centuries to come. People were forbidden to use enchantment, or to consult those who had "familiar Spirits," in fact, such individuals were to be stoned to death.[4] When Saul visited the witch at Endor, he had to promise her immunity from punishment. It is significant that the one he wanted the woman to "bring up" was Samuel, that he might seek his counsel from the spirit world.[5]

With the establishment of the monarchy there was once again a central authority who became the supreme judge. In the country the heads of the families and men noted for their wisdom continued to handle disputes, but there is also indication that the king was accessible to the poorest of his subjects. The people of Israel brought their troubles regularly to David, and Solomon gained a world-wide reputation for his wisdom in handling practical matters.

The prophets, in the main, were concerned with the state

of the nation and the problems of Israel; they spoke to the nation rather than to the individual. It is true, however, that some were concerned with the inner life. Jeremiah has been described as a psychologist by nature.[6] He was interested in the things of the heart, a true pioneer of personal religion. His great letter to the exiles can rightfully be called a letter of pastoral counsel. In Ezekiel we have one who is concerned about the individual. His situation is different from that of the earlier prophets. They spoke to a proud, wayward, often rebellious nation and they uttered the words of warning which were needed. Ezekiel also had a message of warning and judgment, but he was speaking to an exiled people whose morale was low, whose hopes had been destroyed, whose faith had been shaken. He ministered to these people as a true shepherd of souls and has rightfully been referred to as the first pastor in Israel.

There are other sections of the Old Testament that are of interest to the student of human nature. There are passages in the Psalms that are rich in their insight into human personality. Here we find confession, guilt, remorse, frustration, elation, forgiveness—all the range of human emotions and feelings. The book of Job is a dramatic presentation of the thought of one who was grappling with the age-old problem of undeserved suffering. The book of Proverbs is a practical expression of the accumulated wisdom of the "wise men" and their counsel as to the governing of the practical events of daily life. These wise men were teachers but the entire content of their emphases was with the individual in mind. The prophets spoke to the nation; these men spoke to the individual. They are really concerned with the individual welfare. Their authority is the authority of age and experience and common sense.[7] It is safe to assume that such writing was once given as advice to many different individuals in a manner and in situations that would today be described as counseling. They urged the people to be diligent, to respect each other's rights, to care for the unfortunate and the poor, to love their families, to be temperate, self-controlled and chaste. They urged youth to accept the instruction of their parents and made reference to the value of all seeking guidance and counsel. "The way of a fool is right in his own eyes; But he that is wise hearkeneth unto counsel." "Where no wise guidance is, the people falleth; but in the multitude of counselors there is safety." [8]

In the ministry of Jesus is found the source, the inspiration, the ideal for our study. No other influence in the history of humanity has done so much to relieve human suffering, to create a spirit of compassion and to inspire others to give themselves in a attempt to understand and to serve their fellow-men. The records are scanty. There are only about fifty days of Jesus' active ministry recorded. Yet, in these less than fifty days, is contained the record of the most amazing career of human service the world has ever known. The stories and incidents revealed in the four gospels present one who had a unique insight into the needs and problems of people, one who understood with a clarity that has never been equalled or surpassed the meaning of life and human nature. With real significance, the fourth gospel says, "he himself knew what was in man." [9] All of the events of his story, whether it was in dealing with some distracted individual who came to him for help, or whether it was in dealing with his disciples and friends, or when confronted by his enemies, reveal in what a unique sense this was true.

Even more obvious and equally significant is the range of his sympathy, the depth of his compassion, the never-failing concern for people, that dominated his entire life. Whether it was a well-known official who came to him at midnight, a woman taken in adultery, a bereaved mother, or a madman among the tombs, whoever and wherever it was, he was sensitive to the need and desired to be of help. He was moved with compassion by the crowds and, on one occasion, he attempted to withdraw and find rest and quiet by crossing the lake, but, "when Jesus disembarked, he saw a large crowd, and out of pity for them, as they were like sheep without a shepherd, he proceeded to teach them at length." [10] He welcomed a group of children when his disciples thought they would bother him; he wept over the city of Jerusalem.

At the outset of his ministry, in the village of Nazareth, when he was handed the scroll in the synagogue, he selected the passage, "The spirit of the Lord is upon me: for he has consecrated me to preach the gospel to the poor, he has sent me to proclaim release for the captives and recovery of sight for the blind, to set free the oppressed." [11] From the outset, Jesus felt that the primary factor in his mission was to relieve human suffering, for he knew by experience the life of the common people and identified himself with them and sought to alleviate suffering in any manner in which he met it, whether it might be physical, mental, moral or spiritual. In the Sermon on the Mount, he gives his blessing to the poor, the hungry and the sorrowful. So great was his concern, so deep his feeling that the ultimate test he gave to his followers was to be whether or not they had fed the hungry, welcomed the strangers, clothed the needy, visited the sick and imprisoned, and he concluded with the statement, "inasmuch as ye have done it unto one of these my brethren, even the least, ye did it unto me." [12] His concern was not something sentimental or superficial but practical and real. It was in terms of specific people and their individual and particular needs. To meet these needs he gave of the best of his time and strength. In fact, his concern to help the unfortunate on some occasions involved him in considerable difficulty, such as the time he violated the Sabbath law and offended the authorities in order to heal the man with the withered hand. With Jesus human needs took precedence over all traditions and institutions, even the Sabbath.

It is true that he was often followed by crowds, although he did not seek the crowd, the crowds sought him. This was but natural. As the story of his work spread, as people heard of the type of man he was, they came, some out of curiosity, some because of the miracles, many perhaps seeking comfort, assurance, or with a wistful yearning for friendship. His personality being what it was and people's needs being what they were, it was to be expected that he would attract them in great numbers; on one occasion "the whole town gathered at the door," and again, "the people came to him from every quarter." [13] But he never lost sight of the individual within the crowd. His ministry, even when he was talking to the crowd, remained a personalized ministry. Such statements as these cannot help but indicate that there were countless numbers of whom we have no record who sought his counsel—people who, like Nicodemus, sought him out at night, or, like the woman of Samaria, talked to him by the way—unbeknown to the authors of the Gospels, whose stories have never been told. It stirs the imagination as one tries to realize how many lives he must have helped and strengthened.

The records of those particular problems that he did face are all too brief, but they are enough to indicate the attitudes that characterized this field of his ministry. No one came to him and was refused his help or was made to feel that his problem was insignificant. He made no exceptions; to him all men were treated the same. He made no distinction between the high and the low, rich and poor, educated or unlearned, wise or simple. There was no one, regardless of the type of person he was, what he may have done, or what his status in society may have been, but what Jesus felt he was worthy of his consideration. No matter how much a man may have been shunned, condemned or ridiculed before, when he came to Jesus he knew he was being dealt with sympathetically, honestly and sincerely. It was no wonder that the crowds sought him out, or that the common people heard him gladly. The taunt of his enemies, that he was the friend of publicans and sinners, is exactly what he was and what he wanted to be, and history has made it a mark of honor. However, he was not only the friend of publicans and sinners; he was the friend of all who needed his help and, in the course of his ministry, he dealt with the sick and the well, the good and the bad, the educated and uneducated, the old and the young, the rich and the poor, regardless of race or color.

He saw human values where others failed. He saw things in men that others did not see; he saw things in men they could not see themselves. He appealed to one of the strongest motivations in life—he gave to men who had lost confidence in themselves the feeling that someone they trusted believed in them. In lives that had been drifting and purposeless, lives weak and hounded by fear, lives that were dishonest and cruel, lives that had given themselves to lust and passion, he touched inner springs of goodness and power and enabled them to gain a mastery of themselves and to secure a new outlook and a new center for life. His attitude, as has been frequently pointed out, combined the most serious concern for men's needs with an amazing faith in their hidden responsibilities. It is well to stress particularly his patience, for, of all qualities necessary for a counselor, this is one of the most difficult to achieve, and of all problems that confront one who would deal with individuals, none is more difficult to master than that of discouragement or failure.

His plans and thoughts included ideas of infinite proportion and scope but he never lost sight of the value of dealing with people one by one. In fact, it would seem that that was almost his chief concern. While there were many things he wished to accomplish, he was never too busy to face the problems of one individual soul. In so doing he never seemed hurried or impatient, disgusted or offended. He did not shrink from the repulsiveness of a leper or show any fear of the disease. He was of infinite patience. While it is true that he transformed the lives of his apostles, the transformation did not take place all at once. Time and time again they disappointed him almost to the point of breaking his heart, but he never gave up, never lost sight of their need or lost faith in their possibilities. There is nothing more difficult in dealing with people than discouragement or failure. Jesus did not have one hundred percent success. Very often he was disappointed in the very people he would have liked to help the most. A rich young ruler came seeking guidance but was not willing to follow the advice that was given, and Jesus sorrowed greatly for he loved him.

This case of the rich young ruler illustrates a further fact. Jesus, with unerring insight, saw the key to a person's difficulty and demanded that he face it honestly and realistically. In this case the problem was one of wealth which was receiving the first loyalty, and Jesus saw that there would be no ultimate victory until that was eliminated, but he did not make this same demand of everyone. He treated no two cases alike; with the rich young ruler it was one thing; with Nicodemus it was another; with the woman at the well, still another. He never let his sympathy blind him to the necessity of facing the problem honestly and realistically. The noteworthy thing is the spirit in which it was done. He never condemned except in the case of hypocrisy. His attitudes are no better revealed than in the story of the woman taken in adultery, which was inserted into the fourth gospel. After dispersing the crowd that had intended to stone the woman to death, he turned to the woman and said, "Neither do I condemn thee, go and sin no more." Such was his approach to people—not condemnation but understanding and assurance, a recognition that certain demands must be met, combined with the assurance that they could be met. That his methods and his faith in people were justified is a matter of record. Shiftless and purposeless men like Peter became strong and dependable; dishonest men like Zacchaeus became honest and trustworthy; women like Mary Magdalene who lived by her own self-indulgence became self-controlled and pure.

The modern emphasis on psychology and personal work has led to a new appreciation of the insights and methods of Jesus.

Fritz Kunkel writes, "Jesus of Nazareth was the greatest psychologist of all times," [14] and in similar vein, Karl Ruf Stolz states, "Jesus was the greatest personal worker of all time." [15] Such statements could be duplicated many times.

To deal with Jesus' ministry to individuals requires that some consideration be given to the miracles of healing. This is difficult to do adequately in the space at our disposal, but they cannot and should not be avoided and, perhaps, in outline we can point to the chief characteristics. Certain things must be kept in mind in any discussion of the healing miracles of Jesus. First, the attitude toward many types of illness and almost all forms of mental derangement and insanity in those days was described in terms of demon possession or evil spirits. Second, we must keep in mind the findings of modern psychotherapy which reveal how many forms of such illness can be cured. A psychiatrist reminds us that nowadays practically all the healing "miracles" of the New Testament have been reproduced in mental hospitals over and over again.[16] In the third place, we must take into account the tremendous power of Jesus' personality, the faith that the people had in him, and the psychological influence of the crowd which also believed that he was able to heal. In the case of the paralytic, Jesus definitely refers to the faith of the men who brought the patient to him. Where faith was lacking, as at Nazareth, he could do no mighty work. It is also well to keep in mind the fact that Jesus was not the only one who exorcised demons or healed the sick, but his disciples were also given this power and others were referred to as casting out demons. Jesus, on one occasion, defended himself by reminding his accusers that their sons cast out demons. We recognize, further, the fact that our records are very brief and limited and were not preserved as scientific documents to be studied in order that these events could be explained. There are some that, at present at least, we cannot explain, but, in the light of all the factors mentioned above, there are many of those instances that can, perhaps, at least partially, be explained and

understood, such as the case of paralysis, or fever, or even blindness, for we know that all such symptoms can be psychologically induced. Of course, demon possession, as a description
of what today would be diagnosed as epilepsy or mental derangement or obsessions, is easily understood. Klausner, the
Jewish scholar, tells us how widely prevalent and widespread
these cases were in that day due to the conditions of the times
in Palestine.[17] Many of the procedures of Jesus are highly suggestive, such as the time he appealed to the will of the man with
the withered hand, commanding him to arise, stand forward
and stretch out his hand; or the woman with the fever when
he states, "he went up to her and taking her hand made her
rise." [18] Often, in dealing with distraught cases, he began his
approach by requesting the person to "be quiet"; on occasion
he definitely associated the healing of disease, such as paralysis,
with the forgiveness of sins, and again and again he said, "Your
faith has made you well." The tremendous effect of guilt on
personality and the amazing power of faith are now common
knowledge, not only in religious circles, but in scientific circles
as well. Such instances are highly suggestive in the light of
modern knowledge of psychotherapeutics.

Dr. James Mackinnon, in his notable book, *The Historic
Jesus*, describes the situation in these words, "The will of a
God-inspired personality, operating in faith on the patients and,
as a rule, though not exclusively, with the patients' coöperating
will, did achieve the cure of a variety of diseases. The modern
study of psychotherapeutics or healing by mental and spiritual
means, has incontestably gone far to vindicate the reality of
these cures, which an older generation of critical writers, like
Strauss and Renan, too readily assumed to be the creations of
myth or legend." [19] In the case of the Gerasene demoniac Dr.
Mackinnon remarks, "The cure is really wrought in these cases
by a powerful will acting in the strength of a commanding faith
and assisted by the psychic condition of the patient who in his
own deranged fashion has got the conviction of Jesus' power.

There is not necessarily anything miraculous about such exorcisms." [20]

That Jesus healed is one of the best attested facts in history. It is recognized by his enemies as well as by his friends, by the Talmud as well as by the New Testament, although they give different explanations as to how it was done.[21] Karl Ruf Stolz, who has given considerable thought and study to this problem, said, "The personality of Jesus and the application of his insight did directly affect both the minds and bodies of the sick." Then he continues to point out the difficulties with which one is confronted. "The accounts . . . of healing presented by the Synoptic Gospels are fragmentary and pre-scientific. . . . It is simply impossible to reconstruct many of the works of healing which Jesus wrought." [22] Thus it is seen that what Jesus contributed was not a method or a technique but attitudes and a spirit. It was the value of every individual soul and the combination of compassion and faith that he introduced into the world that has been, and is, of such profound significance.

It is well to consider the case of the Gerasene demoniac, mentioned above, for we have more information here than in most cases, and it gives us a striking illustration of Jesus' manner in facing such a situation. In many ways the most significant thing about the miracles of healing is not the fact that Jesus healed but, rather, the way in which he dealt with these people and these situations. In most cases, as in the instances mentioned earlier in this chapter, his response was called out of pity, giving a further testimony of his concern for people. It also reveals other facts regarding Jesus, such as his poise and courage and complete self-control. For example, in this case, we see Jesus, after a busy day, crossing the sea of Galilee seeking rest and quiet, but as soon as the boat has touched the shore he is confronted by this "mad man" from the tombs. This man had been driven from society and was forced to live among the tombs, for they had no institutions in which to care for such individuals in those days. The shouting, the crying out with a loud voice indicate strong emotion and the violence of the case; the cutting of himself with stones indicates the seriousness of the derangement, and the dangling chains at his wrist testify to the abnormal strength sometimes found in such conditions. It is no wonder that the disciples were afraid. In the presence of all this, Jesus remained completely calm and self-collected and asked in a natural tone and manner the simple and sincere question, "What is your name?" Each one can come to his own conclusion as to just how the cure took place, but he should not overlook the result. The man returned and he was clothed and in "his right mind," or, as Dr. Moffatt states it, "clothed and sane." So, however faulty may have been the diagnosis, the result was clear. Nor, should one lose sight of Jesus' statement and its implications, "Go home to your own people and report to them all the Lord has done for you and how he took pity on you." [23] This is, of course, but one incident, while "from many people demons were also driven out." [24] This again appeals to the imagination and one cannot help but wonder how many others are indicated by this word "many" whose fears were relieved, whose tensions were resolved, whose minds were made whole again.

Some mention should be made of the teaching of Jesus. This, too, in a very real sense, can be included as counseling, for very often his greatest teaching was given to but one or two people. Even though he often spoke to groups, most of his teaching was in the nature of an informal conversation which was spoken to answer the questions or to meet the needs of people. His teaching, like his interviewing, was, in the main, informal, natural and spontaneous. Sometimes his teaching was given in a home, or from a fishing boat, or on a hillside, as was the case with the Sermon on the Mount. There is no record of his ever preparing an address or a lecture. His preparation came as he lived, in the world of men, as he walked among them at their daily tasks, as he pondered on the deep meanings of life and the spirit, as he sat in meditation and prayer on some hillside alone, and his teaching was then called forth, as were his acts of healing, by the needs of those before him. It is thus that his teaching is so lifelike, because it was called forth by life, combined with the remarkable ability to illustrate and express profound truths in clear and simple terms. It is also of real significance that he always dealt only with those things that were essential and basic; he did not bother with trivialities but only with those things he thought vital. They can almost be summarized under three heads: those things that deal with human relationships; those things that affect the inner life; and those things that have to do with God. Of course, they all overlap and cannot be confined in any artificial categories. With him religion was not considered as a thing apart, but as life itself. Those who have made a study of the modern emphasis on psychology and mental hygiene have found that, to a large extent, they were but re-discovering the truth of an emphasis Jesus had made so long ago. To quote but two of them, "A careful analysis and comparison of the teachings of Jesus and of the findings of mental hygiene will show a remarkable list of insights which coincide." [25] Another says, "Of all the great teachers of the past none in such outstanding fashion as Jesus represents the teacher as mental hygienist, and the mental hygienist as teacher." [26]

Jesus saw that the chief sources of difficulty, unhappiness and frustration arise in human relationships. He saw what we are just now beginning to appreciate, the devastating effect of hatred, resentment, bitterness, and fear, and so he stressed their opposites—understanding, sympathy, faith, trust, forgiveness and good will. He stressed the attitude and the inner motive rather than the outward act. If men would discipline and purify their inner attitudes and motives, then the outward results could be left to themselves. He saw that men must control their inner thoughts and imaginations, for they are the source of outward behavior that can ruin life. It is from "within, from the heart of man, the designs of evil come: sexual vice, stealing, murder, adultery, lust, malice, deceit, sensuality, envying, slander, arrogance, recklessness, all these evils issue from within . . ." [27] and again "a man's mouth utters what his heart is full of." [28] If one would improve his relations with others, he would do well to begin by "taking heed to himself." An honest evaluation of oneself makes one more considerate in dealing with others. One is not so disturbed by the "splinter" in his brother's eye when he realizes he has a "plank" in his own eye. He taught that men should judge not and they would not be judged; condemn not and they would not be condemned; pardon and they would be pardoned, forgive even seventy times seven, do unto others as they would have other people do unto them, return good for evil, even love their enemies—this is the quality of the life of which he spoke.

Sincerity and humility, kindness, thoughtfulness and good will were the primary virtues of the personal life. The only people for whom Jesus held little hope were the proud and the self-satisfied and the self-centered. The most bitter words he ever spoke were in denunciation of hypocrisy. He saw the deadening, deceiving effect it had on a personality. Over and over again he taught that only he who has a true evaluation of himself, who humbles himself as a child or a servant, who is striving to be genuine and completely sincere, could know the meaning of the abundant life of which he spoke. He also stressed the need of individual moral responsibility. A man reaps what he sows and cannot serve two masters. Therefore, he pled with men to keep alive a true sense of values, for "what doth it profit a man to gain the whole world and lose his own soul." It is the self-controlled that are able to direct their steps on the narrow road and the disciplined with the single eye that find ultimate freedom. He warned against good impulses and pious expressions which did not find expression in constructive action.

Such self-mastery, important as it is, is not enough. There must be a greater incentive than this if one would achieve the highest values as mentioned by Jesus. He condensed this demand into one striking sentence which appears frequently in the gospels, "He that would save his life must lose it." He saw clearer than had ever been seen before or since, the integrative therapeutic power of unselfish love. This is a fundamental law of the mental and spiritual life. The manner in which one gave himself he left to the individual to determine and, again, his understanding of human nature reveals itself. The parable of the talents pre-dates the intelligence test by many centuries. He recognized the relative ability or capacity of different individuals. To this was added the further insight that how much one was able to do was not as significant as the faithfulness with which one used the capacity that he had. So, regardless of how much one could do according to his capacity or opportunity, the fact remains that only those who lose their lives ultimately find them. Undergirding all of this there must be a strong foundation. Life being what it is, storms, stress and strain are bound to come; those lives that are built on superficial foundations will collapse when the time of stress arrives, but those lives that in actual experience have built themselves on the things of which he spoke will stand, they are like a house whose foundation is on a rock.

It was in the matter of faith that he made his greatest emphasis. It was his faith in the fatherhood of God that gave meaning to all of his teaching and was in the background of his entire life. It was thus that he sought to free men from needless anxiety and worry, for, fundamentally, this was unnecessary if one really believed. It was thus that he sought to relieve men from the haunting sense of guilt and to assure them of divine forgiveness, for if one believed that God was like a father, then, like the prodigal in the far country, he could "come to himself," rise up and go to meet him and be welcomed home again. It was thus that he sought to relieve men from fear. Some of the most characteristic words ever uttered by the lips of Jesus were "fear not" or " be not afraid." He saw in numberless ways how men's lives were burdened by fear. He saw, further, that the opposite of fear was faith, so he sought to relieve men of the burden of fear, not by saying it was foolish or unnecessary, but, rather, by awakening in them the power of a living faith, which, once it captured the soul did away with fear. It was thus that he sought to deliver men from frustration, aimlessness and hopelessness, for, if one really had faith in God and his Kingdom, as Jesus presented them, then life was challenging, full of infinite possibilities, fraught with meaning and undergirded with hope.

Perhaps most significant of all in considering Jesus' relations with men was the power of his own personality, that indefinable something about him that challenged and inspired men, that quality of his manhood that challenged Peter and Andrew by the lakeside to leave their nets and follow him, that made Levi "leave all" and become his disciple. It was what made Zacchæus aware that his life had been wrong in a way no one had ever done before and to live a different life from that day on. According to the story, there is no record of any conversation between Jesus and this man except a greeting of friendship. Perhaps even that played its part. Here was one whom everyone had condemned and with whom no one was friendly. So, when Jesus came with understanding and friendship, the contrast between his own life and this life was too much and Zacchæus cried out, repenting of his own sins and vowing that he would make restitution. Thus the influence of Christ's life transformed the lives of those about him. His critics gave him an unintentional compliment when they said, "Teacher we know you are sincere and fearless." [29] He was the master of his own fears; he never lost his poise or self-control. "It seems evident that contact with Christ's personality brought healing in its train. Calm and quiet were brought to the most excited and agitated households. Confidence and hope were inspired in the most despondent and helpless folk. The assurance of God's power and will to heal was made very real to those who were sick and oppressed. Christ brought them a new outlook, and helped them to attain a new attitude of mind." [30]

Furthermore, the power of his personality has not diminished with the centuries, "It is an impressive story, this record of how through him all sorts of people down through the centuries have found health and faith, have faced difficulties with hope and courage, have been freed from fear, have been sure of God's forgiveness for their sin, have been lifted out of discouragement and made strong to start again, have been empowered to face responsibility, have discovered how to pray, and have felt God's presence with them all through him." [31]

THE PASTORAL MINISTRY OF PAUL

The apostle Paul was one of the truly great men of his day—or of any day. A man of rich cultural background and training, of vast interests and titanic undertakings, he was also concerned about the needs and problems of individuals. While he has often been referred to as a theologian, a missionary and an evangelist, he was also a pastor, with a pastor's heart and a pastor's interest. Like so many others we shall discuss later, he also had a problem with himself. He has rightfully been described as a "man of conflict." [32] He was very sensitive, extremely introspective, often to the brink of morbidity; he carried on an intense struggle with himself. In his letters he reveals the emotions, the hopes and fears, the desires and frustrations, anxieties and tensions that distressed his soul. Nowhere does he reveal the struggle of his inner life more vividly than in the letter to the Romans in which he states, "I do not understand my own actions. For I do not do what I want, but I do the very thing I hate. . . . For I know that nothing good dwells within me, that is, in my flesh. I can will what is right, but I cannot do it. For I do not do the good I want, but the evil I do not want is what I do. . . . Wretched man that I am! Who will deliver me from this body of death?" [33] But he was also a man who worked through his conflicts until he could write to his friends at Philippi, "Have no anxiety about anything," and could assure them of the "peace

of God that passes all understanding," and could say of himself,
"I can do all things in him who strengthens me." [34]

Paul's letters themselves are a form of pastoral counseling.
They were not written to form a systematic theology, although
they have often been treated that way. They were written to
meet the practical and religious needs of individuals and of
churches. Several of them were written at the request of some
individual or group of individuals who had written or sent a
messenger seeking his advice and counsel. They were informal
in nature, in the style of spoken language with no thought of
literary ambition or recognition.[35] One New Testament scholar
describes them as "intimate words of counsel which were originally intended only for the ears of his readers." [36] His letters
should thus be seen as growing out of the practical needs and
problems of the everyday life of the people in the churches.
They reveal on the part of Paul a real pastoral concern for the
people in his churches and a familiarity with both their weaknesses and their needs.

These letters also reveal something of the problems that he
faced. It was a time of disillusionment and pessimism; he was
dealing with first generation Christians who faced terrific tensions and problems in their relationship to the surrounding
pagan world and individuals. The Corinthian correspondence
is the classic example. They had written seeking Paul's guidance
for some of these problems which were very real to them. Such
practical matters as whether or not a Christian should purchase
meat which had been offered to idols—which, incidentally, was
the best meat to be had, and whether or not Christians should
indulge in ecstatic speaking or speaking with "tongues"—these
were referred to Paul. The manner in which Paul handled these
questions shows his great insight and wisdom—in one case the
relinquishment of an acknowledged right for a higher social
end, and the other resulting in the matchless expression,
"Though I speak with the tongues of men and of angels, but
have not love, it profiteth me nothing."

In Paul's ministry he faced almost all the problems that a modern pastor has to face—problems of the family, problems of morals, problems of religious belief, the facing of death, and problems of the church. There were questions in the church regarding the place of women, the appearance of factions and divisions, excesses and intemperance even at some of the most sacred observances. He had to give constant warning and advice to keep them from being led astray by the many who would undermine his work and present false views of religion. There were everyday problems such as the relationship of husbands and wives, children and parents, and masters and servants. Oftentimes there were references to personal situations as when he advised the people at Galatia how to restore one who had done wrong, or when he advises two Philippian women to settle their differences, or the little personal letter to Philemon, a letter regarding his attitude and treatment toward a runaway slave.[37]

These letters, which to us are the most significant thing Paul did, grew out of these practical problems that he faced. They were usually written when a personal visit was impossible. It is a safe assumption that if people would send a messenger many miles to seek Paul's counsel, he was much sought after whenever and wherever he appeared, for guidance and advice, both by individuals and by groups. In fact, Dr. Goodspeed refers to them as "incidents" or "by-products" which grew out of his real work, which was personal contacts, his preaching and visiting.[38] This gives some indication as to how great and extensive his personal work must have been. Paul identified himself completely with his people; he rejoiced in their progress; his pain was intense when they failed or fell short. He was at times critical and did not hesitate to rebuke or condemn, but, in the main, he was remarkably patient and, even when most critical, was still affectionate and hopeful. In his attitudes and dealings he showed real insight and rare judgment. He was under no illusions about human nature, as his statements in the Roman

and Corinthian correspondence reveal. Here he referred to all
the known varieties and degrees of perversion, of personality
and character—covetousness, malice, envy, jealousy, anger, selfishness, slander, conceit, strife, deceit, gossip, whispering,
insolence, haughtiness, boastfulness, disobedience to parents,
foolishness, faithlessness, heartlessness, ruthlessness, as well as
drunkenness, impurity, immorality and licentiousness.[39] Yet he
never lost sight of human possibilities, and his emphasis was
always positive in terms of the "new man" who can forget the
things that are behind and look forward to the things that are
before, man who is by nature a son of God and can thus be
more than conqueror.[40] Some of Paul's attitudes toward human
nature would be modified, such as his view of the flesh as evil,
but many of his insights have been validated, or rather, redis-
covered by modern scientific thought, such as the need of
maturity,[41] or that love fulfills the requirements of character,[42] or that centering the thought and attention on that which
is true, honorable, just, pure and lovely is a key to growth and
inner peace.[43]

THE EARLY CHURCH

The same spirit and concern that was exhibited by Paul was
also, no doubt, evident in other leaders of this period, such as
Barnabas or Silas, Timothy or Titus. Of Barnabas in particular
it was said, he "encouraged all the people."

The early church had primarily an itinerant ministry and
depended more upon a mutual helpfulness, especially after the
apostles and immediate followers of Jesus had died. They were
not only limited in leadership but in almost all other aspects
as well; they had no organization, no property, no wealth, nothing but a deep faith and a common loyalty to the Christ. It was
a difficult world in which they lived. It was a world that was
characterized by cruelty, immorality and vice, religious desti-
tution and pessimism. It was a world in which the middle class
had been destroyed, in which there were more slaves than free-

men, where the chief source of amusement was the amphi-
theater where the people gathered to watch human beings kill
each other until it grew monotonous and then men were forced
to fight wild beasts as a novelty. This gives some idea of the
atmosphere in which they lived and the attitudes that were
prevalent among the people. It was a world in which women
and children were often held in low esteem; infanticide and ex-
position were quite general, and the basest forms of vice were
common. It was in this world that the church, a small, scattered,
struggling group of people, attempted to carry Jesus' message
of love and compassion, faith and good will.[44]

Of course, much of the religious thought was cast in an
eschatological setting and the chief concern at first was the
expectation of the imminent return of Jesus; yet, also, and more
permanently, Christianity brought with it a great compassion
for people, a concern for the suffering of the individual, and
a willingness to be of help to the sick and needy. The book
of James defined true religion in terms of visiting the father-
less and widows in their affliction and of keeping oneself un-
spotted from the world.[45] There were many such passages both
in the New Testament and in the writing of the church fathers.

It was to meet these needs of the unfortunate that new positions of leadership were formed. Even before the time of Paul,
seven were appointed to fulfill the practical functions of the
church by administering to the needs of the people, and, by the
time of the pastoral epistles, deacons were taken for granted,
their chief duties being connected with the administration of
charity, visiting and relieving the poor.[46] The influences that
had a bearing on the evolution of the ministry of the early
church were of a very practical nature and they maintained,
in many cases, a very wide and effective program. This program
was conceived primarily in terms of the individual and his
needs. As has been frequently emphasized, the influence of the
spread of Christianity did much to alter social conditions; yet
the aim of the church in these first few centuries was not to

change the structure of society. Their purpose was to prepare the individual for eternal salvation and to take care of the unfortunate and needy while on earth. This aspect of the work has been developed by Shirley Jackson Case, in his *Social Triumph of the Ancient Church*, in which he states, "The homeless were given shelter, the hungry were fed, the naked were clothed, hospitality was freely extended to visiting brethren, the sick and unfortunate were cared for, work was secured for the unemployed, and aid was made available for every form of need." [47] Special attention was given to those who were imprisoned for their faith, to soften the rigors of their imprisonment, if possible and, if they died, to care for their orphans. The extent of this work is indicated in Dr. Case's book in which he states that the church at Rome was supporting from its funds over fifteen hundred persons in distress, while, by the fourth century, the church at Carthage was supporting over three thousand. Basil founded a hospital for lepers and for the sick who were poor, and often ministered to them in person. In fact, his strenuous efforts, together with his physical weakness and severe asceticism, resulted in his premature death, but he was greatly loved and deeply mourned by his people.

As the ministry developed, it was the function of the parish priest to instruct the people, to carry on the charitable work of the church, visit the sick, and, also, to handle the problems of discipline. This involved a wide variety of questions. Since the regulation of Paul that Christians should not carry their differences before pagan courts was quite strictly observed, the church officials were called upon to listen to all kinds of complaints. This was usually done by the bishops, assisted by the presbyters and, down until the second century, the laity also joined in the administering of discipline. For a long time this was done publicly, which, although very humiliating, was felt to be more effective for that reason. Gradually this diminished and there developed the tendency to leave it more and more as a clerical responsibility. [48] The information concerning this period is limited, but what there is contains an abundance of references to the compassion and concern of the leaders for the unfortunate and an occasional reference that would indicate that the pastoral and counseling function was not neglected, such as the statement that "Ambrose was very accessible and affable as a pastor and was much beloved by his people," or that Chrysostom, when in exile, "continued to care for his flock, his benevolences, his missions, and was much sought in counsel." [49]

Chapter II

THE MEDIEVAL PERIOD

THE PENITENTIALS AND THE CONFESSIONAL

During the middle ages there gradually emerged within the Catholic Church the practice known as the confessional which still serves as the method in this large branch of Christendom. The position maintained by the Catholic Church is that the practice of confession was established by Jesus himself, passed on to Peter and the apostles and, through them, to the church which is his representative on earth. It is thus seen as a divine institution which existed in the church from the beginning and is not the establishment of any Pope or council.[1] Since Jesus had the power to forgive sins and passed it on to the apostles and the church who were to carry on his work, it is of the nature of the church to be able to forgive sins also. Even Catholic writers admit, however, that the evidence is lacking to show that there was a practice of private confession during the first centuries that is comparable to the system that is practised today.[2]

The indications of all the early literature are that confession in the first centuries was public. In fact, the clergy opposed private confession and insisted that sins confessed in private should be made known publicly. This included all sins, both those sins committed in secret and those already known to the public. The Didache gave the instruction to the people to assemble on the Lord's day, break bread and give thanks after confessing their transgression in order that their sacrifice might be pure.[3] Origen, said it was the decision of the clergy, who from experience should determine whether or not public confession was necessary. He urged the people to "look about thee carefully for the person to whom thou shouldest confess thy sin. First make sure of the physician to whom thou shouldest lay bare the cause of thine ailment, who knows how to be infirm with the infirm, to weep with those who weep—so that in fine if he shall have given any counsel thou wilt act upon it and wilt follow it: if he have understood and foreseen that thine ailment is such as needs to be exposed and to be cured in the gathering of the whole Church from which it may be that others too, can be edified and thou thyself readily healed, this will have to be arranged with much deliberation and the experienced counsel of that physician." [4]

The church orders for the consecration of a bishop, as early as the third century, contains references to the power to forgive sins. There are also indications that private confession began to replace public confession. Augustine permitted the avoidance of public confession for secret or non-scandalous sins.[5] In the fourth century Ambrose of Milan heard private confessions and "told none but God." Evidence as to just what happened in these early centuries is very uncertain. That confession and penance were demanded is quite established but whether it was necessary to make confession public, whether certain sins must be made public, or whether just penance must be done publicly cannot be established. It was in the fourth century that Basil suggested that the same principles should be followed in seeking the forgiveness of sins that are followed with physical ailments. Just as the individual does not disclose his bodily infirmities to everyone but to the one who is skilled in their cure so he should make his confession of sins to the one who is able to apply a remedy.[6]

In the fifth century Pope Leo the Great wrote a letter to some bishop in which he made the statement that it was sufficient that confessions be made to the priests in secret. He did not forbid public confession but merely stated that a public enumeration of sins was not necessary, and that it should be made first to God and then to the bishop. He felt that the continuance of public confession was dangerous for fear there would be many who would avoid penance if it was required. He urged upon all the necessity of penance, since God had provided but two remedies for sin and two means by which one could gain eternal life—baptism and penance. Those who have violated the vows of baptism could gain forgiveness by confession and penance. He warned against a custom of that day of deferring one's conversion to his death-bed when he might not be able to confess and obtain absolution.[7] St. Caesarius of Arles of the same century in his sermons urged the people to make sincere confessions to the priests and fulfill the penance required in order to escape damnation, since this was God's will by which men free themselves from the results of inevitable sin. The second synod of Davin in Armenia decreed that any priest who revealed what he had heard in the confessional should be anathema, what later became known as the Seal of the Confessional.

The most information that we have of the nature and practice of confession and penance is from the Penitentials which appeared about the sixth century. They were handbooks prepared for the guidance of priests and bishops in the caring for souls. They contained lists of the recognized sins and of necessary penance as well as methods for the receiving and dealing with penitents.[8] They give us not only a picture of society and of the faults of men but the methods and ideals of those who served as their guides and counselors. They were an important factor in the transformation of confession from a public to a private act. Many of them, like later pastoral counseling, used the thought forms and analogies of medicine. The Penitential of Theodore was said to be prepared for "the physicians of souls" while the Penitential of Cummean states, "Here begins the Prologue of the health giving medicine of souls."[9] Priests are warned that unless they have sympathy and feeling for sinners they will not be able to serve effectively in this office.

Many of the Penitentials contained a detailed series of questions that were to be asked and answered by the confessant. The Bigatian Penitential of the eighth century instructs the healer of souls to observe carefully such matters as the age and sex of the penitent, his training, his courage, with what force he was driven to sin, with ·what kind of passion he was assailed, how long he continued in sin and with what sorrow and labor he was afflicted, for the regulating of penance would be determined by such matters.[10] A Penitential ascribed to the Venerable Bede about the eighth century urges the priest to distinguish the sex, age, condition, status, even the heart of the penitent and to determine his penance accordingly. He also used a medical analogy to the effect that as physicians of the body prescribe different remedies depending on the disease, so the physician of souls should make due allowance for different conditions. Even though the fault might be the same, there were other factors that should be distinguished and considered, such as whether the person was rich or poor, freeman or slave, child, youth or older person, stupid or intelligent, layman or cleric, married or single, sick or well.[11] Others expressed similar ideas. The Penitential of Columban also refers to the physician and says, "So therefore the spiritual physicians ought also to heal with various sorts of treatment the wounds, fevers, transgressions, sorrows, sicknesses, and infirmities of souls." [12]

The Penitentials were mainly correctional. Most of them sought to cure by what they termed the principle of contraries, which was that each fault must be replaced by corresponding virtues. Christianity from the first had made strict demands of behavior and had imposed rigid standards of discipline. The penalties demanded in the Penitentials were of a varied nature, some of them being very severe. One of the commonest forms of punishment was the repetition of the penitential psalms, even on occasion, the whole psalter. Fasting also was very common, the severity of the fast ranging from the omission of a meal to living on bread and water for a period of days, or abstinence from meat and wine for a matter of years. There were developed a wide variety of unique punishments consisting of some posture or action that would result in physical discomfort. There are references to sleeping in water, on nutshells, with a corpse in a grave, while flagellation was quite common. Sometimes the freeing of a slave or the giving of alms was demanded, while in extreme cases exile was prescribed.[13]

The Penitentials have frequently been criticized for having an unhealthy moral taint and leaving the way open for later abuses by lax confessors. Yet at the same time, in spite of all this, their main objective, as McNeil points out in his thorough study of the *Medieval Handbooks of Penance*, was the reconstruction of personality. It was their desire to aid in the recovery of spiritual health which had been lost by sin. Their penalties were often inhumanly severe and legalistically applied, yet there is evident within them the desire to help the individual and, in spite of their psychological limitations, they no doubt had much of positive value. McNeil appraises them in this fashion, "Lacking the sensitive humanitarianism generally professed and sometimes practiced today, the authors of these handbooks nevertheless had a sympathetic knowledge of human nature and a desire to deliver men and women from the mental obsessions and social maladjustments caused by their misdeeds. . . . What ever may be found to praise or blame from the point of view of psychotherapy, in the austerities prescribed, there can be no doubt of the presence in them of the intention of a humane ministry. The penitentials offer to the sinner the means of rehabilitation. He is given guidance to the way of recovering harmonious relations with the Church, society and God. Freed in the process of penance from social censure, he recovers the lost personal values of which his offenses have deprived him. He can once more function as a normal person. Beyond the theological considerations, we see in the detailed prescriptions the objective of an inward moral change, the setting up of a process of character reconstruction which involves the correction of special personal defects, and the reintegration of personality." [14]

There can be no question of the profound influence that these penitentials had in shaping the practice of the confessional. Since the time of Leo the Great private confession was accepted and recognized as legal, in the eighth century it was made compulsory. The Council of Liége, which met in 710, decreed that everyone should make confession once a year to his parish priest. The Lateran Council which met in 1215 confirmed what had become an established custom and made it universally obligatory.[15] This Council demanded that confession be made once a year, that penance be faithfully performed and that the priest in the manner of the skilled physician must be faithful, diligent and cautious in the carrying out of this office, fitting the manner of advice to the needs of the penitent and must not in any manner reveal what he has learned in the confessional under penalty of being deposed and doing perpetual penance in a monastery.[16] It was also in the thirteenth century that the formula of absolution was changed from "May the Lord absolve thee" to "I absolve thee." Synods of the sixteenth century suggested that lay people should confess frequently and ecclesiastics weekly. The Council of Trent, meeting in 1551, made confession a divine institution with priests alone having the authority to remit confessed sins. Furthermore, it stated that if anyone denies that sacramental confession was necessary for salvation or was instituted by divine right, or says that the practice of private confession is a human institution and alien from the institution and command of Christ, "let him be anathema." [17]

Out of these developments certain basic principles and regulations are seen to have been emerging, which to a large extent govern the confessional to this day. The confessional was conceived to have been of divine origin and nature. It was inaugurated by Jesus himself and given by him to the church. It was sacramental in nature, a means of supernatural grace whereby the consequences of sin were annulled and the favor of God was recovered. It was not merely the giving of advice, or the enforcing of discipline, although these were a part of it. It was believed that, since Jesus had made the atonement, he also had chosen this way of making forgiveness available to the sinner, by working through the pastors of his church and making them the dispensers of his forgiveness.[18] The confessional is not optional but compulsory and necessary. It must be heard by an authorized validly ordained priest else the absolution given would be null. At first the confessional had to be made to the parish priest but later it became lawful to make it to any duly authorized priest. Certain rules and practices developed. The confessor was under strict obligation to warn the penitent of his obligations. Other rules developed, such as that priests were not to hear confessions outside the church except in case of necessity; they were not to look on the face of the confessant or to inquire concerning others with whom he may have sinned. All that took place in the confessional was to be regarded with the strictest secrecy as was stated by the Lateran Council. This was known as the Seal of the Confessional and was to be observed under strictest regulations, and a violation was punished by the severest penalties. What had been revealed in confession was not to be mentioned either in private conversation or in public discourse. There were to be no exceptions, and a priest must not violate it even to save his life or his good name, the life of another or to advance the cause of justice. In 1828, a Jesuit father refused to reveal to a New York court information he had received in the confessional and since then this practice has been generally recognized by the courts.[19]

AUGUSTINE AND AQUINAS

The common expression, the period of the "dark ages," applies to psychology as much as to anything else. There was little time and no incentive for individual thought; if anything, thinking was discouraged. As one student of psychology put it, "From the standpoint of positive contributions to a scientific psychology the middle ages are relatively unimportant.[20] There are two names that were outstanding in their thought and influence—Augustine and Aquinas. It was Augustine who formulated and systematized the medieval principles of psychology that determined the content and scope of both theology and psychology for centuries. In fact, the two were one.

Augustine was born in North Africa in 354. His mother, the famous Monica, was a Christian but his father was a pagan. His doctrines grew out of his own intense struggle which he described in his *Confessions*. This has been referred to as "one of the most remarkable psychological disclosures in all literature." [21] Augustine was a man of great intellectual power but of a tempestuous passionate nature which caused him great difficulty and extreme suffering. The irregularities of his boyhood and youth were a lifelong source of remorse and regret. He never forgot an incident of his boyhood when, in company with other boys, he stole some green pears from a neighbor's pear tree. When he was seventeen he took a mistress and lived with her fourteen years. In fact he became a school teacher to support the woman and the son she bore him. It was out of his own struggle with temptation and his feeling of helplessness in its presence that his theories of human depravity were derived. In his *Confessions* he spoke of himself as "miserable," "wretched," "soul-sick," "tormented," "filled with shame and fear." [22] Thus, out of the intensity of his own struggle and as a result of his own transgressions, he became convinced that all men were wicked, sinful, guilty by their very nature, incapable of any good except by the grace of God.

Augustine was converted by Ambrose of Milan. He went to hear him preach partly out of curiosity but was captivated both by the man and his message. He greatly desired to be like Ambrose. While in the midst of mental turmoil he heard the voice of a child from a neighboring house saying, "take up and read." Then occurred the famous incident, when Augustine opened his Bible and read, "Not in rioting and drunkenness, not in chambering and wantonness . . . but put ye on the Lord Jesus Christ, and make not provision for the flesh." He closed the book "for instantly at the end of this sentence, by a light as it were of serenity infused into my heart, all the darkness of doubt vanished away." [23]

Augustine truly attempted to explore the paradoxical nature of the human soul. "Behold," he said, "here are two natures: one good, draws this way; another bad, draws back that way." [24] Augustine based his psychology on the Greek background that came to him through neo-Platonism. His psychology was a form of faculty psychology. Augustine felt that man knew the soul introspectively. The soul reveals itself through its functions which are thinking, willing, remembering. Some of his statements sound very modern and reveal his insight as an observer of human nature. He went clear back to his early infancy in his analysis of himself and noticed instinctive selfishness in the jealousy of a baby. In defending the value of confession he compared the sinful conscience to an abscess filled with pus, the priest to the surgeon, and confession to the lancing of the abscess whereby the pus could be driven out.

There have been marked differences of opinion both as to the value of his contribution and as to the nature of his own personality. One historian referred to him as a "neurotic, a psychopath, an irritable sensualist who was incapable of calmness or self-control." [25] While another said, "However he might chastise his early sins, sitting down at forty-seven to write his *Confessions*, one does not feel either that he gloats or sorrows unhealthily about them." [26] Be that as it may, it was Augustine who formulated both the theology and the psychology that dominated the church for several centuries and, to a large extent, is still the psychology of large areas of the world today.[27]

No other name of real influence appeared until that of Aquinas in the thirteenth century. Aquinas was a Dominican friar, a student of Albertus Magnus. Aquinas' systematization of theology and ethics became the accepted doctrines of the church and were of wide influence in the history of psychology. They still form the basis of Catholic psychology today. He created his system of thought based on Aristotle but modified it to fit the thought of Augustine. He discussed the intellectual processes, emotion and the will. He saw that emotions could destroy pure thought but could and should be controlled. The will, he felt, was dominated by the intellect. Like Augustine his was a faculty psychology. He is of importance because he predominated later medieval thought and still has much influence in one branch of the church today.

THE SPIRIT OF COMPASSION

It was not without reason that the medieval period has been termed the "dark ages." It was a time of ignorance and superstition, darkness and fear. As the world moved into the middle ages, the church like everything else was affected. The religion of the average layman was a combination of pagan superstition and such forms of real guidance as he might be fortunate enough to receive. When young Francis of Assisi was troubled and confused he found none who could understand and help him. "No man seemed to care for his soul." He even went to the bishop but found no guidance there.[28] Religious leaders are usually children of their time and, when everything else went into decline during the dark ages, they were not exempt. There are many records of unfortunate, in fact tragic situations growing out of the limited knowledge, the belief in demon possession, the terrible superstition that existed. Epidemics of flagellation swept the whole country, marked by processions marching, singing, bearing crosses and leather thongs, tipped with metal points with which they flogged their bodies, mingling their blood with the blood of the Savior. The primary motive of religion was one of escape; the religious leaders of this period were the monks and friars, and monasticism was the expression of the religion of the day. Yet, in spite of all this, there was preserved a spirit of compassion that was kept alive to bear

richer fruit in days to come and which was not without real
benefit then. In fact it was all that was to soften the harshness,
the cruelty and indifference of these times.

It is beyond the scope of this study to trace the history of
the monastic movement, or even to attempt to evaluate its contribution, although much can be said that is both positive and
negative. There are many examples of the most abnormal behavior by some of the earlier ascetics, such as Simeon the Stylite
who lived for years on top of a pillar. It was inevitable that this
monastic form of life should have unfortunate effects on the
many who participated in it. The psychological effect of a life
of isolation, confinement and self-repression only intensified
some temptations and resulted in illusions, visions, extreme and
eccentric conduct and warped conceptions of religion. The
monotony of life, the attempt to suppress man's native drives
and desires, the rigid discipline, and a strong and exaggerated
sense of sin resulted in intense weariness, irritability, depression
and even insanity. The results on the general attitude of people
toward the home, the family and similar subjects have been
frequently pointed out.

On the other side of the ledger can be listed the fact that the
monasteries were among the most potent factors in civilization
at certain times, and they alone preserved whatever was saved
of Christian tradition and knowledge for a later generation.
Throughout the dark ages they alone provided relief for the
poor, care for the orphaned and sick, and training for the
young. Monasteries along the routes of travel had infirmaries
available for sick pilgrims. About the tenth century many parish
churches, as well as cathedrals and monasteries, maintained
hospitals as well as orphanages and institutions for the care of
paupers. Even lepers were cared for. Special orders and brotherhoods developed, such as the Knights of St. John whose chief
reason for being was to care for those who were sick or otherwise needed help. When the black death invaded Europe, the
Black Friars went into sick rooms and cared for the sick and

buried the dead while others locked themselves in their houses in fear. The Rule of Benedict said, "Before all things and above all things care must be taken of the sick." He himself died of a fever which he contracted while caring for the poor.[29]

The monasteries during this period were almost the sole agencies for human betterment and even made some contribution to counsel and guidance. Bede tells us that wherever a monk happened to appear in a village the people flocked to hear him and that the chief purpose of his visits was to preach, baptise, visit the sick and "take care of souls." He also gives an account of one of the monks, named St. Cuthbert, who would often leave the monastery for a week or even a month and visit the most out-of-the-way and poverty-stricken villages. He was so persuasive in his preaching and so striking in his appearance that "no man present presumed to conceal from him the inmost secret of his heart, but all openly confessed what they had done; because they thought the same guilt could not be concealed from him, and wiped off the guilt of what they had so confessed with worthy fruits of penance as commanded." [30] The story is told of the Curé of Ars who was so besieged by pilgrims who wanted to receive his counsel that he was forced to spend sixteen to seventeen hours a day in the confessional. He would lie down to rest at nine or ten in the evening but begin again at one in the morning rather than disappoint the people who were already forming in line. He would have much preferred a more quiet life of contemplation but his devotion to the people's needs kept him at his post.[31]

It was Francis and his group of followers who changed the conception that it was the first duty of the Christian to shut himself away from a perishing world. His asceticism was of the open road and he carried with him a deep concern for every living creature. He began his new life by changing clothes with a tattered beggar and, with his own hands, washed the wounds of the lepers. It was not without reason that it came to be said of him, "He remembers those whom God has forgotten."

While Francis and his friars, as well as the Dominicans, still held to the ascetic ideal, their object was not so much an escape as it was practical service. Their chief field of labor was among the neglected: they preached to the poor, visited the sick, cared for the lepers and were often licensed to hear confessions.

The order of the "Sisters of Charity" was founded in 1617 by St. Vincent de Paul and Madame Louise Marillac de Gras in Paris. It began with a group of fifteen women for the purpose of visiting and caring for the sick. Originally they were connected with a parish and some of the women were married. The work spread very rapidly and the need of some organization was felt. The woman who was St. Vincent's coadjutator had been left a widow and thus decided to devote her life to this type of service. Concern for her family prevented her from caring for contagious cases and it was felt that unmarried women or childless widows were best fitted for this type of work. The order was established by the Archbishop of Paris in 1663 and was recognized by the Pope in 1668. Those who took the vows of the order pledged themselves to certain personal and spiritual disciplines, also never to refuse to nurse the sick, regardless of how loathsome or dangerous the disease, never to stand in awe of death, always to remember as servants of Christ that, in nursing the sick, they are nursing him. They were permitted no intimacies or special friendship even with each other. They were warned not to feel greater interest in one patient than another but their service was to be like the sunshine and rain which gave of their bounties equally to the agreeable or disagreeable, the just or the unjust.[32]

There never has been a time since the death of Christ that this spirit of compassion, the Christian concern for others has been completely submerged or extinguished.

Chapter III

THE PERIOD OF THE REFORMATION AND THE PROTESTANT PASTOR

The Protestant Reformation brought about many changes. From the point of view of our study the two most important were the emergence of the Protestant pastor and the abandonment of the confessional. The Catholic church continued the confessional as it was; the Anglo-Catholic in a modified form, but Protestantism, in the main, developed a different approach and philosophy toward the needs and problems of individuals. Certain elements of the confessional remained; as we shall see, pastors still faced the private problems of their people and often heard a confession of sin, but the obligatory nature and the supernatural sanctions were abolished.[1] Luther, himself, although disgusted and wearied with much of the superstition that had accumulated around the confessional, did not want to abolish it entirely. He suggested, rather, that it be utilized as an optional and confidential interview between the pastor and the individual. Before confession was made to the minister, however, it should first be made to God. Calvin, in the main, followed the thought of Luther. He felt that confession to God should be followed by confession to men. Both Luther and Calvin discouraged the necessity of scrupulously enumerating one's sins. Calvin based his authority on the passage in James which advocated that Christians should confess their faults "one to another."[2] Calvin thus felt that confession could rightfully be made to any church member, although the pastors were "supposed" to be better qualified than others, and he suggested that one who was in spiritual distress should seek relief and con-

39

solation by a private confession to his pastor, although this was always optional.[3]

Although Luther is remembered chiefly as a reformer, his pastoral ministry was far more extensive than is commonly recognized. August Nebe made a careful study of Luther's attitudes and practices which he published under the title *Luther as Spiritual Adviser*.[4] This volume, which covers the whole range of Luther's work, including chapters on his work with the sick, the forlorn, the erring, the mourning, the tempted and the dying, has many references and quotations from Luther that indicate that, although he was concerned about all Christendom and many evangelical congregations, he "never lost sight of the individual soul," [5] and "No trouble seemed to him so trifling, no sorrow so insignificant, as to be unworthy of his ministry of comfort." [6] He felt that the visits of a spiritual adviser were just as important as the visits of a physician and was quite convinced that many bodily diseases were the result of a morbid spiritual condition. Once, when a noted individual was taken ill, he said, "That is a result of sorrow, which is often a cause of such disorders; for when the heart is troubled and sorrowful, then follows also weakness of the body. The diseases of the heart are the real diseases, such as sorrow, temptation, etc." [7]

Luther, himself, carried out in practice what he advised to others. Even during some of his most trying times as a reformer he continued to care for the sick. During the pestilence of 1527, and later in 1535 and 1539, he went to the homes of those afflicted with the plague and some died in his arms. Furthermore, he urged others to help the afflicted, saying, "We must and are in duty bound to deal with our neighbor in all times of need and danger whatsoever." [8] He said that some died more from anxiety than from the pestilence, but he did advise the taking of every precaution.

It is true that he accepted the idea of demoniacal possession, but so did the medical men of the day. He felt that prayer and faith were a higher kind of medicine which would ward off the devil's pestilence.

He had a deep sympathy for those who were tempted, for he himself had been severely tempted. He said, "I have learned by experience how one should act under temptation." First he suggested that he should seek the comfort of the divine word and then the company of Christian people. He recognized the power of attention; "in these bodily temptations there is only one solitary way to overcome, namely, to turn away from them the senses, the thoughts, and the heart; so also in spiritual temptations there is no other counsel, and no better help, nor more powerful remedy, than that one cast such thoughts out of his mind more and more, as best he can, and think upon the very opposite." [9] He warned the tempted not to spend too much time alone with their thoughts, and said, with real insight, "If we are too much concerned for fear we may commit sin, we shall be overcome." [10]

It was known how willingly Luther helped the unfortunate, and many people sought his guidance and help. In fact, his reputation for helping individuals became so widespread that many wrote him asking him to send them in writing either counsel or consolation, as the case might be, if he could not come in person. Many such incidents and many such letters are included in the book mentioned above. The manner in which he accepted the innumerable appeals and demands made of him, especially in the light of his other interests and activities, indicates an attitude of friendliness and patience that was quite remarkable and a concern for his people that was genuine and real.

Most of the histories of this period are histories of controversy, and most of the preachers referred to are mentioned because of the part they played in some controversy, but, occasionally, one will catch an incidental reference, such as the fact that Zwingli was a good pastor, that indicates that men did not lose the pastoral concern for people even in the midst of such

periods of debate and conflict.[11] Also, we discover that John
Bradford—noted for his remark when he saw a criminal on
his way to be executed, "There but for the grace of God goes
John Bradford"—had a deep concern for his people. In fact,
he was finally imprisoned for his convictions but was so trusted
by his jailer that he was allowed to leave his cell to visit the
sick and the needy, and, after fulfilling his pastoral duties, always returned at the appointed hour.[12] Pattison, in his *History
of Christian Preaching*, tells of one John Fletcher who visited
his parish every Sunday morning at five o'clock, inviting them
to the service, and he adds this significant sentence, "At no hour
of the day or night did misery or suffering knock at his door and
fail of admittance." [13]

One of the earliest men to give special attention to this field
of the ministry was Richard Baxter, a Puritan pastor, whose
ministry at Kidderminster, in Worcester County, England, has
been described as "the scene of a pastoral triumph." [14] In his
book, *The Reformed Pastor*, published in 1656, he stresses again
and again the sacredness and value of work with each individual. Baxter, of course, was concerned primarily with conversion, but he saw the difficulty of dealing with the individual.
"What skill is necessary to deal in private with one poor ignorant soul for his conversion!" [15] Baxter practiced what he
preached. He spent at least one hour with each family in his
parish each year. His clerk arranged the schedule and told every
family what day and hour to come.[16] Baxter regretted the fact
that the size of his parish required that he deal with a whole
family at a time, but he tried to find time to talk with each
one alone, out of hearing of the rest; in the case of women,
though, he advised that others should always be in sight. To any
young clergyman who objected that he did not have time to
know all his flock, he said that, in that case, he should hire an
assistant out of his own salary, for it was better for him to live
on part of his salary than to have any members neglected.

Baxter went to Kidderminster when he was twenty-six years

old. At the time of his coming it had a population of about four thousand people, half of whom lived in town. It was anything but a promising field. His predecessor had been incompetent both in ability and character. Dr. John Brown, in his *Puritan Preaching in England*, said, "If I were asked what in the year 1646, was one of the most unpromising towns in England to which a young man could be sent, who was starting his career as preacher and pastor, I should feel inclined at once to point to the town of Kidderminster in Worcestershire." [17] The people were characterized as ignorant, immoral and irreverent. Baxter himself said that when he came there was about one family on a street that worshipped God and when he left there were some streets where there was not a family that did not. The whole community was literally transformed.

While Baxter's preaching was very effective and was characterized by great earnestness, he himself felt that his success was due to his pastoral labors. He said, referring to his custom of family visitation and instruction, "I find more outward signs of success with most that do come, than from all my public preaching to them." [18] He asked his parishioners to meet at his house every Thursday evening to discuss his sermons, any doubts or questions they had about it, or "any other case of conscience." Monday and Tuesday he and his assistant took between them fifteen or sixteen families for private catechising and instruction. This enabled him to get over his entire parish of some eight hundred families once a year.[19] His wife also was of considerable help in this work. He admitted that, except in cases requiring learning in theological difficulties, his wife had better judgment than he and, except for cases requiring complete secrecy, he submitted them to her for her counsel and advice. This parish work he called his recreation; his only regret was that it limited his time for study.

Since the community had no physician, he also served as a doctor for a period of five or six years. He entered this work not by choice but by necessity. Advising one family in a period of illness, he soon found that others sought his help. Since he charged no fee, he was often besieged by patients, as many as twenty standing about his door at once. Partly because it interfered with his other duties and partly because he feared he would do more harm than good, due to his lack of knowledge, he secured a "godly and diligent" physician to come to the community. After that he refused to practice any more except in consultation with him.[20] He had a peculiar success with melancholy persons and they came from all over the country to consult him. Many of his remarks on the subject are in close agreement with what psychoanalysts were saying many years later. He carried on an extensive correspondence with those who sought his help in the facing of their troubles and perplexities. He was also the friend and counsellor of some of the most influential people of his day.

Out of such a vast experience of contact with personality, he developed a real insight into human nature. His recognition of the subtleties of evasion and rationalization has a peculiarly modern tone and flavor. He said, regarding his experience with men, "I now see more good and more evil in all men than heretofore I did. I see that good men are not so good as I once thought they were, but have more imperfections. . . . And I find that few are so bad as either their malicious enemies or censorious separating professors do imagine . . . even in the wicked usually there is more for grace to make advantage of, and more to testify for God and holiness, than I once believed there had been." [21]

His success is even more remarkable when one considers the fact that all through his life he suffered from poor health; he consulted no less than thirty-six doctors and was the victim of the doctors' medical experiments as well as his own. From the age of twenty-one his life was uncertain, and he said he never knew a working hour that was free from pain. Even so, he felt that his weakness and his pain had some value, for they prompted him to think in terms of those things which were essential and caused him to speak "as a dying man to dying men." Many new methods and techniques have been developed; theology has been changed and clarified, but, in terms of devotion to the pastoral task, Richard Baxter has never been surpassed. When he was too old and sick to continue his ministerial tasks, he still opened his doors morning and evening that people might come in to him.[22]

John Wesley was not a pastor in the sense of one who lives in a community with his people—the world was his parish. His ministry deserves much consideration because of the profound psychological implications of both his message and his societies in the lives of the people. He appeared at a time when social conditions were intolerable and the state of the church was such that it had little to offer. Poverty, ignorance, immorality, vice and degradation were everywhere. The Industrial Revolution was upsetting the whole life of the people. They were crowded together in the cities, working hours that today would be thought impossible, for a few cents a week. At the same time these people, who were forced to live exposed to all the hardship and disease that are a part of poverty and the slums, were aware of the extremes of wealth that were enjoyed by the privileged. The sense of frustration and resentment, a lack of moral values, resulted in crime and drunkenness that has seldom been equaled. The conditions were intolerable and have been described in detail in many volumes; we cannot devote more space to it here. The life of the individual of the masses was almost unbearable. It was in this situation and to such people that Wesley began to preach. He himself was a man of many contradictions, defending witchcraft with the same vigor with which he appealed for repentance; yet the total value of his preaching cannot be overestimated. His message was an appeal for a new life, a new character, a new experience. He stressed the divinity which he felt was in every human soul. This was something new to the people to whom he was preaching. The courage and efforts of the man are unparalleled in history. Time and time again he thwarted mobs by the calm courage of his own manner, and often the bullies themselves were overcome by the spirit of the one they intended to mob. Driven out of the church, he preached to thousands of people at a time out of doors, on the streets, and at the mouths of coal pits; he also visited the jails. Wesley saw that more than preaching was needed, for a man once converted needed further help, or the influence of his former associates and surroundings might tempt him back to his former habits. To counteract this and to provide for further development, Wesley organized "class meetings" of groups of twelve members who would meet once a week to strengthen each other by telling of their trials, confessing their failures and testifying to their victories. One historian describes the results of his work on the lives of the people: "And that was why Wesley succeeded. The poor folk resorted to violence and debauchery because they knew no better way of relieving their thwarted souls. . . . They relieved their sense of pent-up frustration in 'revivals' rather than at hangings. Assured that they could be accepted in heaven, they no longer cared that they were rejected on earth. They gave up their dram-drinking and other vices, and deadened themselves to the black anguish of life by steeping themselves in faith. The opiate was not altogether compounded of delusions. The converted joined 'societies,' and in these societies they found a comradeship which destroyed the anonymity that had blighted their lives. They were no longer bits of refuse floating along in the gutters; they were persons now, with names that were known and sins that might be confessed aloud." [23]

Wesley was also concerned about individuals. The list of his private charities is quite amazing. He distributed all his wealth among philanthropies and personally founded orphanages, Strangers' Societies, refuges for widows, medical dispensaries and inexpensive libraries for the poor. When extreme manifestations of emotion occurred during his meetings he undertook a course of visiting to study the cases of those who had cried out in the meeting. At first he attributed such expressions to God, but, later, to Satan also, and as time went by he tended more and more to discourage them altogether. His journal reveals many instances when he was called to homes to see individuals who were in a serious condition, shouting, screaming, requiring several people to control the distortions of the body.[24] In spite of his acceptance of such ideas as demon possession he also attained a conception of the power of faith to influence the personality and even health. Writing in his *Primitive Physick*, he said, "The love of God, as it is the sovereign remedy of all miseries, so in particular it effectively prevents all bodily disorders the passions introduce, by keeping the passions themselves within due bounds; and by the unspeakable joy and perfect calm serenity and tranquillity it gives the mind it becomes the most powerful of all the means of health and long life." [25]

John Frederick Oberlin, French Protestant pastor in the Vosges mountains, is another who transformed the complexion of a community as a result of his pastoral labors. Here for over fifty years he ministered to five little villages that comprised his parish, although he had many much more attractive offers which he might have accepted. On one such occasion he refused to leave because, he said, it had taken him ten years "to learn every head in the parish" and now it would take another ten to use the knowledge. He kept a book of records which contained an inventory of the moral, intellectual and domestic wants of each; it included the ancestry, hereditary tendencies, characteristics and deeds of every member of the five villages under his care.[26] He not only studied them, he served them. President Wilkins, of Oberlin College, in his Bicentenary Address on the birth of Oberlin, described his work as a pastor. ". . . he was tireless, resourceful and fearless; going on horseback, by day or by night, regardless of season or weather, to points of need, and ministering with charity or with medical or surgical help as readily as with religious comfort." [27] Like Bax-

ter, he found it necessary to act as physician since the parish had
no physician, nurse or pharmacist—consequently he acted as
all three. He gave instructions in first aid, trained some women
as nurses and finally arranged for one of the parishioners to go
to Strasbourg to study medicine and then return to practice in
the parish. He recognized that to deal with the individual was
not effective unless one also dealt with his community surroundings. Consequently, he took an active part in all types
of community reforms and progress. He was interested in
everything for the good of the people from the building of a
better road, on which he worked with pick and shovel, to the
building of a church. He was a pioneer in such matters as primary and secondary education and in the scientific study of
agriculture. The parish register for him was more than just a
record of his people. He kept it before him daily. At a certain
hour of the morning he prayed for his individual parishioners
by name. It is said that the people of the village knew this and
would pass the house in silence during that hour, and to a large
extent it created the bond of fellowship that existed both between the pastor and the people and between the people and
the pastor.

Glasgow was the scene of the unusual practical ministry of
Thomas Chalmers. His sermon, "The Expulsive Power of a
New Affection," is commonly recognized as one of the great
sermons of the century and contains ideas that psychologists
were later expressing in a different terminology.[28] He was also
a great teacher and reformer, but it is his work as a practical
pastor that concerns us here. This practical interest was not evident in his early ministry. In the first seven years of his first
pastorate at Kilmany he did not care for personal contact and
made little or no attempt at pastoral work. A series of events,
chief of which were the deaths of his brother and sister, a
serious and confining illness of his own which kept him in his
room for four months, together with a reading of Wilberforce's *Practical View of Christianity*,[29] combined to produce

a revolutionary change amounting to a conversion in his attitudes and activities. The first thing he did was to visit all the sick, bereaved and dying in his parish.[30] It was in Glasgow that he sprang into the limelight. He was especially concerned about the poor and the submerged. His organizations of charity to meet the problems of some ten thousand poor people by utilizing volunteer workers is worthy of careful study today. One historian has described his varied pastoral work of "organizing a system of parochial visitation, grappling with the sins and sorrows of the great city, pondering over the economic problems which faced him in the teeming tenements, and carrying the hand of the philanthropist, the mind of the statesman, and the heart of the Christian pastor from floor to floor and family to family in the tall houses where his parishioners lived and labored." [31]

There are many others who could be mentioned, such as Robert Hall, of whom it was said, "No man was easier to approach," or Reginald Heber, noted as the author of the hymn, "Holy, Holy, Holy," whom Thackeray described as, "the beloved priest in his own home of Hadnet, counseling the people in their troubles, advising them in their difficulties, kneeling often at their sick beds at the hazard of his own life; where there was strife, the peacemaker, where there was want, the free giver." [32] Charles Haddon Spurgeon, although unable to do much visiting, had the same deep interest in people and was consulted by large numbers. He refers to one day in which he received over thirty individuals for conferences at the chapel, consuming his entire day from the time he arrived in the morning until time to conduct a prayer meeting at night. On this particular day he did not even take time for lunch, having forgotten about it in his interest in the people.[33] Another described him as a "master physician in the troubles of the soul."

One of the greatest pastors was the Reverend John Watson, better known as Ian Maclaren. He won notable distinction as an author and also as a preacher, but, in the eyes of many, he was best known as a pastor. His Yale lectures, published under the title *The Cure of Souls*, was one of the first books to bear this title and reveals his interest in and mastery of this field. This volume describes his own methods which we will discuss in another section. Suffice it to say that he applied what he wrote; he was tireless in his efforts, not only dealing with people in conference but writing innumerable letters of counsel and comfort. His favorite motto, "Be kind for everyone you meet is fighting a hard battle," reveals the key to his attitude. His thought was not to condemn or judge, but to understand, comfort and help. Late in his ministry he said that if he could live his life over again he would give his people more consolation. His biographer, W. Robertson Nicoll, points out the significant fact that, great as his success had been, the pastoral work had been very difficult for him and he had to school himself to it.[34]

One of the strongest advocates of personal work and also the most successful was Henry Drummond. In a letter, dated 1882, he said, "I must say I believe in personal dealing more and more every day, and in the inadequacy of mere preaching." [35] In the fall of 1893, he read a paper entitled "Spiritual Diagnosis," in which he advocated some form of clinical training for theological students. The first sentence was, "The study of the soul in health and disease ought to be as much an object of scientific study and training as the health and diseases of the body." The minister as a spiritual adviser should be as thoroughly acquainted with the soul as the physician is with the body. "He should know every phase of the human soul, in health and disease, in the fulness of joy and the blackness of sorrow." This, however, he did not find easy. "A friend is in trouble, we are in trouble. But how are we to proceed? What guide have we in ministering to a soul diseased?" He appealed for others to take an interest and to attempt this deep and difficult study of human life and character. He presented it as a possible life mission opening up a field of life-long study and effort.[36]

Drummond first came into prominence while working as a student with Moody. Moody put him in charge of the inquiry rooms, which was exactly to Drummond's liking, for here he had the opportunity to work with the individual, as he had always advocated. Here, in these inquiry rooms, he came face to face with thousands of men and women in crisis moments of their lives; here he faced every form of suffering and problem imaginable. It was here that he gained his understanding of human nature, his insight into character, his knowledge of life, both at its highest and its lowest levels. Some of the experiences he ran into appalled him. Once he said to a friend, "Such tales of woe I've heard in Moody's inquiry room that I have felt I must go and change my clothes after the contact." On another occasion, returning from a meeting, he said, "I am sick with the sins of these men! How can God bear it?" All of his work was not done in the inquiry rooms. He was well known and justly famous as a speaker, but it was in his dealings with individuals that he was peculiarly effective. One biographer refers to him as a speaker and then continues, "Off the platform his work was even more effective. In a moment he could put himself alongside the most hopeless, the most desperate, of human souls, woo from them secrets that no ear had ever heard, and lead them again into a 'larger place.' But for one confidence that he sought, a score were thrust upon him. Strange individuals of every calling, honorable and the reverse, felt that they could trust him, nor was their trust misplaced." [37]

George Adam Smith, in his thorough biography, *The Life of Henry Drummond*,[38] tells of the many types of tragic cases that were brought to his attention and how deeply moved Drummond was by every case presented to him. He continues with this description, ". . . to associate Henry Drummond only with meetings and addresses would be to misrepresent him. Had he ever been carried away with the size and success of these, had he ever been tempted to swerve from his own principle that the individual was the aim and object of religion, he must have been brought back by one element of the meetings themselves. At each of these there were handed up to the chairman a large number of requests for prayer, which in nine cases out of ten had to do with the darkness of the tragedy of some individual life. Carefully preserved among his documents are some scores of these anonymous scraps of paper, shabby, soiled, and often misspelt, each of them the confession of a fallen soul, or the sob of a broken heart, or the cry for warmth of a cold and starving one. From vice or servitude to some besetting sin, from long doubt and vain struggle to the light, from wrecked and dreary homes, or wasted by love and fear that battled for years over the characters of those who were dearest to them, they had crept to the meetings, and felt the strength of the faith that was present, and cried to be lifted upon it as their last chance. Drummond sought out many of these, and was sought by many more. He worked hard in the inquiry room, but shy men, who would not stand up in a meeting, nor enter an inquiry room, waited for him by the doors as he came out, or waylaid him in the street, or wrote, asking him for an interview. He took trouble with every one of them, as much trouble and interest as if each one was a large meeting. His sympathy, his leisure from himself, his strength, won their confidence, as his personal charm on the platform had first stirred their hope, and he thus became acquainted with the secrets of hundreds of lives. Men felt he was not a voice merely, but a friend, and on his arm they were lifted up. He was always hopeful about the most hopeless, picked out some good points in the worst, and sent a man away feeling that he was trusted once more, not only by this friend, but by Christ, by God." [39]

The publication of his book *Natural Law in the Spiritual World* [40] and its immediate popularity made him even more in demand as a counsellor for those who sought spiritual guidance. He followed a very heavy schedule and, when he did have a free evening, it was usually taken up by "inquirers, of whom there are always one or two somewhere." He wrote, in one letter, of scheduling interviews until eleven o'clock, and one of his hosts tells of his having worked all night with men in trouble. Wherever he went he was sought out by people who had heard about him. His ministry to individuals became world-wide, extending to the continent, the United States and even to Australia. While conducting meetings at Melbourne and Sydney, he did much personal work; many hours a day were given to private interviews, and he continued to receive correspondence from young Australians seeking spiritual guidance after he had returned to Scotland. He was interested in every type of personality, especially the handicapped or unfortunate, and almost any sincere story of distress could consume the time that had been allotted to other things. Often he declined an attractive speaking engagement to go and encourage some individual.[41]

It is difficult to determine the reason for his success. If anything, it was a combination of attitudes. The naturalness of his personality, the earnestness of his manner, his courtesy and sympathy drew men to him and, perhaps, account for something of his power over them. Marcus Dods, in a memorial address on the Sunday following his funeral, said, "To anyone who had need of him, he seemed to have no concerns of his own to attend to, he was wholly at the disposal of those whom he could help." [42] He had a genuine interest in others and a deep faith in the sacredness of human nature; in spite of all the grossness of human nature with which he was confronted, he felt it was capable and worthy of redemption. Men intuitively felt that they could trust him with their deepest problems. George Adam Smith said, "He never betrayed, either on or off the platform, one secret of the many hundreds" that were confided to him.[43] The influence of such a personality attracted men to him and drew from them confessions they had never felt free to express to any other man. The methods which he advocated were in accord with those which were emphasized much later, after the development of the new psychology had exerted considerable influence, such as his suggestions that the counsellor should let them "talk . . . clean out of themselves." [44] Very few men have ever entered into the problems of so many individual lives.

He was peculiarly effective with students. He had successful missions at Smith, Wellesley, Williams, Amherst, Harvard, Dartmouth, Yale, Philadelphia, Princeton and the Medical Schools in New York. One student said, "We could tell him as we could not tell others, the worst about ourselves,—the worst, and just as easily also, the best, our ideals, and ambitions, of which men are often as ashamed to speak as they are about their sins." [45] In Edinburgh his meetings were crowded to capacity but after the meeting he was often seen late at night walking the street with some student, wrestling with intellectual or moral difficulties, or found two or three flights up in an informal discussion in the students' quarters.

He seldom spoke of his own struggles, but, as George Adam Smith said, we assume that he had them. He could not have shown the interest and insight into the problems of others without knowing something of it from personal experience. Smith points out that he was so absorbed in his interest in others that he forgot about himself.[46] He was afflicted with a malignant disease of the bones and the spine which caused him extreme suffering. At times he could not move so much as his head for the pain. Even so, while in this condition, he maintained his interest in world events, in politics and literature, but, especially, in his friends, and on more than one occasion he brought encouragement and counsel to others.

Chapter IV

THE PROTESTANT PASTOR IN AMERICA

Such men as those we have mentioned in the preceding section made a great record. They helped countless individuals in the crises and difficult moments of their lives; they served as an inspiration and a guide to other pastors who were not so well known but who were also carrying on a faithful ministry to individuals. While these men were fulfilling their duties in Europe, there were others in America, equally devoted and equally successful. One of the greatest was Horace Bushnell. He spent all his ministry in one parish, but his influence, through his writing and lecturing, became world-wide. During his long pastorate he developed a deep concern for his people which they, in turn, felt for him. Bushnell was a man who knew the meaning of struggle and suffering from personal experience. Late in life he published a book entitled *Moral Use of Dark Things*. Four dark things which he had to face and use were doubt, sorrow, unfair opposition and poor health. Although he was a man of profound faith, he went through an intellectual struggle so intense that he referred to it as a period of "agonies of mental darkness and confusion concerning God," [1] and once said that his religious life was utterly gone. The death of his little boy and infant daughter influenced his whole life and character. From this experience he said he learned more of experimental religion than from all his life before. Because of his theological position he was much misunderstood, bitterly opposed and unfairly condemned. As a result, he felt very much alone. Ministers in his own denomination and in his own city refused to exchange pulpits with him. In a letter to a friend he said, "I know what it is to have the purest motives, most fervent prayers, and most incessant labors misapprehended and misrepresented." [2] Along with all this was a life-long struggle with ill health. He suffered from a chronic bronchitis and frequently had to leave his work and seek a warmer climate. For years his work was done in spite of pain and suffering and a cough which prevented any continued sleep. Thus "he could live in the struggles of others because he knew the meaning of struggle himself." [3]

As with Watson, his pastoral duties were not easy for him but he fulfilled them faithfully and well and, as the years progressed and his own experiences deepened, they became more effective. He visited all of his people once a year and more often if occasion demanded. His concern for the sick and the distressed is revealed in one letter which was written by a member of Dr. Bushnell's church, a Mr. Thomas Winship, "In our time of trial and affliction, Dr. Bushnell would, if at home, be sure to be on hand; and those seasons, sometimes of long continuance, were frequent with me. My daughter, after several severe illnesses, was at last a confirmed invalid, confined to her bed for nearly nine years. When at home, he used always to call upon her every week, usually on Monday morning. It did not seem to me possible for any man to manifest more tender sympathy and care for her spiritual interests than he did. He was always faithful, always true, to me and mine." [4] Such faithfulness and regularity were displayed with all such cases. Another chronic invalid was visited each week at the same day and hour; she came to expect it, always prepared for his visit and was never disappointed. Once, while visiting a blind man, he found the room chilly, for no one had been found to set up his stove. Before he left, he put the stove in place and had the fire going. Even when he was the busiest with his writing and other responsibilities, he did not neglect this work and in some letters he expressed the wish that he could devote more time to it.

It was Dr. Bushnell's custom to spend one evening every

week in the church office, at which time he was available to anyone who might wish to consult him on any matter. It was noted that young men, in particular, took advantage of this opportunity.[5] There was one man who came to see him every week, seeking aid in overcoming a bad temper. There was another whom he tried to free from a morbid conscience. There was a woman who was having great difficulty about religious questions; there was a friend who sought his advice about a nervous and flighty child. These are but a few examples of many who sought his help. His daughter tells of an old Negro who came with a "message from the Lord." [6] He was received in the same gracious manner as all the rest.

Like others whose names became well known, he received many appeals for advice and guidance through the mail. His daughter, in her *Life and Letters of Horace Bushnell*, includes many examples of the voluminous correspondence he carried on with people who were in trouble. There are letters of advice, letters of consolation, letters of encouragement. There are letters to those who were sick, to those who were in pain, and to those who were facing death. There is one account of a correspondence he maintained for several years with a stranger in a distant place, a man he had never seen, who had "appealed to him for the secret of strength and peace." [7] A study of these letters would repay anyone who faces the responsibility of bringing others consolation and hope.

His interest in people was exhibited in his preaching. It was said that he lived in an age when men usually approached life through doctrine but he, rather, approached doctrine through life. He preached, Theodore Munger said, "always to life." For some time he maintained an informal "Meeting of Inquiry" on Sunday nights. Questions which people had on their minds were dropped into a box at the door and then were answered by the minister from the pulpit.

His most significant contribution, and that for which he is best known, was his justly famous book *Christian Nurture*, published first in 1847.[8] It was a protest against the prevalent Calvinism which allowed little or no place in the church for children and which considered all human nature as depraved. His thesis was that the child should grow up a Christian and "never know himself as being otherwise." The book was not only a new emphasis in theology; it did much to influence the educational psychology of his time and was a strong influence which turned the attention of the church toward a more adequate training of youth. The book truly had a far-reaching influence. A psychologist, writing many years later, said that his contribution to the idea of conversion did much for the mental health of adolescents.[9] He pointed out the fact that the family and the community and the nation as well, all furnished an environment which determined the character of souls and were, therefore, within the realm of the church's legitimate interest.

Much space could be devoted to the ideas presented in this most significant book. Many of them were far ahead of their day and are being emphasized now, due to the influence of modern psychology. It was some time before Freud that Bushnell said, referring to a child, "more . . . is done or lost . . . in the first three years of his life than in all his years of discipline afterwards." Therefore he advises, "Let every Christian father and mother understand, when their child is three years old, that they have done more than half of all they will ever do for his character." [10] Thus he stresses, again and again, the significance of the attitudes of the parents, the atmosphere of the house which the child takes over unconsciously. He said, "If the child is handled fretfully, scolded, jerked, or simply laid aside unaffectionately, in no warmth of motherly gentleness, it feels the sting of just that which is felt towards it; and so it is angered by anger, irritated by irritation, fretted by fretfulness; having thus impressed just that kind of impatience or ill-nature which is felt towards it, and growing faithfully into the bad mold offered, as by a fixed law. There is great importance, in this manner, even in the handling of infancy. If it is unchristian, it will beget unchristian states, or impressions. If it is gentle, even patient and loving, it prepares a mood and temper like its own. There is scarcely room to doubt, that all crabbed, hateful, resentful, passionate, ill-natured characters; all most even, lovely, firm and true, are prepared, in a great degree, by the handling of the nursery." [11] This quotation is given at some length but it reveals how practical in nature and how modern in tone his thought was. Other passages could be selected which point out the effect on the child if it lives in an atmosphere of anxiety, extreme nervousness or fear; or such a statement as this, "Nothing wounds a child more fatally than to see he is not trusted." [12] All in all, it was a significant book which has had a remarkable influence on American Christianity and which reveals the practical insight which Bushnell had into the meaning of human nature and the development of human personality.

Another book which reveals his interest in the problems of personality is his *Moral Use of Dark Things*,[13] in which he is willing to face its deepest issues although he recognizes that with some things—such as dealing with the problem of pain—he can offer no complete solution. He does attempt to offer, insofar as possible, some practical suggestions that may be useful. He also recognizes the effect of the physical on the mental attitude and, also, the effect of the mental attitude on one's physical condition. He said, "There is a pain which belongs to the mind itself." [14] In a chapter on "Insanity," he states that all men are more or less abnormal; the wise man is one who recognizes it and understands himself well enough to make due allowance for it. "These frequent exhibitions of insanity appear to be quite indispensable, as revelations carried to their extremity of something that is working more latently and gently in us all. We are not all insane, but we are in a kind of incipiency that must be recognized, if we are to exactly understand ourselves." [15]

Finally, because of continued ill health, he had to present his resignation, in spite of his people's protest that he should reconsider, or maintain some partial connection with them. In his farewell sermon he said, "With you thus for twenty-six years, in all the tenderest issues and subtlest windings of your life; by you in your disasters and troubles, and in your holidays of success; close enough to you to feel the touch of your anxieties and tremblings for your children, and the throb of your private thanksgivings on account of them; at your weddings; by you in your sick-chambers and your funerals; with you in your struggles under and with and out of your sins; sometimes' crossing you a little and sometimes a little crossed by you,— with no other effect than that pulling the cord has tightened it, —in this manner my ministry among you has been a kind of course in trust and well—experimented affection; a good element for courage and growth, an element, at once, of stimulus and rest for the heart." [16]

This same concern was also in evidence in others. Theodore Parker was best known as a reformer but his biographer includes this paragraph, which reveals a great many things that must have taken place. "In the privacy of the study many sorrows and anxieties were poured into a patient ear; many failures were confessed and many burdens were relieved. We read of a husband and wife going to him separately with their domestic trouble and finding out long after that both had got the help that made them one again from the same friend; . . . The book, the pleasure, the sermon was put aside to answer any human cry." [17]

Henry Ward Beecher was especially noted as an orator and a preacher. He did not do pastoral work in the customary sense and he did very little house-to-house calling. However, he did have a "combination of sympathy and strength" that "drew to him the troubled and distraught." [18] He held a prayer meeting every Friday evening which lasted just one hour, but after the meeting he would stay in the front of the room to answer questions or to converse with those who were seeking counsel, either for themselves or others. If the situation was a private one, he would sit in a pew by the individual until he had heard the story. Then he would give advice if possible, but often would make an appointment for another interview when more time would be available. He often referred them to assistants or other counsellors, both men and women, in whom he had confidence. Speaking to young ministers, he urged them to study human nature. He said, "You must go into a parish and say to yourself, 'There is not a man, woman or child within the bounds of this parish to whom I am not beholden. . . . I am to get thoroughly acquainted with them. . . . I am to prepare them to hear me preach by gaining their confidence outside of the church and pulpit!' You must meet them in their everyday life, in their ruggedness and selfishness. You will find one man a laughing stock in one neighborhood, and another as an odious man in another. Nobody can be a laughing stock or odious to you, you are like physicians who attend the inmates of a hospital; it matters not to them from what cause the patients are lying hurt and wounded there. Sick men belong to the physician's care, and he must take care of them. Do not pick out the beautiful and good, or those who suit you. Select from your parish those who NEED you most, and if you cannot be patient with them, if you cannot bring your soul to be a sacrifice for others and bear with them, how can you make them understand what Jesus Christ did for the world?" [19]

One of the greatest—if not the greatest—preachers ever produced in America was Phillips Brooks. He was equally great as a pastor. In Allen's massive two-volume work, *The Life and Letters of Phillips Brooks*, are many references to Brooks' deep sympathy and amazing success in dealing with people. Dr. Allen writes, "In his large parishes, as well as in the outer world, he was constantly confronted with the problem of sorrow and suffering. His own personality attracted as by a magnet those who were in trouble. He suffered with them through the immeasurable tenderness of his own soul and his vast outflow of sympathy. What the meaning of it all might be, in a world which was beautiful, which God had created and loved, was the problem which haunted him. He did not undertake to solve it by any dogmatic principle. He waited for the growing light. But of one thing he was sure, that the only consolation was in God." [20] He had a great love for humanity and it was said he "had a genius for friendship." The power of his own personality is legendary. One of the most familiar stories of Brooks tells of the man who went to see him about a certain problem and came away so obviously relieved that his friends asked him what solution he had received. The man's reply is often quoted. He said, in effect, that he had not received a definite solution to his problem; that what he had received was more; it was the "contagion of a triumphant personality."

He spent his mornings in his study and his afternoons calling on his parishioners and the sick. He went to all but had a special concern for the poor and unfortunate. Allen speaks of the "healing power he carried with his presence" [21] when he went through the wards of a hospital. "A mysterious influence seemed to go forth from him for good, for strength and for life, even when he sat down in silence by the bedside and no need was felt for words." [22] He apparently practiced "creative listening" that is now stressed by the authorities on work with the sick and distressed. "When people were in trouble he would go and sit with them without saying anything, and let them talk." [23] Bishop Lawrence tells of one particular parish call which Brooks described to him years later, for it caused much comment in the congregation at the time. In Brooks' words, "I gained more people and loyalty by one call than in any other way. I found a young mother, tired out and almost ill with the care of her sick baby. I told her to go out, get some fresh air, see her friends, and I would look after the baby. She went and, I suppose, told of it afterwards." [24]

As with Drummond and others who reveal an understanding of life, countless people sought him out, often after the services, but more often at home. He gave himself to the demands of people without reserve. The Reverend Leighton Parks, who spent several weeks with him on one occasion, was astounded at the number of callers that began coming early in the morning. Out of curiosity, he began to keep a record and found he averaged one every five minutes. But Brooks refused to seclude himself or to establish hours, for he said it might not be convenient for some people to come at the hour he might set. It was a common situation to find someone in the reception room, another in the dining room, while he would be talking to a third in the study.[25] His house was described as a refuge for anyone in trouble. Bishop Lawrence spoke of the rectory as a place where "friends, parishioners, and seekers for advice, help, jobs, or the truth, or inspiration and comfort, found him. He was open at any and all hours to them all. How he ever wrote his sermons was a constant wonder to his friends." [26] Allen states, "People from far or near, in critical moments when the issues of life were in the balance, thought of Phillips Brooks. It made no difference whether they were connected with the church in any of its forms or not, whether they knew him or not, his name carried with it some magical appeal; they called for his aid; and it must be said he never disappointed them." [27] When these people would come, Brooks would drop whatever he had at hand, make them feel at ease quickly and they would proceed with the individual's problem as though Brooks had nothing else to do and that was for him (as at the moment it was) the one thing in the world he was the most interested in.

There are many stories of the people who were strengthened, whose spirits and hopes were renewed by his sermons or his influence. "He had a great gift for inspiring people who were depressed or who had lost heart for their work. A word from him would send them back to their tasks again, with renewed energy." [28] He was often called on by other clergymen for counsel in their own lives or in their work and they would tell him of their difficulties and of their problems. Parents and pastors of every denomination wrote him innumerable letters requesting that he look after some young person from their home or parish who had gone to Boston—nor did he neglect such commissions, for he knew what they meant to those who sent them.[29] He surprised a physician by calling at the hospital on a colored man who had been injured. It was known that Brooks was due at a reception, but Brooks said that the man had sent for him and he therefore could not send an assistant.[30] A workingman in one of the suburbs of Boston was informed that it was absolutely necessary that he have a serious operation the next day and that there was only a chance that he would recover. He and his wife had only the evening before them and they decided to spend it in going to see Phillips Brooks, although neither of them knew him personally. Mr. Brooks received them, as they had felt he would. He reassured them and promised to be with them the next day.[31] If at all possible, he always answered the calls in person, and "wherever he went his personality carried power, courage and hopefulness." [32]

Brooks preached regularly at Appleton Chapel in Harvard and then for three hours he consulted with the students in the chaplain's rooms at Wadsworth House. The students took quick advantage of this privilege and came in increasing numbers. One undergraduate said of Brooks, "More than any man I have ever known, Phillips Brooks possessed that which commanded instant trust, complete confidence." [33]

In his preaching he had the individual in mind. Lord Bryce said, "He spoke to his audience as a man might speak to a friend." [34] There are many references to the way his sermons brought consolation, faith and hope to many who found life difficult. Many of his subjects were what was later called "Life Problem Preaching," such as "The Purpose and Use of Comfort," "The Withheld Completions of Life," or "The Consolation of God." [35] The publication of such a volume of sermons, which was widely circulated, was followed by a flood of letters seeking guidance, comfort and counsel. Like others we have mentioned, he carried on an extensive correspondence giving counsel, consolation or encouragement, as the case might require.

One man said to him, "I cannot understand how you, who have such perfect health and happiness, can know so much about the condition of those who have neither." [36] The truth of the matter was that Brooks knew the meaning of struggle from his own experience. When he was but a young man his ambition was to be a teacher but he failed. The humiliation and sense of shame was so intense that his father had to make excuses for him as he refused to see his friends. All his life there was a note of loneliness and sadness in the background of his life. He was a keen student of human nature; while walking the streets, attending a social function, or in a meeting, he was observing and noting the life about him.[37] It was claimed that he made what could almost be called a scientific study of the art of consolation. He neglected no source of information but, most of all, he studied his own soul.

His concern for people never left him. When he was finally elevated to the bishopric he expressed concern that he should not have to discontinue the work with individuals which he had enjoyed so much in the pastorate. Referring to the many people who needed help, he said, "I hope that there will be a good many of these who in one way or another will find me out and will give me the privilege of hearing them and helping them." [38] He need have expressed no concern. They continued to seek his help "in a steady stream" from morning until late at night. When the day for his funeral came his body was placed in the vestibule of Trinity Church at eight o'clock in the morning. A continuous line, numbering many thousands, filed past, and there were many thousands still waiting when the hour for the service arrived. After the service another was held in the open air for the thousands who could not get in, then the body was carried by Harvard students through Harvard yard while the students and citizens stood in solemn silence and watched the procession pass. One wonders how many of those who viewed that procession had at one time been in his study or had been visited by him in the hospital or helped by him in some fashion in their hour of need.

PART II

FROM THE TWENTIETH CENTURY
TO THE FIRST WORLD WAR

Chapter V

THE NEW PSYCHOLOGY

One of the many manifestations of the late nineteenth and early twentieth century was the scientific mode of thought which characterized the intellectual world. One of the primary features of this development was the appearance of the new psychology. Psychology, prior to this time, had been subject to philosophy and had been considered as a branch of philosophy; now it emerged claiming to be a science in its own right. More than any factor or development since the Reformation, this had a profound influence on the more thoughtful clergy and religious leaders. It necessitated a re-thinking and a re-evaluating of their historic function of the "cure of souls" in the light of the new insights and discoveries that were being uncovered. An adjustment to the findings of science was nothing new to the church. Religion had had a long life of conflict and adjustment to the findings of the scientists, as President White has well shown in his monumental two volumes, *The Warfare of Science with Theology*.[1] But psychology was different. It invaded the very area of the soul; it dealt intimately with the inner life of the mind and personality. There was no evading of the issue. As Harrison Elliott expressed it, "the fact is that the development of psychology has more bearing upon religion than any other scientific advance." [2]

Of course, it cannot be said that psychology is a product of either the nineteenth or the twentieth century. Its history can be traced back to the early Greeks as is done in any valid history of psychology.[3] It has been truly said that psychology is the oldest and the youngest of the sciences, or as Ebbinghaus

put it, it has a long past but only a short history.[4] Men such
as Plato and Aristotle, Descartes, Locke, Berkley, Hume, Kant
and many others, who worked primarily as philosophers, made
important contributions to psychology. It is beyond the scope
of this volume to trace or even list the essence of their thought.
While these men did have a profound and far-reaching influence
on the thought of religion, they did not influence the practical
work of the pastor nearly as much as the men who came later
and who worked strictly as psychologists. It was in 1879 that
Wilhelm Wundt at Leipzig founded the first official psychological laboratory in the world. This laboratory was of supreme
importance because it became at once the center of experimental research in the new psychology and because of many
of the students who were trained there.

In America, William James at Harvard was the pioneer and
father of the new psychology. No other individual had a greater
influence in the popularizing of psychology than did he. Prior
to his time there were others who had written on psychological
subjects, but nothing that equaled the work of James in quality
or even touched him in popular appeal. It has often been said
that William James wrote psychology like a novelist while his
brother wrote novels like a psychologist. His *Principles of
Psychology* has been called the most interesting book on psychology ever written. William James came from a family of
great learning; he traveled widely, and had a rich and varied
education. He finally received an M.D. degree but never practiced medicine. He became very much interested in the physiology of the nervous system and, in the late seventies, in connection with his classes, he began experiments, and, as a result,
according to some, he can be credited with the first psychological laboratory in America. In fact, this very informal work
in his laboratories antedated Wundt's. He was appointed assistant professor of philosophy at Harvard in 1880, and in
1889, professor of psychology. It was his *Principles of Psychology*,[5] which he published in 1890, that gained such immediate

attention. He had intended to write this book in two years, but it finally took him twelve years to complete it. Professor Boring said of it, "No other psychological treatise in the English language has in the modern period had such a wide and persistent influence." [6] This book was followed by a *Briefer Course*,[7] which contained much of the larger work condensed, and his *Talks to Teachers on Psychology*.[8] His *Varieties of Religious Experience*, his contribution to the psychology of religion, will be described in connection with that field. James shifted his emphasis from psychology to philosophy and his later writings were in that field, but no man has had a greater influence on the development of psychology in America than he.

The writings of James were widely read by the clergy. His chapter on "Habit," which was included in his *Principles*, *Briefer Course* and *Talks to Teachers*, became the source of illustrations in many sermons. His article, "The Energies of Men," which contains the thesis that there are sources of energy within men on which they can draw in time of need, was similarly used. In this article he made his famous statement that most men do not live within sight of their limitations. This article, which James said he wrote in a few hours' time, had a wider response than any of his other writing. Elwood Worcester credited it with saving his own life and, with James' permission, distributed several thousand copies through Immanuel Church in Boston.[9] His theory of the "stream of consciousness," the power of attention, and what has been termed the James-Lange theory of the emotions all had a great influence.

James was closely akin to the clergy in his motives and his general attitude. When asked what was his chief desire in his work, he replied, "To find a balm for the human soul." [10] William James' thinking came as the result of an intense personal struggle. While still a young man he suffered an almost complete breakdown resulting in backache, insomnia, eye trouble, deep depression, inability to work and study and even, at times, to read. He confided in no one and suffered intensely from shame, insecurity, doubt and fear. This continued over a period of some twelve years. His letters, edited by his son, reveal times when he seriously considered suicide, some of the sections even being deleted because of the depth of despondency and despair expressed.

Dr. Norman Cameron, in an address at the Centenary of James' birth, described the extent and severity of these struggles. Then he continued, "This is the picture of a young adult in serious difficulties with life. The celebrated autobiographical passage speaks of a 'general depression of spirits about my prospects' and of 'horrible fear of my own existence.' After recalling the appearance of a psychiatric case he had once seen he 'became a mass of quivering fear,' the world changed for him, and he awoke every morning with a horrible dread. For months he was unable to go into the dark alone; he dreaded to be left alone at all; he wondered how other people could live so unconscious of the 'pit of insecurity beneath the surface of life.' His ultimate improvement—'Then so hypochondriacal and now with my mind so cleared up and restored to sanity'— he ascribed partly to what he found in Renouvier, to his new attitude toward the doctrine of free will, and to the conclusion that mental disorder need not necessarily mean brain disease. Nevertheless, even when he was thirty-six years old, he still spoke of himself as suffering from a sense of his own inadequacy to his tasks, 'both intellectual and corporeal!' " [11]

That William James was able to master his own difficulties, and attain the freedom of personality that he did, has been an inspiration to many people and, of course, did much to mold and temper James' own attitudes. As Dr. Cameron stated in the same address, "I believe the world owes a great deal to these personal misfortunes of William James. . . . James was thrown heavily upon his own resources; his incapacities and frustrations at such a time gave him an intense and intimate appreciation of the deepest philosophical and religious problems; his illness clearly developed and deepened the bed in which the stream of his philosophic life was to flow." [12] James was one of the first to recognize the value of studying the abnormal to gain an understanding of the normal. He felt that the morbid and the unusual had much to contribute to general psychology. However, he never limited himself to the abnormal; he never limited himself to anything; he was intensely interested in everything and ruled out nothing as impossible until he had first closely examined it. He cannot be confined to a system; he never founded a school, but he will always remain one of the most influential and unique personalities in the history of American psychology.

The other name that had a large influence in early American psychology was that of G. Stanley Hall. He was a contemporary of James and studied under him for a while, but they were different in temperament and drew farther apart and carried on their work quite independently. Hall was a country boy who was dissatisfied with the farm and who vowed he would be something. His driving ambition never left him. With his mother's approval and his father's opposition, he decided to go to college and prepare for the ministry. While at college he became interested in philosophy, especially in John Stuart Mill, and developed a fascination for the theory of evolution that remained with him all his life. Leaving college he studied theology at Union Theological Seminary but tells in his *Confessions* that when he preached a sermon in the class of homiletics, the professor, instead of making his customary suggestions, knelt and prayed for his soul.[13] It was Henry Ward Beecher who advised him to go to Europe and study philosophy. In fact, he arranged with a wealthy member of his parish to make the funds available so he could do so. He returned from Europe, took his degree in theology and preached in a little country church for ten weeks. Then he became a tutor in a private family and later a professor in Antioch College.

It was the appearance of Wundt's *Physiologische Psychol-*

ogie that turned Hall's attention to psychology. He wanted to go to Europe again at once and study under Wundt himself. He was side-tracked by an offer to teach English at Harvard which he did for two years. It was here that he had his relationship with James and received what is considered the first doctorate in philosophy in the new psychology. Then he went on to Germany where he became Wundt's first American student. He also studied under Fechner, Helmholtz, von Kries, and Kronecker. When he returned to America he was given a lectureship at the new graduate university, John Hopkins, and later he became head of the department of psychology. It was here that he founded the first genuine psychological laboratory in America in 1883. In 1887, he founded the first psychological journal in America, the "American Journal of Psychology." Here he had such students as Dewey, Cattell, Sanford, Burnham, Jastrow and others. Hall was blessed with good health and carried on a terrific schedule. He was interested in everything and, like James, excluded nothing from his investigations. He visited poor houses, asylums, morgues, meetings of revolutionists and eccentric groups, just to understand human nature. He urged his students to work till a "second breath" came, for he felt that out of such efforts great discoveries are made.

While things were at their height at John Hopkins, Hall received the unexpected offer to become president of the new Clark University at Worcester, Massachusetts. Believing in the possibilities of such a venture, he accepted, a decision that was to cause him much unhappiness later. At Clark he founded the "Pedagogical Seminary," the second psychological journal in America. The American Psychological Association was organized in his study in 1892 and he served as its first president, being elected for the second time in 1924. The only other man to serve twice was William James. Hall is generally credited with being the one who developed the questionnaire, a method of psychological investigation peculiarly American. Here he completed his famous work, *Adolescence: Its Psychology, and*

Its Relations to Physiology, Anthropology, Sociology, Sex, Crime, Religion, and Education.[14] Following the publication of this book Hall became more and more interested in child study. His biographer said of him, "He strove to understand the history of mind that he might understand the possibilities of a single child." [15] He did much to introduce psycho-analysis to America, sponsoring a conference at Clark which was attended by Freud, Jung, Brill, Meyer and many others. It was here that Freud delivered his famous *Introductory Lectures on Psycho-Analysis,* which marked the first real impact in America. Hall was one of the first in America to recognize the significance of Freud's psychology and he accepted many of his doctrines.

His books were well received and, through such activities as those mentioned above, he achieved rather wide recognition, causing many to approach him about their personal problems. Literally thousands wrote him seeking advice and counsel, feeling that here was one who could understand their problems. From time to time he burned these letters so that they would not fall into the hands of someone after his death. Of course, he also counseled his own students. In his study he "had examined students privately, by the hour, probing delicately into the secret places of their minds. . . . Here he had listened to confessions from hundreds of troubled men and women." [16]

Like James, he knew the meaning of suffering and frustration from personal experience. As a boy he was very shy and introverted but, to a large extent, he mastered this handicap, although late in life he confessed that he was never able to do justice to the spirit of good fellowship that he really felt. While at Clark his wife and child died in a tragic accident in the home. After this tragedy he lost himself in work. His second wife became demented, a source of much sorrow, care and difficulty. The story of his disappointment at Clark is too extensive to be included here. The funds which he had been led to expect would be available were not forthcoming; the whole enterprise was involved in much misunderstanding, frustration and some bitterness. As an old man he was even driven out of the library he had built, but he defended the man who caused it to be done and even included him in his will. In the midst of all these difficulties he showed real courage and never lost sight of his search for truth. When he finally faced the problem of retirement, he met it by writing *Senescence*,[17] an attempt to understand old age psychologically.

Like James, Hall founded no school and established no system. He admitted that his life had been a series of "crazes." He would become interested in some idea that he thought had promise, study and read exhaustively about it, present it in a book or a lecture, and move on to something else. In spite of all his "foundings," his greatest contribution is recognized as his capacity for stimulating in others an interest and a willingness to work. He died still dreaming of books he was never to write.

There were other men who also pioneered in psychology and made significant contributions in these early days. George Trumbull Ladd, of Yale, came into psychology by way of the ministry. He graduated from Andover Theological Seminary and preached for ten years in the Middle West before he went to Bowdoin College in 1879 and later to Yale. He founded one of the early psychological laboratories at Yale and wrote one of the first textbooks. Laboratories began to spring up throughout the country; many other journals and societies were instituted and, by the 1890's, professors and departments of psychology were added to most schools. Due to the support of the universities, experimental and applied psychology began to develop very rapidly in America. Edward L. Thorndike, who had formerly worked in James' laboratory and who took his doctor's degree at Columbia in 1898, marked the beginning of the modern laboratory approach to the problems of learning and habit formation, with his studies in animal psychology.[18] Later he worked almost entirely in the field of educational psychology. Pavlov, the great Russian scientist, began his famous experiments on the conditioned reflex in 1904. Pavlov's famous experiment with the dog began with a well-known and frequently observed occurrence, the fact that saliva drips from a dog's mouth as it waits in anticipation of food. Pavlov, however, worked with greatest care and precautions. He worked in specially prepared, windowless, sound-proof rooms, built of walls of turf two feet thick. His success in conditioning the dog so that the saliva appeared at the ringing of a bell is familiar to all, and the significance of his experiments are recognized by all students of psychology.[19]

Meanwhile important developments were taking place at the University of Chicago. In 1894, James Rowland Angell, although only twenty-five years of age, went to the new university as head of the department of psychology. The same year John Dewey went to Chicago as professor of philosophy. Dewey had studied with Hall at Johns Hopkins, and Angell had studied with James at Harvard. Due primarily to the influence of these two men, the University of Chicago became a center of psychological study and was instrumental in the forming of a new school of psychology, known as functionalism. Advocates of functionalism, from the first, were interested in utilities, joined hands with common sense, and were interested in mental processes, not merely as contents but as operations. They faced and asked such questions as, "What do mental processes accomplish?" Such a psychology could not avoid questions of value and had much in accord with the thoughts and purposes of the ministry. It produced many books that were to prove of real significance such as Angell's, *Psychology*, or Dewey's *Human Nature and Conduct*.[20] When Angell left Chicago the department was carried on by Harvey Carr who continued in the same tradition.

In 1903, John Watson, who was later to achieve so much fame as the founder of the rival school of Behaviorism, received the first doctor's degree in psychology ever granted from the University of Chicago. The extreme views of Watson and the behaviorists need no elaboration here. They attempt to make psychology a science in the strictest sense of the word; they discarded and rejected the notion of mind and consciousness or mental processes completely and unequivocally as a superstition and unfit for scientific investigation. Man was seen as an animal species, as one among many species who must be studied as a living organism reacting to his whole natural environment, both physical and social. All was considered to be stimulus and response. "Laryngeal habits" was the definition of thinking. It need not be described further. The appearance and development of behaviorism has a part here because it attracted so much attention from the clergy and because so much of it was in such direct and open opposition to everything for which the church stood. If it was right, the church was wrong. There could be no reconciling of the two. It did arouse much opposition, and stimulated much new investigation by the clergy into the meaning of human nature. This does not mean that there was no value to be derived from behaviorism and its concept of the C-R, some recognized, but as a total system it had to be opposed.[21]

Another development of these years that was to prove of considerable value was the development of psychological tests. In 1904, the French Minister of Public Instruction appointed a commission to formulate methods for improving the instruction of feeble-minded children. The most outstanding member of the commission was Alfred Binet, director of the psychological laboratory at the Sorbonne. As an outgrowth of this study, together with Theophile Simon, he published his first scale for the measurement of intelligence in 1905. Binet developed his tests on the principle of estimating intelligence by measuring the combined effects of attention, imagination, judgment and reasoning by the ability to perform certain fairly complex tasks. Then by giving them to a group he determined how many tests and answers to questions a normal child of a certain age could accomplish succesfully. In 1908, he revised his scale and arranged it into groups. Here, for the first time, was used the concept of mental age irrespective of chronological age. In 1911 he revised and enlarged his tests again. This scale has been continually studied and has been revised many times since and is used all over the world. The revision of L. M. Terman of Stanford University, made in 1916, is the most widely accepted in America. It was Terman who introduced the expression, "intelligence quotient" commonly referred to as "I.Q.," which is the ratio of the mental age to the chronological age. Since then many other tests and similar approaches have been developed, not only of intelligence but of aptitudes, personality and emotional stability. Their influence for all who deal with human nature has been very significant.

MEDICAL PSYCHOLOGY

The development of medical psychology influenced the ministry even more than the regular academic psychology discussed thus far. This was certainly true in the more practical area, the actual techniques of dealing with people. Psychiatry and medical psychology were developed by men who were motivated by very practical purposes as they sought to meet definite life problems on which they were consulted. In the main, it can be said that this science developed independently of academic psychology. General psychology had a background of libraries and laboratories, it was associated with the lecture platform and the academic world. Psychiatry and psycho-analysis grew out of clinical practice and medical experience. This, too, has a long history. Gregory Zilboorg in *A History of Medical Psychology* [22] fills 484 pages with the developments of psychiatry before he comes to the work of Freud. It is shown that very early in the development of primitive man, among Siberian tribes, in China and the Malay Archipelago, a form of hypnotism was used as a treatment for the sick. Hippocrates had a very rational classification of mental diseases, while Asclepiades, as early as

150 B.C., differentiated between delusions and hallucinations and used music for therapeutic purposes. Weyer, in the sixteenth century, was the first physician whose major interest was in terms of mental illnesses and thus foreshadowed psychiatry as a medical specialty. He did as much as any one man to liberate the treatment of the mentally ill from political prejudice and superstition. Langermann, as early as 1797, divided mental diseases into functional and organic, and insisted on the psychological origin of physical diseases. He thus stressed the need of the development of psycho-therapy. Ferrus, in the middle of the nineteenth century, was the first to inaugurate what today is called occupational therapy. There were many others whose stories reveal a genuine effort to be of service to the mentally sick, and often a real understanding.

In America the story would have to go clear back to Dr. Benjamin Rush of Philadelphia, signer of the Declaration of Independence and generally credited with the title of Father of American Psychiatry. He spent over thirty years of service to the mentally ill, he was the first to attempt a systematized study of mental disease and wrote the first general volume on psychiatry in America, a book which was accepted as standard for over seventy years.[23] Many of his methods were crude and would even be considered cruel from a modern point of view. He utilized a gyrator and a tranquilizer which he invented. He frequently used blood letting and emetics and advised the use of fear. Even so, in comparison with his day, he was far more humane than the average and much ahead of his time as to general procedure. He did more than any one individual to cut away superstition and ignorance and point medical psychology in the direction of a scientific basis. The first organization in the United States was the Association of Medical Superintendents of American Institutions, formed by thirteen Superintendents of Mental Institutions in 1844. Later the title was changed to the American Psychiatric Institution. Also in 1844 was established the "American Journal of Insanity," the first journal in the English language devoted to medical psychology.

It was in France that the major emphasis was upon psychiatry and the predominant interest was in abnormal phenomena. No story is more dramatic than is the story of Pinel's efforts to take the chains off the inmates of the Asylum of Bicêtre. Pinel had been influenced to study mental disease because of a tragedy that occurred to a young friend of his. This young man suffered a mental breakdown, rushed into the woods and his body was later discovered torn to pieces by wolves. Pinel began an intensive study of all that had ever been written on mental disease and, as early as the 1790's, was telling the world that the insane were not demon-possessed but sick. The conditions that existed in the asylum when Pinel took it over are almost indescribable. The lunatics who were considered as desperate, dangerous animals, worse than criminals, were lying about chained, raving, tortured. They were unkempt, filthy, nails long, hair and beards matted, driven to violence by the cruelty and neglect to which they were subjected. Pinel was himself a very small, shy, retiring personality yet, against the advice and warning of all his contemporaries, he stood in the midst of a group of "violent maniacs" and ordered the locksmith to strike off their chains. Before he was granted permission to remove their chains he was told that he was mad himself for wanting to unchain these "animals." Pinel contended that much of their violence was due to the very chain, and said, "The mentally sick, far from being guilty people deserving of punishment, are sick people whose miserable state deserves all the consideration that is due to suffering humanity." [24] He also introduced the taking of psychiatric case histories and the keeping of case records. Esquirol, who succeeded Pinel in 1810, continued his reforms and gave the first course of lectures in psychiatry ever to be offered.

Bernheim and Liebault utilized hypnotism or mesmerism and contended that it was nothing more pathological than suggestion and thus, with Braid of England, contributed much to the birth of psychotherapy. Liebault was a French country doctor who practiced at Nancy, which he was to make famous. He was very much loved by the poor people of the community who were his patients. He often used hypnosis, although he refused to take a fee when he did, for he did not want to capitalize on a method that was so new.[25] In the middle of the nineteenth century Charcot was recognized as the leading neurologist of the day. He was the head of the Salpêtriere in Paris where he devoted much study to hysteria and to the investigation of hypnotism. Charcot was a noted teacher and received much publicity. He is best remembered for the fact that he attracted Sigmund Freud of Vienna who was greatly influenced by one statement that he made. Pierre Janet was a student of Charcot's and also noted as a teacher. He carried on an extensive private practice dealing with nervous diseases. He devoted himself intensely to the study of neurosis, hysteria and dissociation; he also used hypnosis and discovered that an emotional shock, though entirely unavailable in the waking condition, could be readily remembered and described during hypnosis. He further discovered that certain suggestions made by the physician, to the effect that these shocks were "past and gone now," had a decidedly helpful effect on the life of the patient. He felt that neuroses were due to a lowered state of nervous tension which was not sufficient to enable the individual to overcome the problems of life. His findings were published about the same time as those of Breuer and Freud. They were very similar in many points, although Freud was soon to take the leadership of the whole movement, and the center of the interest in abnormal phenomena was to shift from Paris to Vienna.

There are others who could be mentioned. Vincenzo Chiarugi in Italy had removed the chains and torturesome devices from his patients even before Pinel, but his work was not as well known and received less publicity. Kraepelin, a contemporary of Janet's, was a doctor of medicine but had studied empirical psychology under Wundt. He was dissatisfied with the vagueness and confusion which marked the classification of mental diseases. He made an intensive study of thousands of case histories. He saw that mental disease was not an isolated incident in a man's life, and that it was not enough to study him just as he was, but the study must include his background clear back to his childhood. As a result of his studies, he developed the principle that mental diseases must be classified, and he distinguished twenty-two major pathologies. He gave the name manic-depressive and dementia-praecox to two types of disorders.

It was Sigmund Freud of Vienna, however, who caught the attention of the world—not just the medical world, but the general public as well. Freud was guided by very practical motives as he made his investigations and published his findings. He was born in 1856, studied medicine in the university, worked for some time in the physiological laboratory and in the hospital, specializing in the anatomy and diseases of the nervous system. Hearing of Charcot and his outstanding work, Freud went to Paris in 1885 and studied with him for a year. He was very much interested in Charcot's use of hypnosis and, also, in a statement that he made that always, in all cases of neurosis, there was some difficulty in the sex life of the individual. Freud returned to Vienna and began active practice of his own, using the methods of hypnosis. He faced the difficulty that some of his neurotic patients could not be hypnotized and, even when they were, the percentage of cures was not too large. Anxious to discover some further understanding, he went again to France to study the work being done at Nancy, but was somewhat disappointed and returned to Vienna to continue his efforts, but still with only moderate success.

He then began his famous association with Josef Breuer, who probably had more influence on Freud than any of the others mentioned. They began to coöperate in their study of neuroses. Breuer was following a new method which had been suggested to him by one of his patients, which was to let the patient "talk out" her difficulties while hypnotized. She talked freely, displayed much emotion and could remember events that otherwise were forgotten. As a result she was much relieved. The original patient was thus able to return to normal life by no other apparent treatment. This method was tried with other patients and the results were favorable. It was discovered that many of the things they spoke of were lost to the normal state of mind, especially events that caused feelings of guilt and had been completely repressed or forgotten. Freud and Breuer published their findings jointly.

Breuer became dissatisfied with the new method, and Freud was left to work alone. He gathered around himself a group of his own students who met in a room in his home, where they discussed actual cases and his developing theories. Freud felt that many mental disturbances that were not due to actual organic causes were due to emotional conflicts that took place below the conscious level. These impulses and desires that were thus repressed and refused expression still found expression in some other way, which was often an abnormal one. Freud began to dispense with hypnosis as a method and, instead, had his patient completely relax, usually in a reclining position, and tell of his difficulties including anything that came to mind, even of the minutest detail. This method was termed free association, for all restraints were taken off; the patient was to tell everything, no matter how trivial or embarrassing. The next development in his approach was to include the patient's dreams which were used to discover some clue to the original source of the complex. This was followed, further, by analyzing slips of the tongue or lapses of memory, all of which were said to have some meaning. He noticed that all of these expressions of neurotic symptoms revealed something of a sexual nature. This, of course, is the emphasis which brought him so much attention from the general public and also so much criticism, although

Freud's conception of sex was of a much broader nature than is in the average person's mind when he uses the term. In fact, for Freud sex complexes began in infancy and included almost everything in the experience of the individual.

Freud came to America in 1909, at the invitation of G. Stanley Hall, to give a series of lectures on psycho-analysis at Clark University. His visit to America did much to stimulate interest in this country and of course as in Europe, aroused much opposition. His theories did gain the support of a group of men in this country, such as A. A. Brill, Smith Ely Jelliff and William A. White, as well as Dr. Hall. We cannot trace all the developments of his work. The final result, Woodworth says, can be summarized under three heads. The fundamentals of Freud's psychology were the importance of repression, the importance of the sex drive, and the importance of the infantile period.[26] The significance of such findings to the religious worker are obvious at once. Many ministers naturally revolted against Freud's extreme emphasis on sex, but others recognized that if these theories of repression, the expression of the sex drive, and origin of complexes during infancy were true, they explained many of the behavior problems that they had been confronted with that were often of such a baffling nature. Freud was both a genius and a pioneer. It many ways he was one-sided and intolerant. His extreme views have, in the main, been modified and greatly changed. Nevertheless, he developed a field the final results of which are not yet known.

Freud had many followers, as well as much opposition, while he was alive. It was possible to have an International Congress of Psychoanalysts as early as 1908. It was inevitable that there would be breaks in Freud's group because of some of his extreme theories and his demand of complete acceptance of his views. His two most famous disciples, and the ones who have had perhaps an even greater influence on the work of the clergy, were Alfred Adler and J. C. Jung, both of whom separated themselves from the movement and founded schools of their own. Both men have been rather widely read and are frequently quoted.

While not the first to separate from Freud, yet one of the most noteworthy, Alfred Adler founded a rival school which he called "Individual Psychology." He recognized the importance of the sex drive, but felt that Freud greatly over-emphasized the part it had to play. Adler felt that the basic factor in all neurosis was a feeling of inferiority. This may be caused by any one of a number of things, but it is always a source of difficulty, for Adler said that everyone had a will for power, an innate desire to excel, to achieve dominance and superiority. Where this is denied, either through some physical defect, because of situations in his environment, or because of some other reason, the individual compensates in some manner to secure his feeling of superiority. Where this native desire is not achieved by normal means, it is secured by abnormal ones. Adler claimed to be the "legitimate father of the inferiority complex." It may be some outward expression of conduct of an extreme form, or it may be an inner expression of fantasy or reverie. This self-assertive impulse, Adler said, was the dominant force in life, rather than the sexual impulse. Adler also stressed the importance of the period of infancy and childhood but from a viewpoint different from Freud's. To him the important thing was to discover the "style of life" which the child had developed; the goal of superiority he sought and his manner of securing it. He made much of the child's position in the family. To help an individual he must be led to recognize his own situation, to understand himself, what he is trying to do or to avoid, and, thus, to adjust or develop more acceptable expressions of his style of life. Adler's system is much simpler than Freud's and much more acceptable to the minds of many of the clergy. Examples of people suffering from these feelings of inferiority were evident in the congregations of every minister who happened to read Adler's books.

Adler's psychology, like perhaps the psychology of all men, grew out of his own experience. When he was five years old he had a serious illness and a doctor told his father that he could not live. This experience intensified his fear of death and caused him to study medicine. Jealousy of his mother's attention to his brother, an early struggle with an organic inferiority and a striving to keep up with an elder brother did much to influence his later theories.[27] He frequently spoke of the ability to turn a "minus into a plus" as the foundation of all his work.

There have been much discussion and various versions of Adler's relationship to Freud. Adler himself claims that he was never a pupil of Freud's but a member of his discussion group, joining at Freud's invitation in 1902. He never attended Freud's classes and was never psychoanalyzed, although he was a member of the editorial staff of Freud's journal. When Freud demanded complete acceptance of his sexual theory, Adler and nine others resigned in 1911. The whole controversy was marked by much bitterness and jealousy, attitudes unbefitting scientists, a misfortune in the development of the whole movement.

Adler was very sensitive by nature. Reading accounts in the newspapers of suicide, delinquency and divorce, he asked himself the questions, Must these things be? Are they unavoidable? Then he set himself to determine their cause and reason.[28] His biographer said that no one ever went to him for help and was refused.[29] On one occasion, when a colleague referred to a character in a story as a worthless type, Adler replied, "There are no worthless types." He taught that there were three common life tasks set before every individual—(1) work or employment, (2) love or marriage, (3) social contact. The latter he referred to as the necessity to love one's neighbor.[30] In speaking of his psychology, he said its only proper goal was to bring "peace to every human soul." It is obvious that such attitudes were attractive to the clergy. Adler himself was a Jew by race but united with the Protestant church, although he could rightfully be called agnostic in his views. He recognized any form of real religion as of great value to the individual and said that the idea of God was the most enlightened thought that had occurred to mankind. He enjoyed speaking to groups of clergy and said he felt they might be the best to spread his psychology, for their profession was already one of good will. He felt the clergy had a distinct advantage over the psychiatrists for no question of a fee was involved with the person they were helping.

When political developments in central Europe became more and more totalitarian, he came to the conclusion that the hope of the world was in America. He made several lecture tours in America and, in 1932, he occupied the first chair of medical psychology in the world at Long Island University. He dropped dead on the street in 1937, while on a lecture tour in Scotland.

Jung was also an early disciple of Freud and many say the most brilliant of his early followers. He was, for a time, president of the International Association of Psychoanalysis. However, he, too, separated himself and developed the school which he called "Analytical Psychology." Jung is most noted for his concept of the racial unconscious and the development of the idea of psychological types. He would not reject completely the ideas of either Freud or Adler. Briefly summarized, the two main types were the "introvert," whose interest and attention turned inward or were centered on himself, and the "extravert," whose interest and attention were turned outward to the social or physical environment. These terms have now become household expressions. Jung also spoke of the "ambivert" whose interests combined elements of both. His concept of the unconscious which, he feels, includes not only experiences that have been repressed but other matters that have been forgotten or acquired unconsciously, and also the collective or racial unconscious, which is inherited and goes clear back to primitive life. Jung has attracted much attention from the clergy because much of his writing has dealt with religious subjects and some of his statements have given a tremendous place to religious values.[31] He has written several significant volumes, but the one which attracted the most attention was *Modern Man in Search of a Soul*. In this volume he made the statement that has been quoted literally thousands of times, "Among all my patients in the second half of life—that is to say, over thirty-five—there has not been one whose problem in the last resort was not that of finding a religious outlook on life. It is safe to say that everyone of them fell ill because he had lost that which the living religions of every age have given their followers, and none of them has been really healed who did not regain his religious outlook." And, speaking of the minister, he said, "Here, then, the clergyman stands before a vast horizon. But it would seem as if no one had noticed it. It also looks as though the protestant clergyman of today was insufficiently equipped to cope with the urgent psychic needs of our age. It is indeed high time for the clergyman and the psychotherapist to join forces to meet this great spiritual task." [32]

The implications of the findings of such men were profound and far-reaching, affecting every area of life. The reactions of the clergy were varied. There were a group that bitterly opposed all psychological developments and discounted all of its values, often without proper study or evaluation. There were others who opposed certain expressions, such as the complete sexuality of Freud or the extreme behaviorism of Watson. Such conceptions could not be reconciled with religion. The psychologists also opposed such positions. Some of the psychologists, such as Watson, Janet, Freud, were outspoken in their contempt and opposition to religion, picturing it as a superstition or neurotic expression of life. Such conceptions were, of necessity, opposed.

The great majority of the clergy were perhaps indifferent. They were aware that developments were taking place; they would have recognized such names as those mentioned above; they knew that courses in psychology were being included in the college curriculum; they might even have used psychological terms, but they made no attempt to study, to evaluate, to understand this body of knowledge as it related to their own work or to their own parish problems. There were a few, however, who recognized the significance of these developments. They did not agree with all the theories of Freud or Watson or of anybody else. They saw that Freud and some of the others, in spite of their understanding of human nature, did not have an understanding of real religion, but were merely describing a neurotic expression of religion. At the same time, the psychologists were uncovering facts about human nature that could not be denied and must be faced frankly and honestly—facts which were extremely important and could be very useful. How the clergy utilized and applied this new knowledge to the age-old function of the "cure of souls" occupies a major portion of the remainder of this book.

Chapter VI

PASTORAL THEOLOGY
AND THE PSYCHOLOGY OF RELIGION

PASTORAL THEOLOGY

As has by now become apparent, the church has always had a concern for the need of the individual. There have always been men who sensed its great significance and some who have made it their major concern. Nor did the schools for the training of ministers ignore it completely. It is true that it received minor attention in comparison with other subjects. The instruction given was included in a department or a course that was usually listed as "Practical Theology." This covered the whole field of the practical work of the minister—preaching, homiletics, liturgics, the operation of a church, and other related subjects. In most schools and in most books on the subject there was included a section on the method of dealing effectively with the individual. The knowledge of human nature was based on the personal experience of the instructor or the writer; the motives, purposes and procedures grew out of the theology of the time. Some of these men achieved real insight in dealing with people and some of the volumes in this field have much that is worthy of study today. One of the best ways to review this field is to consider some of the volumes that have become classics. They express the thought, the instruction and the experience of their authors.

Richard Baxter, whose amazing success as a practical pastor has already been referred to, published his *Reformed Pastor* [1] as early as 1656. He wrote it because he felt that pastors should be reformed in this matter.[2] It deals primarily with the minister's work with individuals. He lists various groups that should be given attention, such as the unconverted, those under conviction of sin, and those already partakers of divine grace, and he urges careful oversight of families and diligence in visiting the sick. In referring to those who come with "cases of conscience," he said, "A minister is not to be merely a public preacher, but to be known as a counsellor for their souls as the physician is for their bodies, and the lawyer for their estates; so that each man who is in doubts and straits may bring his case to him for resolution; . . . But as the people have become unacquainted with this office of the ministry, and with their own duty and for the future, and see that you perform it carefully when they do seek your help. . . . One word of seasonable, prudent advice, given by a minister to persons in necessity, may be of more use than many sermons." [3]

For this reason he stresses the fact that the minister must consider "all the flock, or every individual member of our charge. To this end, it is necesary that we should know every person that belongeth to our charge; for how can we take heed to them, if we do not know them? We must labor to be acquainted, not only with the persons, but with the state of all our people; with their inclinations and conversation; what are the sins to which they are most addicted, and what duties they are most apt to neglect, and what temptations they are most liable to; for if we know not the temperament or disease, we are not likely to prove successful physicians." [4]

With Baxter the primary thing was conversion. The "misery of the unconverted" should fill the minister with such compassion that it should impel him with all his might. For this reason he advised beginning an interview with the most basic issues, such as questions regarding the individual and the future life. He recognized that the minister must vary his approach according to the character, age and condition of the individual with whom he is dealing. He urged men to study the method of dealing with people as they studied their sermons. The attitudes were important. "We must feel toward our people as a father toward his children; yea, the tenderest love of a mother must not surpass ours." [5] But the first requirement of those who would care for the souls of others it to take heed to their own souls.

Baxter's book had a wide influence. Daniel Wilson wrote an introduction to a revised edition which appeared in 1829; he again called the attention of men to the concern for the individual and urged them to study Baxter's book. "In a crowded congregation numbers do not understand, do not give attention, do not apply. It is when we come to them in private and individually, and with all the influence which affection, and character and official station give, that we touch the conscience." [6] It was not only those who come to church who need the pastor's guidance, but the masses of people in every community that should be sought out by the minister—the ill and the infirm, the sinners, the skeptics, or those detained by bad family arrangements or other reasons. He questioned whether the pastors had been "true shepherds of their flocks." "Have we looked after each individual sheep with an eager solicitude? . . . What do the streets and lanes of our cities testify concerning us? What do the highways and the hedges of our country parishes say as to our fidelity and love of souls? What do the houses and sick chambers of our congregations and neighborhoods speak? Where have we been? What have we been doing? Has Christ our Master seen us following his footsteps and 'going about doing good'? Brethren, we are verily faulty concerning this. We have been content with public discourses and have not urged each soul to the concerns of salvation." [7]

The Schaff-Herzog *Encyclopedia of Religious Knowledge*, published in 1883,[8] included an article entitled "Pastoral Theology." It divided theology into two divisions, theoretical and practical. Under the second is included Homiletics, Catechetics, Liturgics and Poimenics. The author stressed the fact that "The pastor needs not only power in the pulpit, but also power to reach and sway men by personal contact and influence. . . . The large and general relation of the preacher to his congregation as a whole becomes in the pastor a personal and an individual relation to each member of the flock, without regard to condition or character. This involves the dealing with a great variety of natures, each one of whom is a separate and a sacred responsibility to the pastor. The work is endless. There are always some souls in need of personal ministrations. Men are reached and saved one by one, and not in mass. The preacher must be a pastor to gather in one by one the souls to whom he has spoken from the pulpit the words of truth." [9]

In the remainder of the article many practical and valuable suggestions are made that would not need to be changed appreciably in the light of later knowledge, such as the influence of the pastor's own personality. "What he is will condition what he says; his character and life will help or hinder his work." The work should be systematized and adequate records kept. The pastor should not always be preaching. His purpose is "to enter into the sympathies of the people," to know them and to gain their confidence. He should inform himself concerning the spiritual condition of every member of his congregation, giving special attention to the sick and afflicted. In the later case his calls should be brief and his words few and carefully chosen. He must be aware of the great variety of temperament, disposition, character and condition, and must make allowances for differences that come from nature, education, antecedent or circumstances. In order to do this, he must be "a many-sided man," always studying "the endlessly varied manifestations of human nature." [10]

In 1896 John Watson, better known as Ian Maclaren, was invited to give the Lyman Beecher Lectures on Preaching at Yale University. He chose to consider the practical work of the ministry and entitled his lectures, which were later published, *The Cure of Souls*,[11] one of the first of several volumes to use this title. He discussed the genesis and technique of a sermon, theology and the new dogma, the machinery of a congregation, but he included one chapter which he entitled "The Work of a Pastor." He compared the work of the pastor to that of the physician and divided it into two divisions: visitation and consultation. He stressed the fact that for the "true pastor, visitation is a spiritual labour, intense and arduous, beside which reading and study are light and easy. When he has been with ten families, and done his best by each, he comes home trembling in his very limbs and worn-out in soul." [12] He advocated the keeping of two books of records, one that would contain all the data regarding each family in his parish; the other that would be kept locked in a drawer, shown to no one and destroyed at death. This second book was to contain the spiritual history and character of each of his people. It had the results of the pastor's diagnosis which was changed and added to from time to time. He said the pastor should visit every home at least once a year and go at once when any time of need arose, regardless of what other work he was doing, the presence of contagious disease, or any other factor.

The five rules of consultation which he advocated were: (a) never press for confidence, but receive only that which is offered freely, (b) urge the person to reveal nothing more of any painful secret than is necessary, (c) regard every confidence as absolutely sacred, (d) give such practical advice as he can, especially urging restitution, reformation or watchfulness, (e) never fail, so far as possible, to lead every person who consults him to accept Christ as his Saviour and Friend. His spirit is indicated in the following statement, "It is a hard fight for everyone, and it is not his to judge or condemn; his it is to understand, to help, to comfort—for these people are his children, his pupils, his patients; they are the sheep Christ has given him, for whom Christ died." [13]

Washington Gladden contributed the volume, *The Christian Pastor*,[14] to the International Theological Library. He covered the whole range of practical theology and also included discussions of The Pastor's Work with Young Men and Women, The Pastor and the Children, The Mid-Week Service, Revivals, The Institutional Church, and The Care of the Poor. The most significant chapter, from the standpoint of this study, is the chapter entitled "The Pastor as Friend." His approach was what the title would indicate. The minister ought to be "the one man in all the vicinity to whom the heart of anyone in need of a friend would instinctively turn." [15] To serve thus as "friend, counsellor and guide" is a heavy responsibility. If the minister is "the kind of man that he ought to be, a great many stories of doubt and perplexity and sorrow and shame and despair are likely to be poured into his ears. The cure of souls is his high calling; it invokes for him what tenderness, what dignity, what sympathetic insight, what sanity of judgment, what love for men, what faith in God!" [16]

He then indicated those who need the minister's friendship, the great number in every community—the anxious, the sorrowful, disappointed, of whom "the gossiping world knows nothing at all"; those who are troubled with doubt, those who have wandered away, those who have given in to despondency and despair, the sick and the bereaved. He advocated coöperation with the medical profession but recognized, on the other hand, that there were some things "the doctor with his drugs can never cure but that would be quickly put to flight if the load of shame and remorse that are resting upon the heart could be removed. The utmost wisdom is needed in dealing with such cases; . . . If by gentle questioning he can draw forth the rankling secret, and convince the troubled soul, by his own forgiveness, that the Infinite Love is able to save to the uttermost all who trust in him, he may prove to be the bringer of health and peace. The cure of souls is a phrase with a deep and real meaning." [17]

William A. Quayle, beloved bishop of the Methodist Episcopal Church, presented his suggestions in a volume entitled

The Pastor-Preacher.[18] The book is what the title implies, but it is significant that he placed the word "pastor" first. He covered a wide range of subjects, including preaching, the devotional and intellectual life of the pastor, the example of Paul and Christ, but in the heart of the book is a significant section on The Pastor, with such discussions as The Pastor and the Sick, the Child, Youth. His practical nature can be seen from his list of fourteen rules to govern the Pastor and the Sick, as follows: 1. Pay much heed to the sick. 2. Call immediately as soon as notified. 3. Call often. 4. Do not stay long. 5. Do not, as a rule, talk about their sickness. 6. Do not always talk about religion. 7. Do not always pray. 8. Take with you an atmosphere of health. 9. Bring good and sunny weather. 10. Sometimes read a little portion of God's word but not a hackneyed portion. 11. Draw conversation to holy things, but not with funereal air. 12. Never let the sick person feel it is a burden for you to call. 13. When you pray, pray briefly and tenderly. 14. . . . study to drop a helpful word, the Christ word, and never be mechanical about it.[19] His spirit is revealed by this statement about the child, "We misconstrue him when we think slightingly of his troubles and his joys. A child's troubles are very real and very bitter." [20]

In 1912, Charles Jefferson delivered the George Shepard lectures on preaching at Bangor Theological Seminary which he entitled *The Minister as Shepherd.*[21] This little book, like Baxter's, has become a classic. Also, like Baxter, he made a great appeal for the significance of this part of the minister's work in a day when he felt its value was not recognized, was sometimes ridiculed and looked down upon and often avoided. Presenting the whole subject from Jesus' analogy of his own life to that of a shepherd, he liked to think of the minister in terms of a shepherd and preferred this title to any of the others: preacher, priest, clergyman, rector, parson or minister. He felt that this term, when used in the sense in which it was used of Jesus, had the best connotation for what he felt was the most

vital and permanent form of a minister's task. Jefferson said
that Jesus liked to think of himself as a shepherd; it was with
this attitude that he looked upon people and it was to this task
that he called those who were to carry on his work. Jefferson's
conception of the work is best described in his own words. "It
is the mission of the pastor to 'minister to minds diseased; to
pluck from the memory a rooted sorrow; to raze out the written troubles of the brain; and, with some sweet oblivious antidote, to cleanse the stuff'd bosom of that perilous stuff, which
weighs upon the heart.' There is always someone ailing in the
parish, not physically only, but mentally, morally, spiritually.
The diseases of the soul are multitudinous, and the remedies
provided by the Almighty are efficacious only when applied
by a skilled practitioner. There are soul diseases peculiar to
certain ages and certain temperaments, and certain callings and
certain environments, and the minister ought to know the
symptoms of these diseases, the stages of their development,
and the hygienic processes by which they may be cured. . . .
Here is a field in which the minister is called upon to put forth
his skill and strength. His mission is to the sick, and all sick
people are not sick with the same sickness, nor do they all require the same remedies or the same kind of nursing. Nowhere
else does the minister need such piercing insight, such fine
powers of discrimination, such skill in diagnosis, and such ability to cope with subtle and mysterious forces, as here. There
are ministers who hardly enter into this great realm of pastoral
service. Such consciences are in their parish, but they do not
know how to treat them. Wounded hearts are bleeding but they
do not know how to staunch the flow of blood. Bereaved and
other grief-stricken souls are mourning, but they do not know
how to speak the healing word. Spirits are sick unto death, but
they can bring them no relief. There are those possessed of
demons, and the pastor does not know how to cast them out.
The whole science of spiritual therapeutics is unknown to him,
and followers of Jesus in many cases suffer on for years with

diseases from which an expert spiritual physician could have delivered them. There are in many a parish cases of arrested religious development, instances of moral paralysis, sad attacks of spiritual prostration which could be relieved and cured if only the minister understood better the nature of the soul and the remedies offered to human minds in Jesus Christ." [22] In this manner and in this spirit he speaks of the Shepherd's Work, the Shepherd's Opportunity, the Shepherd's Temptations, and the Shepherd's Reward.

A practical book, one frequently used as a text-book and written for that purpose, was *The Work of the Pastor*, by Charles R. Erdman, professor of Practical Theology of Princeton Theological Seminary.[23] Like the other authors, he includes the whole range of a pastor's duties but also includes a chapter entitled "The Cure of Souls," a task which "cannot be accomplished by dealing with them in the mass, but only by individual and personal treatment." [24] He recognizes that no two cases are alike and divides them into fourteen common classes—the irreligious and the indifferent, the professed skeptics, the inquirers, the new converts, those with doubts and difficulties, the despondent, the deluded, the backsliders, the sick, the bereaved, the afflicted, the erring, the perplexed, the mature Christians. He advocates "some acquaintance" with the principles of modern psychology, but is inclined to depend on proof texts in dealing with "professed skeptics" and "inquirers."

Many such books continue to appear. The more recent volumes have shown an interest in the findings of the psychologists as they apply to pastoral work. A book written definitely with the "pastoral" approach in mind was a little volume *The Pastoral Ministry* by Hampton Adams.[25] He deals with the traditional subjects of pastoral calling, helping the bereaved, dealing with adolescent boys, etc., but is well aware of the findings of psychology. Albert Palmer's *The Minister's Job* [26] includes a chapter on "The Minister as a Personal Counselor" and takes into full account the whole field of psychology, psychiatry and social case work. One of the most recent of such books is *Pastoral Work* by Andrew W. Blackwood.[27]

STUDIES IN THE PSYCHOLOGY OF RELIGION

A field of investigation that was to have considerable influence in the "care and cure of souls" was the rise of the science of the psychology of religion. It was largely an American product. It is true that there were forerunners in Europe in such men as Hume, Comte, Kant and Schleiermacher, but, in the sense that we are thinking of it here, it was an American movement. It began in the closing years of the nineteenth century after the field of general psychology had attracted much attention and had gained a place of some significance. In the main, it was an application of the findings of general psychology to the field of religion. No one can rightfully be called the founder of the psychology of religion, but as much credit is due G. Stanley Hall as to any one individual, not only for his own efforts, but also for the fact that he was the type of personality that inspired others to take an interest in the field.

The two major areas of interest and investigation in the first decade were conversion and adolescence. Hall was studying the place of religious conversion in the awakening of adolescence as early as 1881. Others were also examining these fields. Their findings were expressed in a series of articles that appeared toward the close of the century. Hall wrote on "The Moral and Religious Training of Children and Adolescents"; J. H. Leuba presented an article on "A Study in the Psychology of Religious Phenomena," which dealt mainly with conversion; W. H. Burnham wrote on "The Study of Adolescence," and E. D. Starbuck on "A Study of Conversion." All of these men were students of Hall.[28]

The first important volume which appeared was *The Psychology of Religion* by E. D. Starbuck.[29] It appeared in 1899, the year that Dwight L. Moody died, and, in a sense, marks the transition point from the period of revivalism to a more psychological interpretation of religion. Starbuck was a brilliant and thorough student. He was trained in both philosophy and empirical psychology and was vitally interested in religious problems. He entered Harvard as a graduate student where he studied under William James and where he began his investigations of conversion and religious growth. He later transferred his research to Clark University where he secured the interest and support of other graduate students as well as that of President Hall himself.

Starbuck proceeded by circulating two rather extensive questionnaires—one on conversion and one on religious growth. James, his teacher, gave only half-hearted support to this procedure, for he questioned the value of such findings. Later, in his introduction to the book, James admitted his own doubt of the worth of such data in the beginning, but also admitted the value of Starbuck's findings. In his questionnaires, Starbuck included questions that would give him information in such general areas as the age of conversion, the motives and forces leading to conversion, the experiences preceding conversion, the mental and bodily affections accompanying conversion, the feelings following conversion, the character of the new life, as well as questions to discover the experiences of those who had an experience of growth rather than conversion. He received 192 returns complete enough to be used; almost all of them from people of the Protestant faith. He organized, summarized and evaluated these findings. His conclusion was that conversion is primarily an adolescent phenomenon, although he distinguishes three types: the positive or volitional, the negative or self-surrender, and the spontaneous awakening type. He recognized the limitations of the psychological approach but felt it had great value. His volume holds a significant place as one that serves as an introduction of a method and an area of investigation that would bear much fruit.

Meanwhile, George A. Coe, then a professor at Northwestern University, was doing considerable research and, in

1900, published *The Spiritual Life*.[30] He also gave much attention to Conversion and Adolescent Difficulties, as well as to a study of Divine Healing and the meaning of Spirituality. He also used the method of the questionnaire for securing his data. His book was quite practical in intent. In the Introduction he refers specifically to the "care of souls" in terms that foreshadow much that was to be emphasized in the new century. "Why should not the care of souls become an art—a system of organized and proportioned methods based upon definite knowledge of the material to be wrought upon, the ends to be attained, and the means and instruments for attaining them? Such an art would require scientific insight into the general organization of the mind, and especially into the particular characteristics of the child mind, the youth mind, and the mature mind." He continues to point out the need to be able to discriminate between the normal and the morbid states, to understand the intimate relationships between the spiritual and the physical, and to be able to recognize individual differences of temperament and personality.[31]

In 1902, William James was invited to give the Gifford lectures at Edinburgh University. He chose the Subject *The Varieties of Religious Experience*. The basis of his treatment was not the questionnaire but the biographical study. It was an exhaustive study of religious experience. He divided the religious into two groups: those who had a religion of "healthy-mindedness" and those who were morbid-minded or who had a "sick soul." He gave innumerable examples of each. He also discussed the process by which the divided self becomes unified. His definition of conversion as "the process, gradual or sudden, by which a self hitherto divided, and consciously wrong, inferior and unhappy, becomes unified and consciously right, superior and happy," is perhaps quoted as frequently as any passage from American religious literature.[32]

The chief criticism of the work was the fact that he selected for his examples those who were the extreme or abnormal, but he said he did not want to study those who were just following a pattern someone else had set; he wanted to study those whose religious experience was original. Furthermore, he always held that the abnormal was the exaggeration of the normal and, therefore, gave us information a bit more clearly defined. The book as were all of James' works, was written in good literary style, achieved almost immediate popularity and had gone through thirty-six printings by 1928.

The first decade was marked by quite an advance. In 1905 Davenport published *Primitive Traits in Religious Revivals*, as the title would indicate, a study of the revival movement.[33] In 1906 Wundt published his *Folk Psychology*,[34] which dealt with religion in its general cultural setting. In 1907, James Pratt brought out his *Psychology of Religious Belief*.[35] He dealt with a field hardly touched up to this point. He discussed the nature of belief, its expression among primitive peoples in India, in Israel, Christian belief and the development of belief in the periods of childhood, youth and maturity. In 1908, George B. Cutten presented a comprehensive volume, The *Psychological Phenomena of Christianity*,[36] in which he attempted to make a summary of the conclusions made in the other detailed studies. He took in the whole range of phenomena—abnormal and normal, and presented chapters on a wide variety of subjects, such as Mysticism, Ecstasy, Glossolalia, Visions, Dreams, Stigmatization, Witchcraft, Demoniacal Possession, Religious Epidemics, Revivals, Faith Cure, Christian Science, Miracles, as well as Conversion, Sex, Intellect, Knowledge, Prayer, Denominationalism, Immortality and many others.

About 1910 the "Psychology of Religion" began to appear as a separate subject in colleges and universities. There also appeared an attempt to systematize the findings that had been made in certain areas. One of the first of these generalizations, and one of the first to be used as a text, was *The Psychology of Religious Experience*, by Edward Scribner Ames, of the University of Chicago.[37] Rather than being subjective and inward, with Ames the psychology of religion became objective and social; it was a sociological interpretation of the origin, nature and function of religion. This was followed in 1912 by James Leuba's *Psychological Study of Religion*,[38] which was completely humanistic in its conclusions. In 1916, Coe, who was now at Union Theological Seminary, published his *Psychology of Religion*,[39] which indicated the broadening of the field that had been taking place.

With the coming of the third decade of investigation a great variety of studies were made. More volumes began to appear in specialized areas. Sanctis and Underwood presented volumes on Conversion; Otto and Leuba made studies of mysticism; Stolz and Strong wrote on the Psychology of Prayer; Bundy and Hall made psychological studies of Jesus. Hall's volume, *Jesus the Christ, in the Light of Psychology*,[40] was a great disappointment to him for he expected it to receive a much more favorable reception than it did. In 1904 Hall founded a Journal of Religious Psychology which was later discontinued. Niebuhr, McComas and Clark made psychological studies of denominationalism and the cults. Others made investigations in each of these fields. These names are but a few who achieved some prominence. Many general, rather comprehensive volumes appeared. Pratt published his *Religious Consciousness*; [41] Thouless, *An Introduction to the Psychology of Religion*; [42] Josey, *The Psychology of Religion*,[43] and Conklin, *The Psychology of Religious Adjustment*.[44]

Such volumes varied in value. Most of them were intended as text-books and, no doubt, grew out of class-room lectures. In the main they surveyed the earlier literature and discussed the earlier findings with little new in the way of emphasis.

The psychology of religion up to this time had been largely an academic discipline. Its contact with the problems of people was through such methods as the questionnaire and the biographical study. The later books in the psychology of religion still included the traditional investigations of Adolescence, Conversion, Mysticism, etc., but they also began to devote more space to the "cure of souls" and have more material that comes to bear directly on pastoral counseling.* Walter Marshall Horton wrote a volume entitled *A Psychological Approach to Theology*.[45] It was his feeling that theology and psychology should join hands so that they might together promote the development of human personality. He criticizes theology because it has "so far failed to furnish the minister with any adequate general theory of spiritual diagnosis. Such a theory should be based upon a body of exact knowledge concerning the varieties, symptoms, and causes of human ills and perversities, and should enable the minister to fit his gospel to human needs with precision, as the skilled physician fits his remedy to the disease. . . ." He feels that this theory must be built on a vast number of case studies, carefully analyzed and classified. Perhaps some day the ministry will develop specialists in certain types of disorders, but, in the main, the minister's specialty would be the field of the milder disorders of personality—a field which, he feels, presents in itself a task that is almost staggering.

Anton T. Boisen published an original and unique contribution entitled *The Exploration of the Inner World*.[46] It is based on his own experience of mental distress which necessitated his being placed in a mental hospital. As a result, he made a most thorough study of himself and of the others who were there, both while he was a patient and, later, while he was a chaplain. He came to the conclusion that what had happened to him had been, essentially, what had happened to them, "their inner world had come crashing down." As a result of this experience, and of his later study and work, as described in another chapter, he wrote this book. He gives some very thorough case studies of others he dealt with in the hospital, and includes analysis of such experiences as those of Paul, Bunyan and George Fox.

* I am aware that these go over into the next period, between the Wars, but it seems more logical to complete this field here than to include another section on the psychology of religion later.

With the case of Fox, he gives an imaginative description of him in our present day, and describes how his case would be handled today if he were to present himself before the doctors of divinity, philosophy or medicine. The book contains a study he made, with a young minister, of a typical small-town congregation, showing the wide range of the needs of the people and the inadequacy of modern agencies to meet them. He includes a discussion of the distinctive task of the clergyman in meeting these needs.

Later studies in the psychology of religion began to give specific place to counseling as such. Dr. Henry Nelson Wieman, professor of the Philosophy of Religion at the University of Chicago, and his wife, Regina Westcott Wieman, who had formerly taught psychology, served as dean of women and been active in clinical psychology, collaborated to write *A Normative Psychology of Religion*.[47] This is a comprehensive volume and includes such chapters as "Personal Problems of Religious Significance," "Psychotherapy and Religion," and "Counseling Procedures." K. R. Stolz published *The Psychology of Religious Living*,[48] and included a chapter on "Religion and Mental Health," which included a special reference to the religious counselor. In 1940, Ernest M. Ligon presented *The Psychology of Christian Personality*,[49] a psychological interpretation of the Sermon on the Mount. He feels that psychology has much to contribute to the interpretation of religion that would make for mental health and would make it the power in human life that it ought to be. The same year Professor J. G. McKenzie presented *Psychology, Psychotherapy and Evangelicalism*,[50] which also gives a psychological interpretation of religion, especially of such concepts as salvation, conversion, sin, guilt, forgiveness and atonement.

The most recent volume has been Paul Johnson's *Psychology of Religion*.[51] He was influenced by contemporary personality psychology and has been active in the counseling and clinical movement. He includes a section on Normal Personality and emphasizes the therapeutic values of religion, such as the worth of every person, the fellowship of the church, the invisible companionship and faith, worship, devotion, confession, forgiveness and discipline.

The subjects these men have investigated have been numerous and varied. Many of them have had a bearing on the counseling function of the ministry, both directly and indirectly. Such emphases as the significance and problems of adolescence and the therapeutic power of religion are seen at once to have a direct bearing. Some would put all counseling as only a branch of the psychology of religion; others would say it is an outgrowth; still others would say that they are two parallel movements that touch at certain points. Certainly they are closely related and later counseling knowledge and procedures were advanced and improved because of the efforts of such men as these.

Chapter VII

MORE GREAT PASTORS

One of the primary concerns of the true pastor has always been the individual needs and problems of his people. He has always sought to give guidance, comfort and encouragement to the perplexed, the wayward, the unfortunate, the sick and bereaved—to anyone who might need or seek his help. Preaching and the pulpit have received the major attention of the historians and biographers, but we usually discover that most great preachers also spent much time and had a deep and genuine concern in meeting the individual problems and in helping in a personal way to meet the needs of their people. Of course, there have been men—and there still are—who thought primarily in terms of crowds and a public meeting and discounted the value of such a personal ministry. There are others who resented the impositions that it made upon their time and patience and who closeted themselves against it. In the main, however, such men would be the exception and, we find that most men who were successful in a public way were also very faithful in trying to be of help whenever they were approached or needed. It is true that many were limited to a certain extent by theological pre-suppositions which greatly influenced their approach to human nature. In the majority of cases, the primary concern was to "save the soul," thinking only in terms of a future state and chiefly in terms of theological and biblical concepts, overlooking emotional and environmental conflicts which were the real sources of the difficulty. This criticism cannot be applied to the ministry alone. The same situation existed in the attitudes and procedures of both the medical and teaching professions in years gone by. They were both subject to the same limitations and errors in dealing with the personality problems of their patients and pupils. At the same time, we often find an amazing insight and understanding into the problems of human nature on the part of some of these pastors. Just as fine parents have used child psychology for years, and great teachers have used educational psychology long before there were any texts by such titles, so great pastors have been using pastoral psychology since long before the present-day emphasis and terminology became so prominent. Behind many of the more or less scientific terms that are so common today are principles which these men discovered and utilized. Their psychology grew out of their own experiences but they often had an unusual effectiveness and a high percentage of success in their work. Their procedure and methods, and especially their spirit of devotion and their attitudes, are worthy of much study and consideration.

Two men who gained a world-wide reputation as preachers were Alexander Whyte of Scotland and Peter Ainslee of Baltimore, Maryland. Both did very significant work as pastors. Dr. Whyte worked indefatigably as a preacher. He worked and toiled over his sermons faithfully, patiently and, at times, painfully. He was no less thorough as a pastor. His elders at St. George's told him his chief task was to preach and that visitation and pastoral work were not necessary. He knew, however, that real preaching could only be done as an outgrowth of pastoral work. It was said that more important than the books and other furnishings of his study were "two deep armchairs that rested, one on each side, by the spacious fireplace. In one of them sat this great specialist in sin, in the other a long succession of men who believed that no other doctor could understand their case. Here broken hearts were mended, here despairing souls got their glimpse of a new hope, here the chief of sinners saw the prospect of his final triumph through grace. The stories told in that sacred chamber are buried now with the physician." [1]

Peter Ainslee was recognized as Baltimore's most distinguished citizen where he served for forty years as the minister of the Christian Temple. He was also recognized throughout the world as a preacher, author and editor; he was one of the most eminent apostles of Christian unity; he was noted as a crusader for social justice and world peace but, like Whyte, he recognized the value of personal pastoral work. His diary records the fact that in one month he made three hundred and twenty-five calls. He refused to give up this work even when it overtaxed his strength and was definitely against his physician's advice. In his own words, "I learned at the very outset of my ministry that the one fundamental method of pastoral visitation is a definite and personal concern for every member of the flock, . . . As the physician goes on his rounds, believing he has the cure for most ills of the body, I go on my rounds with no less confidence, believing the gospel of Jesus Christ is the one cure for all the ills of the soul. If in the preparation of an article or a sermon my mind did not work with ease, I would put on my hat and make a round of calls to come back with messages seething through my brain." [2] Needless to say, a man with such an attitude was sought by many. His biographer said of him, "With an all but infinite patience he listened to the endless confidences poured into his receptive ear. The fortunes and misfortunes, the least joys and sorrows of all his people became his own." [3] And again, speaking of him as an administrator, he says, "His reverence for the individual always got in the way of his efficiency. One human appeal anywhere along the path could always stop him. One inconsequential but importunate questioner could prevent him from being punctual on a platform where he was to address a thousand. No place to which he was going was ever so important as the person who just now had broken into his presence. People were always more important to him than organizations." [4]

Washington Gladden, famous as the author of the hymn, "O Master, Let Me Walk with Thee," recognized as a social prophet, preacher, author and poet, was also one of the greatest of pastors. Luther A. Weigle described his personality in these terms, "Far-sighted, broad-minded and independent in judgment, he labored tirelessly for social righteousness and the common good; yet never seemed hurried or worried. He possessed the imperturbable calm of one who is a friend of his fellows, at peace with conscience and at home with God." [5] Such serenity of spirit was not always a characteristic of his personality. He achieved it as the fruit of much struggle. Sadness came early in his life. He had a vivid memory of childhood experiences and, in his *Recollections* describes with great feeling the close relationship he and his father enjoyed while he was still a very small child. They were the closest of companions, but while Gladden was still a child his father died after a brief illness. He describes the extreme sorrow and sadness of the experience and comments, "Childish sorrows are short-lived, we say, but this one was not. It has never let go of my heart; the pain of it is poignant yet." [6] His religious struggles were of equal intensity and, like his childish sorrow, he could describe them in great detail more than fifty years later. He said the business of religion in his day was to fill men's hearts with fear.[7] In his case it succeeded. He describes the efforts that were made to frighten sinners with the fear of hell, and said, "That fear was always haunting me in my childhood; my most horrible dreams were of that place of torment." [8] He tells of his boyhood struggle, how he kept trying for years to gain some assurance of the favor of God; he tried a thousand times to give himself to God as they said he should but, when no emotional or ecstatic experience resulted, he felt that he had failed and was still under the wrath of God. To quote again his own words, "That little unplastered room under the rafters in the old farmhouse, where I lay so many nights, when the house was still, looking out through the casement upon the unpitying stars, has a story to tell of a soul in great perplexity and trouble because it could not find God." [9] "It was not until my eighteenth year that a clear-headed minister lifted me out of this pit, and made me see that it was perfectly safe to trust the Heavenly Father's love for me and walk straight on in the ways of service, waiting for no raptures, but doing his will as best I knew it, and confiding in his friendship." [10]

It was out of such experiences that Gladden developed his conception of religion and the ministry. They were both summed up in the word "friendship." "Religion," he said, "is just being friends with the Father above and the brother by our side." [11] The relationship of pastor with his people was not that of "teacher with pupil nor of master with servant, but of friend with friend." [12] He expressed his philosophy in *The Christian Pastor*, which is discussed elsewhere in this volume. He is no doubt speaking out of personal experience when he writes, "There is, however, in every congregation enough of real trouble to tax the minister's resources of sympathy and wisdom. How much there is, in every community, of anxiety and disappointment and heartbreaking sorrow that never comes to the surface, of which the gossiping world never knows anything at all! A great deal of this trouble comes to the minister; he must always be the sharer of many burdens which are hidden from the public gaze. This is just as it ought to be; the pastor has as little reason to complain of it as the doctor has to complain of a multitude of patients. But it is apt to be the most exhaustive part of the pastor's work; the drafts made upon his nervous energy through the appeal to his sympathies are heavier than those which are due to his studies. . . . Every pastor must be ready for a great deal of that kind of work. . . . There is less of what is known as pastoral visiting, but there is more of demand upon the pastor for counsel and help in all sorts of personal troubles." [13]

He served three years as one of the staff of preachers to Harvard University. This consisted of conducting prayers in Appleton Chapel every morning, leading a vesper service every Thursday afternoon and preaching in the chapel on Sunday evening. Every week-day he was to be in Wadsworth House for two or three hours to meet students who might wish to call and discuss personal problems. This latter part of the responsibility, he felt, was the most significant of all. They came to him with all sorts of problems. Many, of course, were of an intellectual nature, like that of one boy, whose case he described as typical, who was attempting to reconcile the first chapters of Genesis with his course in geology, an issue that was causing much concern in those days. The majority, however, did not come for theological instruction but to discuss problems of a more personal nature. He said that such experiences made him understand the value of the confessional. One of the largest groups of students who desired to talk to him came to discuss the question of the selection of and the preparation for their life work.[14]

This concern for individuals permeated and undergirded all of Gladden's interests and activities. It was the basis for his preaching and, as we have said elsewhere, was a determining factor in his interest in social causes and movements. It was fundamental in his charitable work. He saw the psychological implications behind poverty and relief work. He saw that to provide food, clothing or coal was the easiest and most superficial of contributions. He felt that the deepest need of the poor was "manliness and self-respect," which can even be destroyed by the charity improperly applied and which are always more difficult to provide. Most of his writing grew out of his concern for the problems of people. He wrote a book, *Being a Christian: What It Means and How to Begin*, as a result of his own painful experiences as a boy, and was able to say, "I have been comforted in knowing that out of the perplexities of my boyhood, help has come to many who were seeking the way of life" [15]

Gladden felt that every minister should center his thought upon two main areas, the problems of the soul and the problems of society. He saw clearly that man must be studied in his social relationship. He urged all pastors to become original investigators to make a patient and thorough study of the men, women and children of their parishes until they had a first-hand knowledge of the facts of human nature. This "most fascinating study" would "uncover many painful facts; it raises many hard questions, but it is more interesting and more significant than any other subject which can engage the human intellect." [16]

Among the various programs attempted by churches, none has received such wide publicity as has that of the Emmanuel Episcopal Church in Boston, which is usually referred to as the Emmanuel Movement. The name was coined by the newspapers and was not suggested by those participating. Dr. Elwood Worcester, the leader of the so-called movement, served for several years as rector of St. Stephen's Church in Philadelphia, where Dr. S. Weir Mitchell, the noted psychiatrist, was a parishioner, and he became his close friend. Dr. Worcester says it was from Dr. Mitchell that he received the first impetus for his later work. In 1904, he became rector of Emmanuel Church in Boston and Dr. Samuel McComb became one of his associates. Neither of these men had ever studied medicine but Worcester had studied psychology under Wundt and had taught it for several years at Lehigh University, and McComb had studied psychology at Oxford. Both of them were intensely interested in the subject and in the whole field of mental therapeutics. They sought the advice of Boston specialists, among them Dr. Richard Cabot, of the Harvard Medical School, and Dr. Isadore Coriat, of Tufts Medical School, and before announcing any program consulted some of the leading neurologists of New England to see whether or not they would have their approval. The result was that, since their purpose was to deal only with those situations where the disorder was of a functional nature and where religious faith would play a definite part, the medical men gave their sympathy and coöperation.

From the very beginning of his ministry Worcester was dissatisfied with the quality of the work done by the church and the ministry. As he studied the New Testament and the history of the early church, he felt that something valuable had been lost from the Christian religion which it once had possessed in dealing with the illness and the problems of human nature. He did not feel, however, that he and his associates could return to the first century but, rather, that they must combine the findings of modern science with the disposition and power of Jesus.[17] He felt, further, that he had something to contribute to troubled people and set out to prepare himself and discover the methods and techniques by which it could be done. He described his attitudes as he attempted the venture. "I was prepared to descend into the depths of human personality and to dwell amid the abnormalities of human nature and, so far as opportunity was given me, to explore, with a calm, clear mind, the mysteries of the spiritual world." [18] Later, as he looked back upon it, he said, "We little imagined the length, breadth and depth of the abyss of human sorrow we were about to explore when we undertook to deal with the spiritual maladies of mankind. . . . Had we known the abuse, the misunderstanding, the notoriety to which we were subjected, I fear that we would not have had the courage to undertake the task." [19]

Emmanuel Church started with a tuberculosis class under the supervision of Dr. Joseph H. Pratt, for the poor people of the Boston slums who could not afford to go to the Adirondacks or to a sanitarium. They were taught how to sleep in the open air, how to avoid contacting or communicating the disease, and given general instructions in health. Also, they were given an added emphasis on discipline, encouragement and hope. The results were very encouraging and led them to widen the scope of their classes. In the fall of 1906, after consulting with leading neurologists, they instituted a similar class for the nervous and morally distressed and discussed such questions as worry, anger, habit, suggestion, prayer, nervousness and similar topics. These classes were often addressed by leading specialists in the field of medicine and psychology. Dr. Worcester and his associates stated their belief in a book which they published to make clear to the public just what the nature of their work was. "We believe in the power of the mind over the body, and we believe also in medicine, in good habits, and in a wholesome, well-regulated life." [20]

Needless to say, with the publicity that such a venture received, they were deluged with people seeking help. Worcester described these days when "a constant procession of men and women passed through my study. I ate when I could. I tried to give myself to each of these persons as if I had nothing else to live for, to put them at their ease, to enter into their problems and sufferings with understanding and sympathy, not to hurry them and not to allow them to waste my time. . . ." [21] A series of articles in the Ladies' Home Journal brought more than five thousand letters from people seeking help, in spite of the fact that a notice had been included that they could not be answered. In the introduction of the book *Religion and Medicine,* which he wrote with Dr. McComb and Dr. Coriat, they expressed the hope that other churches would take up the work because of the great need for it and also so that it might relieve them from the pressure of those who came from distant cities. The class was supported by voluntary offerings taken at the meetings. They did not ask or accept rewards for their services. Morning and evening clinics were held as well as the mid-week health class and the Sunday service of worship.

They continued their close relationship with the doctors and refused to treat a patient until he had had a thorough diagnosis from a competent physician indicating that there was nothing that demanded medical or surgical treatment. They recognized that their greatest benefit was given in the realm of functional nervous disorders because such problems are so closely associated with the moral life where the possibilities of drugs and medicine are extremely limited and the personality of the physician and attitudes of the patient are all-important.[22] Most of their treatment was in the nature of suggestive therapeutics, although they frequently used deep relaxation and hypnosis if the patient consented. The books describing their work [23] are filled with cases of the most striking cures, such as cures of "psychological blindness," or paralysis, insomnia, or of such success with people with whom psychiatrists and specialists had failed. Worcester tells of using the methods of relaxation and suggestion to provide serenity and calm before an operation literally hundreds of times. He also, on occasion, used suggestion during sleep and cites some interesting cases of its use with very small children to cure certain habits or personality abnormalities. On one occasion Dr. Cabot made a careful study of one hundred and seventy-eight cases over a period of nine months. In the eighty-two cases of neurasthenia, twenty showed marked improvement, sixteen slight improvement, seventeen no improvement and the rest were unavailable for checking. In the twenty-two cases of alcoholism, eight were much improved, which is a good record. Also, good results were revealed in cases of fear, hysteria, obsessions, as well as with those addicted to drugs. Added to these acute cases should be listed many discouraged, tired, despondent people who found new courage and hope.

In October, 1929, Dr. Worcester resigned from the rectorship of Emmanuel Church to devote his time exclusively to work with individuals. He worked with Mr. Courtenay Baylor, a man who had once come to him for advice but had become so interested in the work that he gave up his insurance business to work with Dr. Worcester. They dropped the name Emmanuel and incorporated their work under the laws of Massachusetts, with the title, "Craigie Foundation." [24] They moved their headquarters to a residence in Boston secured by Mr. Baylor. Dr. Worcester spent some time in other cities, one day a week being spent in Grace Church in New York. The only thing he asked to be permitted to take with him from Emmanuel Church was an old Morris chair in which he said he had treated "thousands of men, women and children." [25]

Just a year after Dr. Worcester went to Emmanuel Church,

there was organized "The Guild of Health" in the Church of England. It was composed of both laymen and clergy and stated as its objective the study of the influence of the spiritual upon the physical, the possibility of healing by spiritual means in full accord with scientific principles, the use of united prayer on behalf of the sick, and the development through spiritual means of both individual and corporate life. They distributed many pamphlets and sponsored group conferences besides providing opportunity for individual consultation. Under the leadership of Rev. F. C. Sherman, there was developed in the Protestant Episcopal Church of America "The American Guild of Health." They made a greater emphasis on religious education than did the Guild of Health in England, conducting many study classes and teaching missions. The work was done in full coöperation with the medical profession and by staff workers who were carefully trained.[26]

It should be recognized that the program of the Emmanuel movement was an exception. Nor was it always well received. Some opposed it bitterly and others, such as C. R. Brown, warned that it would be both unwise and dangerous if it were extended to other churches and attempted by men who were not trained for it. He further questioned the wisdom of having a regular church service for the consideration and treatment of nervous troubles for fear it might develop an epidemic of nervous and mental troubles.[27]

Far more expressive of the point of view of the majority of men in this period would be Jefferson's conception of the "minister as a shepherd." His book by this title expresses his philosophy and is described elsewhere in this study. He carried on this type of a shepherding ministry even in the "Skyscraper Church," as the Broadway Tabernacle was frequently called by the New York papers. He saw men everywhere, old and young, who were bewildered and discouraged, disillusioned, despondent and cynical, broken in health and hope. The privilege of ministering as a shepherd to such people was the minister's great opportunity, primary responsibility and richest reward. "It is a work which requires extraordinary wisdom, unfailing patience, plodding fidelity, unfaltering boldness, a genius for hope, abiding faith, and boundless love, but there is none other that is more clearly the work that Christ just now wishes done, and upon the faithful performance of which the future of humanity more manifestly depends. The cities must be saved, and they are to be saved by shepherds." [28] "He must live with the people, think with their mind, feel with their heart, see with their eyes, hear with their ears, suffer with their spirit. He must bear their grief and carry their sorrows." [29] This was the shepherd's great privilege. There was no satisfaction from a public meeting that could compare with "the satisfaction of knowing that by an act of yours one human life has been changed forever." [30]

Another man who thought in terms of the pastor as a shepherd was George W. Truett, famed pastor of the First Baptist Church in Dallas and world figure, especially in Baptist circles. On one occasion he was given a tempting offer to become the president of a university, but, after serious consideration, he declined, saying, "I have sought and found the shepherd heart of a pastor. I must remain at Dallas." [31] In spite of his innumerable responsibilities he ever retained the "shepherd's heart" and was considered an "easy mark" for all who were in trouble. He was the "confidant of storm-vexed human souls," [32] who sought his counsel in increasing numbers.

He had a tragic experience early in his career which influenced all of his later ministry. While hunting quail with a friend his gun accidentally discharged; the load struck his friend in the leg and he died a few days later. Truett's grief was intense; he condemned himself for his carelessness and told his wife he could never preach again. After much agonizing, Scripture reading and prayer, he did return to his pulpit. A member of his church described the result of his ordeal. ". . . there is no doubt it is the crucial experience of his life. It is the event that has molded him more than any other. No one can come to him with a sorrow greater than his sorrow. His vast capacity for helping people in trouble, as well as his power in the pulpit, is born of the tragedy which re-made him." [33]

His "capacity for helping people in trouble" was not confined to his own parish, although this was in itself tremendous. (The membership of the church when he arrived in 1897 was 715; after forty-four years it was 7,454—in all a total of 18,124 persons had been added to the congregation in forty-four years). [34] Dr. Truett conducted many revival services and, during such meetings, always had many conferences with individuals about personal and religious matters, either in the inquiry rooms or in private conference. Every year for many years he spent a week with the cattlemen of the West. Here, among these men of the out-of-doors, he was sought as much as by those in the cities. Once, while on shipboard, he was asked to preach at a Sunday morning service. It was a mixed and heterogeneous congregation, representing many nationalities, faiths and all walks of life. He spoke of the knowledge of God that was available to all men. In the days of the voyage that followed many sought him out to discuss their own problem and their own desire for a knowledge like that of which he had spoken. During the first World War Dr. Truett was one of twenty American preachers selected to go overseas and preach to the members of the Allied armies, under the auspices of the Young Men's Christian Association. Here he spoke daily in camps, hospitals, tents, huts, in the fields, woods or streets, wherever the men were stationed. After speaking he was almost always sought for interviews by the soldiers. Frequently he spent an eighteen-hour day speaking and interviewing. Once, after an address in a hospital, he wrote his wife, "I could wish that I were a thousand men, that I might tarry beside every bed for a personal interview." [35] Another form of counseling that increased with the years was his counseling with other pastors and preachers. A great many came from all denominations—especially young men—seeking help in the problems of their work and in their personal problems. Mrs. Truett said that this was one of the deepest and most abiding interests of all his efforts.[36]

Similar in spirit, though from a different section of the country, was Charles S. Medbury, the pastor of the University Church of Christ in Des Moines, Iowa. For more than twenty years he ministered faithfully and often sacrificially to the needs of the people in his church. At his death a professor in Drake University, located just across the street from his church, wrote this tribute, "His radiant personality, his sincerity and his gracious smile put at ease not only the joyous and the self-confident, but also the shy, the awkward and the wayward. When those who had sought his counsel left his presence they went out with a new courage and a stronger grip upon themselves because of his faith in the high purpose of youth. . . . Through the years a path grew to his office door. Students sought him for counsel, for hope and for strength." [37] A former student wrote from England, "He had the ability to put one at perfect ease from the first moment of the interview, and before it was ended one was willing to entrust him with the intimate secrets of one's life." [38]

Here was one who, without technical knowledge of psychology, met the needs of many. After Medbury's death there was found in his desk, in his own handwriting, a statement entitled "My Creed." It expresses very eloquently the pastoral attitude which many such men carried into their work. It had been written only for his own use, with no intention of its ever being seen or used for publication.

"To this day that is mine, my country's and my God's I dedicate my all. My talents, every one, shall be held subject to the sight draft of the emergencies of others. I will enlarge my soul by cultivating love for those from whom I find myself recoiling. No man shall ever feel his color or his caste in my presence, for within my heart of hearts there shall be no consciousness of it.

"The man who has fallen shall find in me a friend, the woman down, a helper. But more than this, those falling shall have my trust that they may stand again. The cry of every child shall find my heart whether the cry of need or of aspiration. Not one of all the nation's 'little ones' shall be despised. Cherishing every life of whatever land or race and mindful of hidden struggles in all things I will strive to help and to serve.

"No words shall ever pass my lips that hurt another in things of face, form, station or estate. My own weaknesses, my foibles and my sins shall chasten speech and spirit and deny my pride. My life shall be a dedicated thing. I shall count it desecration to pervert it. The vandal hands of lust and hate and greed shall not be permitted to despoil.

"And thus I resolve, not because I am good, but that I want to be; not because I am strong, but that I feel weakness; not that I feel above others, but with all my soul I long to be of humankind, both helped and helper. So do I dedicate my days. So do I set apart my culture. So do I receive but to give to others. So do I press humbly into the presence of the sacrificial Son of Man, crying out in eager consecration, 'Let me follow Thee, Master, wherever the world still needs ministry, wherever life is still to be given for many.'

"Help me, Thou whose manger cradle brought democracy to light, to meet in my own worth democracy's final test and to my own great day to be true." [39]

Thus it is obvious that men have always been called upon to provide pastoral guidance and have done so—sometimes with outstanding results. Their psychology in the main grew out of their own experience. Their successes were due to their genuine concern for people, the earnestness of their desire to help, the sincerity of their sympathy, the faithfulness with which they discharged their duties, the practicalness of their procedure and the depth and quality of their faith. This fact should also be emphasized: we have but referred to a few whose names have been remembered because they achieved sufficient distinction to

have their names well-known and the events of their lives recorded. There have been hundreds—in fact, thousands—of pastors in cities, villages and towns whose names will never be
listed in any book but who have also been faithfully striving
to meet the needs of their people and, to a large extent, have
done so in the same spirit as the ones mentioned here. If the
story could ever be told of the millions who have been strengthened in time of need, comforted in time of sorrow, reassured in
time of failure and guided in time of perplexity, it would be
one of the greatest stories in the world.

PART III

SOME ALLIED MOVEMENTS

Chapter VIII

REVIVALISM AND MISSIONS

REVIVALISM

The most prevalent expression of Protestantism came to be an evangelistic one and the most common method was the revival. The revival, like the monastic movement, mysticism and other religious expressions, can be shown to have both positive and negative results. It is evident that there were many tragic results. The combination of the theology of the day, the appeal to fear, the personality of the preacher, the illiteracy of the people, the atmosphere and monotony of the times, plus the powerful effect of crowd psychology did produce mental and nervous disorders which ranged from the swoon to insanity and suicide. The picture of the revival at its worst has been ably presented in Davenport's study, *Primitive Traits in Religious Revivals*. Here is described in some detail the "emotional epidemics" that occurred in various places. When these meetings were characterized by intense appeals to the emotions rather than to the intellect, and when the motive of fear was coupled with mass suggestion of the crowd, they became quite naturally "a very hotbed of disorder and mental disintegration." [1]

While the dangers and negative aspects of the revival are very evident, yet on the other hand, there were many values that resulted. Even Davenport, speaking of the extreme type, says, "In spite of an unbridled religious method which gave free rein to human weakness and human passion and which did an incalculable amount of harm, there were still enforced in a very large number of cases true rational principles of living. And it is due to the straightforward manliness and moral sanity of many of these rugged pulpit personalities that a multitude in their day and generation did not sink to the level of the savagery with which they were surrounded." [2] Groves and Blanchard, in their *Introduction to Mental Hygiene*, recognize its weaknesses and faults and then add, "It was a crude process of therapeutics because it used mass suggestion and played upon primitive emotions, but it did influence a multitude to face squarely the realities of their time and place, leading to moral strengthening of character and more wholesome standards of living. . . . If it taught a harsh theology and built up fears of a wrathful God, it also furnished an antidote for the feelings it created by offering a salvation which restored the lost soul to the heavenly fellowship from which he was estranged. In the days when the revival flourished, every community had its repeaters who again and again made public confession. . . . The notoriety that they received has tended to obscure the fact that a larger number continued their professions and made an honest effort to live up to their ideals." [3]

The first of the great revival movements in America is termed the "Great Awakening" and dates from about the year 1734 and the preaching of Jonathan Edwards. Edwards was minister at Stockbridge; he was a man of marked personal magnetism and spoke with great force and conviction. He was a thorough Calvinist and preached unconditional election with all the fervor he possessed. His most famous sermon was entitled, "Sinners in the Hands of an Angry God." Other themes were, "Wrath upon the Wicked to the Uttermost" and "The Eternity of Hell's Torments." One of his best known illustrations was to picture man as a spider hanging by a slender thread over the flaming pit. The agonies of hell were described with great vividness and in gruesome detail; then the congregation was warned that there might be some of them who would be in hell before the year was out; in fact, some sitting in the meeting might be there before morning.[4] The results of such preaching, coupled with the fact that the people already accepted these ideas, were that many fainted away in sheer terror; many became hysterical, weeping, crying and shrieking. Some of them never fully recovered, but others actually gained a new unity and peace. Edwards was a man of balance himself; he had not anticipated such experiences and could not explain them. He was not sure whether it was the work of the devil or of the Holy Spirit, but he finally decided it was the Holy Spirit and justified it. Later he regretted that he had not discouraged such expressions.

Edwards was subject to his theology but, as A. C. McGiffert has pointed out, he was by nature a psychologist and, in many aspects, reveals a modern insight into human nature. In his biography of Edwards, McGiffert refers to the fact that Edwards was aware of "rationalizations" before psychologists invented the term and quotes his Journal in which he determines to search "out all the subtle subterfuges of my thoughts." In his effort to understand himself, he examined his dreams every morning, for here, he felt, he might discover what were his "imaginery actions and passions" and he could discern what were his "prevailing inclinations." [5] He not only analyzed himself but gave himself to the precise description and discriminating classification of the "frames of mind" of his people. He noted the vast differences in the nature and circumstances of people and thus he opposed those who insisted that conversion should always be of the same pattern. His purposes were practical; he did not observe and classify for the sake of observation and classification but for the practical purpose of gaining knowledge that would enable him to save souls who were "in the enemy's territory." [6]

Many revivalists followed Edwards and, in almost every case, there were some of these abnormal expressions. Some favored them and some opposed them. The results would indicate that the preacher's attitude was a large factor in their occurrence. Davenport went after such excesses for their own sake and was especially successful in producing tremblings, shriekings, fallings and faintings. On the other hand, the Tennant brothers, Gilbert and William, felt that they were a hindrance and had these people removed from their meetings. Whitfield, who initiated field preaching in England, came to America and had the same tremendous following in this country that he had had in England. He had a dominant personality and a magnificent voice and people came to hear him by the thousands. Although he spoke enthusiastically of Davenport's work, he did not encourage excesses to the same degree and, while he did work people up emotionally, he had less of the actual fainting and trembling than did some of the others. The Wesleyan Revival in England has been frequently reported and is mentioned elsewhere in this volume. Wesley was not sensational but he was so intense and impressive that he did kindle the emotions of his hearers with the same results that occurred in the meetings of these other men. Wesley had read of Jonathan Edwards' approval of these extravagances and he, too, gave them his sanction, but later he reversed his opinion and revealed marked control and good judgment for the day in which he lived. The most extreme examples came from the Kentucky Revivals of the late eighteenth and the early nineteenth centuries. Kentucky was a raw, unorganized frontier, and life was crude and simple. The families were widely scattered and developed what was termed the "Camp Meeting." They came from many miles; literally thousands were in attendance and the meetings continued for days—morning, noon and night—and did not break up until the food ran out. Many of the people were illiterate and, perhaps, more than in any other meetings, they were characterized by intense appeals to feeling and imagination rather than to the intellect.

The most notorious example of the development of the psychological crowd is furnished by the Cane Ridge camp meeting of August, 1801. Barton W. Stone, a pioneer in the movement of the Disciples of Christ, went to witness it and wrote in his biography that it defied description. People fell on all sides and would lie in an apparently breathless and motionless state for hours, broken only by occasional sobs or groans, and then they would arise to shout "deliverance." At night developments reached their height. The setting of the campfires blazing around the vast throng of worshippers, casting weird shadows against the darkness of the woods and forests may have made some contribution, but the psychology of crowd emotion can be the only final explanation. As the preachers—and there would be several of them working at once—became more fervent, all the bonds of self-control were released. As one after another would fall or begin to shout and shriek, whole areas would give way to "laughing, leaping, sobbing and shouting." Those who fell, and the estimates range from one in six to one in three, were carried to the meeting house where some would lie prostrate, others roll over and over and others jump up and run jumping over benches and stumps shouting "lost! lost!" [7] There are many stories of scoffers who came to observe but who were seized by the spell. It was estimated that in one meeting at least six thousand fell helpless, while others gave way to what was known as the jerks, shaking, twitching or writhing on the ground. Many expressed themselves in "the holy laugh"; others by "barking" at the foot of a tree and they were said to be "treeing the devil." Many would leap, sob, shout or swoon, and, if the proceedings were dull, one such victim could often set a whole section into action.

Of a very different type and nature was the work of such men as Nettleton and Finney. Nettleton still appealed to fear but he objected to any startling manifestations and told the people to go home and think it over. The result was an almost complete repression of any reflex phenomena. To his pulpit preaching he added house-to-house visitation, personal conferences and individual instructions.[8] Finney was trained as a lawyer but felt the call to preach and became one of the most influential evangelists, especially to professional groups. He was the inventor of the "mourner's bench" and the "anxious seat." Of a very forceful personality, he had great success. In a meeting in Rochester, New York, when Rochester had only ten thousand inhabitants, he had over one thousand converts. He was a Calvinist but not of the rigid type of some; he rejected the doctrine of predestination and insisted that salvation was for all. He made a great emphasis upon righteousness and upon the ethical demand of God for a pure life. He used the motive of fear but said he did so for the good of the sinner. He felt that to comfort the sinner was doing him an injustice, but to appeal to fear was a favor, for it might save him from the abyss.

During the latter part of the nineteenth century there is no name in religious evangelism that stands above that of Dwight L. Moody. No man had a greater influence on the next generation than he, touching the lives of such men as Grenfell, Eddy and Drummond, to mention but three of hundreds. Some of these men recognized the limitations of his theology but they were captivated by the sincerity and earnestness of the man. His message was not so much an appeal to fear as to love. His decision to become an evangelist was made not because of the desire to address a crowd, but simply by "deciding that since he was going to talk to people about the salvation of their souls, he might as well talk to a good many of them at once." [9] He was joined by Sankey in 1871 and they started their evangelistic tours that had such amazing success. They first came into prominence in England and then came to America where they continued their work for many years. Moody had a unique quality as a speaker; he was an expert at suggestion and made a tremendous impression upon his hearers. He would not tolerate any excess of emotionalism. His meetings were attended by great throngs; as many as six thousand converts were reported in a meeting in Chicago alone. In spite of his great public success, his interest in the individual was always evident, not only in his message but in his life. He once said, while visiting the dying during a small-pox epidemic, "Wherever doctors will go to save men's bodies I will go to save their souls." When he first started his famous Sunday School class in Chicago that had such unusual success, he knew every boy and girl by name, visited them all in their homes and knew most of their personal problems. Recognizing the need of a deeper approach as well, he established his schools, and most of the money which he raised was turned over to the Young Men's Christian Association.

Most of the later American evangelists represented variations of Moody. William A. (Billy) Sunday is, perhaps, an exception. Sunday's fame as an athlete gave him a unique appeal to the public. After his conversion he spent three years with the Chicago Y.M.C.A. where his work was of a personal nature; he advocated individual work as being the most effective. He used more than any other the methods of big business in organizing and promoting his campaigns. Very large sums of money were subscribed to carry them forward; he appealed to the sensational and was much in the headlines. He claimed to have preached to over eighty million people in all.[10]

There were many others but the influence of the large meetings began to wane after the first World War. The influence of such meetings may be attributed to a combination of factors; the cultural level of the people had much to do with the forming of the psychological crowd. Also the theological ideas accepted and the general notions and beliefs held by the people were decidedly different. The attitude and personality of the leader, the motive of fear, the power of mass suggestion all were a strong influence. In the main it may be said that the best of the revivalists were sincere men. They were motivated by a great desire to save individual souls and were guided by the theology of their day.

As was stated earlier, from a psychological point of view they can be shown to have had both positive and negative results. The extreme appeal to the emotions, the attempt to pour all—men, women and especially children—into one mold and the creation of a sense of guilt and the appeal to fear in so doing had many harmful results. On the other hand, they did appeal to the conscience and many lives were on a higher level of character and conduct. Sweet, in his book *Revivalism in America*, feels that too much emphasis has been given to the excesses of camp meetings and too little to the routine work of the frontier churches and preachers. They all stressed conversion and all were very individualistic in their dealings with their people. Among the Presbyterians only those properly qualified were permitted to take communion. Each individual was examined and only those who were worthy were given a token which was collected by the elders. The frontier Baptist churches had monthly congregational meetings when the life of each member came under the scrutiny of the church. The Methodist method of dealing with individuals was through the class meeting. Every member was assigned to a class and placed under the supervision of a Class Leader. This class met once a week and each member was expected to stand and give of his experience.[11] The primary thing is that it was personal in emphasis, dominantly personal in emphasis and intent.

MISSIONS

It is impossible to include the story of missions except in the briefest fashion. Some mention must be made, however, for it is certainly a part of the total picture. There is no group of people who have given themselves more completely to the relief of human suffering than have the missionaries. The great career of David Livingstone is an outstanding example. For more than thirty years he served as physician, scientist, minister and reformer, in a life of courage and hardship that has rarely been equaled. Of equal consecration was Father Damien who served in the leper colony on Molokai Island. His motto was the verse of scripture, "I was sick and ye visited me." He lived by this motto among the lepers for ten years and then, as the story goes, no longer said "my brethren" but "we lepers." He ministered to the people, raised the moral standard of the community, opposed the lawlessness, improved the water supply and sanitation and lived to see the establishment of hospitals with resident doctors and nurses to carry on the work. The frontiers of the United States and Alaska was the field of Sheldon Jackson. He was small of stature but great in energy and faith, and "wherever he heard the cry of need," he went to help. Such was the spirit that characterized the work of these missionaries.

Missions have had a relatively small influence on the pastoral methods of this country, but in the countries they have served they have been the one great influence that has introduced not only the Christian religion with its spirit of compassion, but also the whole field of scientifice medicine and nursing. Even to this day in many sections of the world the only humanitarian help offered to the masses, the only ministry of health and healing centers in the Christian missions. It was as early as 1793 that a ship's surgeon, John Thomas, was overcome by the suffering in India and joined the English Baptist Missionary Society and went out as a colleague of William Carey.[12] In China the first scientific medicine was introduced by Alexander Pearson, a ship's surgeon, and Thomas R. Colledge opened the first hospital in China in 1827. The man generally considered the founder of medical missionary work in China was Peter Parker who founded his hospital in Canton in 1835. Almost a century later, in 1931, nine-tenths of all the nurses in China were Christian.[13] From these beginnings it has grown until in 1943 there were more than nine hundred Protestant missionary doctors in the field and more than twelve hundred nurses.

The objectives of early medical missions were to heal the sick and to serve as an auxiliary to evangelism. They were motivated by a spirit of compassion—to save the souls of those who had never had the privilege of Christian teaching and preaching and to relieve the suffering of those who did not have the benefit of medical care. They made little, if any, emphasis upon the relationship of religion and health. This, of course, was also the case with both ministers and physicians in

England and America in that same day. It was not until recently that any statement was made concerning the relationship of "body, mind and spirit." The Jerusalem Conference of 1927 declared, "man is a unity: and his spiritual life is indivisibly rooted in all his conditions, physical, mental and social," therefore, "missionary work must be sufficiently comprehensive to serve the whole man in every aspect of life." [14] In the Layman's Report of the Commission to Re-study Missions, published in 1932, under the title *Re-Thinking Missions*, it says that the welfare of the individual's soul cannot be secured separately from the welfare of his body, his mind or his general social context. Speaking of the medical missionary in particular, it says, "It is not possible always to dissociate bodily from spiritual requirements; the wise physician, responsive to the unspoken needs of his patients, is often able through intimate conversation to enlarge and enrich the professional service he has given, and to convey hope and assurance to troubled minds." [15] In speaking of India, this report refers to certain native family customs which lead to definite personality disturbances and neurasthenic states, and recommends, "Since the influence of a good central mental hygiene clinic working together through the medical centers and the church is almost the only way successfully to combat these conditions, we urge that the need of such a clinic be recognized." [16]

The Madras Missionary Conference, held in 1939, made this significant statement in its report. "In the relationship of religion and health lies an imperative call for pioneering. The scope of the hospital's ministry will be enlarged by using specially trained members of the staff to inquire as to the economic, social, mental and religious background of every patient, so that both bodily and spiritual ministration may be provided in ways adapted to the special needs of the individual, both while in the hospital and after leaving it. The hospital would thus become a center where search could be made for ways in which spiritual ministry might aid in bringing full health to patients. We have scarcely crossed the threshold of such a quest as this. We need fuller understanding of the inter-relationship of body, mind and spirit. We need continued study and development of the contribution that faith and prayer and religious practice can make to the maintenance of mental and physical health and to the cure of disease. We ask the churches and hospitals to undertake together in selected centers continued inquiry in this significant field." [17]

The truth is that in the mission field, more than any place else, men have been ministering to the "whole" man, physically, mentally, socially and spiritually. This is seen in the heroic work of Wilfred Grenfell in Labrador, where he served as doctor, teacher, counselor and preacher with such monumental efforts that he not only helped countless individuals, but almost single-handed transformed this vast section of the country. The keynote of his preaching was "courage."

Perhaps the most dramatic and unusual record of all missionaries has been the work of Albert Schweitzer in Africa. His story is well known. Before becoming a missionary he had already achieved eminence as a scholar and an author, a lecturer and professor, an artist on the organ of real distinction, an authority on organ construction, as well as a preacher. It was no wonder that his friends and the world at large were startled by his decision to study medicine and to go to Africa as a medical missionary. He said that since boyhood he had been concerned because he had been granted such a happy life while there was so much suffering in the world. Many times he had tried to determine what the words, "Whosoever would save his life must lose it" meant for him specifically. He tried two projects—caring for abandoned and neglected children and for tramps and discharged prisoners—but in neither case with much success. It was while reading a missionary magazine which told of the need in Africa that he reached his decision,[18] which led to such amazing success in Africa. His doctor's dissertation for his medical degree was on the mental health of Jesus, in answer to those who, at the time, were claiming he was subject to delusions of persecution and grandeur. To write this dissertation he found it necessary to make a thorough study not only of Jesus but also of the medical problem of paranoia. While he was in Africa he had a great concern for the mental patients and constructed for them special rooms, separating them from the other patients. It was while he was at the height of his work in Africa that he formulated his philosophy in terms which satisfied him, a quest he had begun long before. It is summarized in the phrase, "reverence for life." For Schweitzer this was all-inclusive.

The missionary who has done more than any other in the realm of pastoral counseling, as such, is Dr. E. Stanley Jones. Dr. Jones is a man of world-wide reputation; his books have had a wide circulation and he has spoken to thousands from the platforms of almost every country in the world. As he has traveled about the world people have gone to him by the scores. His books are full of references to individuals who have come to him with their problems. He has been very much interested in the findings of psychology and the growth of pastoral counseling; he has read widely and has consulted with many authorities. He expresses his conclusions in a book entitled *Is the Kingdom of God Realism?* [19] In this book he speaks about what doctors and others have said about the relation between religion and health, and says, "These clues set me on a quest— the most rewarding of my life—a quest to find the Kingdom written within us." [20] As a result of his reading and his own personal experience "with hundreds of cases," he discusses the effects on the personality of hatred, guilt and inner conflict, and deals with such problems as anxieties and illness, the self-centered and the self-disrupted, etc. It is his conclusion that all the phychologists are saying that the four great enemies of Christian human personality are resentment, fear, self-centeredness and guilt, and Jesus emphasized their opposites—

love, faith, unselfishness and moral rightness with God and man.

In another volume, a companion book designed to be read as a daily devotional guide, he states, "We have handed the body over to the doctor, the mind to the psychiatrist, the soul to the minister, treating these three parts as separate entities. They are not separate. Life is a whole. You cannot affect one part without affecting all three." [21] These books have had a wide circulation and have done much to interest many people in the subject of the relationship of medicine, psychology and religion.

Chapter IX

HUMANITARIANISM
AND THE SOCIAL GOSPEL

Clara Bassett, in her book *Mental Hygiene in the Community*, states, "History will show that almost every important social reform has originated in the church or been initiated by individuals in whom the religious motivation was the factor of paramount importance." [1] She continues to mention the various fields, such as prison reform, orphanages, child-caring institutions, hospitals, care of the insane, and other areas where this has been true. Space does not permit a detailed account of all the movements or individuals who have participated in these programs. Only a few of the outstanding can be mentioned. These and many others who are not included have had a profound though indirect influence on the work of the pastor because of the ideas they stood for, because of the inspiration of their own lives and the work of others whom they stimulated which led to later developments and reforms they instituted and the institutions they established.

HUMANITARIANISM

The church has always been concerned about the sick. Richard Baxter, in his autobiography, tells how the ministers, remembering the words, "Inasmuch as ye did it unto one of the least of these ye did it unto me," cared for the sick and the dying during the plague of London when most people remained behind shut doors in terror and fear.[2] Such has always been the case. It was this spirit of compassion that led to the founding of the first hospitals. For centuries the establishment of hospitals was the result of religious motivation. Among the early fathers, Basil established a hospital at the gate of Caesarea; St. John Chrysostom at Constantinople, and, under the guidance of Jerome, Fabiola built the first general public hospital at Rome. Hospital orders were formed as early as 1113, when the pope recognized the Friars of the Hospital of St. John of Jerusalem who maintained hospitals for the pilgrims to the Holy Land. There were other brotherhoods which had a special concern for the sick and unfortunate, such as the Franciscans, founded in 1208, or the "Sisters of Charity," who were organized and trained especially to care for the sick and to aid the poor.[3] In the thirteenth century Pope Innocent III, summoned Guy of Montpellier to build a model hospital near the Vatican. When bishops would come to visit the Holy See, the Pope would call their attention to this hospital and suggest that they might have a similar one in their dioceses. The result was a great increase in hospital building throughout Europe.[4]

The same spirit of compassion later led Protestant churches to establish hospitals. There are more than four hundred and fifty hospitals in the United States that were established by various branches of the Protestant Church, as well as many homes for children, the aged and other groups. The flag of the American Protestant Hospital Association contains a shield, quartered by the Latin cross which symbolizes Christianity and one of Christianity's many benevolent outgrowths, the Christian Hospital. In the upper left quarter of the shield is the Greek Cross, the international symbol for the relief of the sick and wounded; in the lower right quarter is the Lorraine Cross, since medieval times the symbol of relief to the unfortunate; in the upper right quarter is the Urn Lamp, the emblem of the Florence Nightingale Nurses, symbolizing the knowledge of nursing; in the lower left quarter is the Wand of Mercury and the Serpent of Aesculapius, symbolizing the art of healing; surrounding the shield is a grapevine, symbolizing sacrifice and the teaching of the Minister of Healing: "I am the vine, ye are the branches." Underneath the shield is the motto, "Numquam Non Paratus" (Never Unprepared).[5]

It was also the church and the religious motivation that inaugurated the first concern for the mentally ill. The first hospital in America to admit the mentally ill was the Pennsylvania Hospital, established as a "religious duty" by the Quakers in Philadelphia.[6] It has the significant distinction of being the first hospital in which cure rather than custody and repression was the underlying principle. It is true that practice, at times, was far behind principle, and they still continued the practice of exhibiting patients for a fee, but, nevertheless, it was far beyond the common practice of the time and was still the first public institution where the mentally ill were "not to be confined as malefactors but to receive curative treatment as sick patients." It was also the Quakers—to whom too much credit cannot be given—who established the second institution for the mentally ill in America, the Friends Asylum at Frankford. The plan originated with a Quaker minister, Thomas Scattergood, who had traveled in Europe and had seen a similar institution, "The Retreat," established by the Quakers at York in England. These Quakers in Philadelphia made major emphasis upon providing a religious atmosphere which they felt would have a large influence upon the ultimate recovery of the patient.

The largest name in the concern for the mentally ill was Dorothea Lynde Dix, a retired school teacher, a woman who was quite frail and sickly, and yet for forty years she carried on her monumental efforts, leaving over thirty mental hospitals as a testimony of her great work. It all began on a winter day in 1841, when a young theological student, who had been assigned to teach a Sunday School class in the women's division of the local jail, felt incompetent for the job and went to Miss Dix for advice. She replied, "I will teach them myself," which she did. She was shocked by the filth, the dirt, the brutality and the negligence to which the inmates were subjected. She was especially concerned about the presence of insane persons, who were innocent of any crime but who, nevertheless, were being treated as criminals. Although Miss Dix was almost forty years of age, this marked the beginning of one of the most outstanding careers of all humanitarian efforts.[7]

Her childhood was far from happy; she said she never really knew the meaning of childhood. The conditions in her own home were so intolerable that she ran away to live with her grandmother. Here she received only a little of the love and affection she had missed at home; instead, she was subject to a Spartan discipline which frowned on all emotion and whose one great virtue was summed up in the word "Duty." At the age of fourteen she started a school for little children, dressing herself to appear older than she really was. The enterprise failed, chiefly as a result of her stern discipline, but a later school for older children and a charity school for the poor were quite successful. Her health was never very strong and on one occasion she suffered such a severe physical collapse that her friends gave her up as gone.

A powerful influence in her life was that of Dr. William Ellery Channing, a liberal churchman and an inspiring humanitarian. He invited her to tutor his children, which she did for several summers, staying in the Channing home. Miss Dix admired him very much and his lofty ideals of service to one's fellow men did much to stimulate her personally and, no doubt, were a large factor in the choice and carrying forward of her later career. It was the incident in the East Cambridge jail which launched this later career. It would be difficult to describe the cruelty and brutality, the neglect and indifference, the degradation, filth and actual torture, both physical and mental, to which the insane were subjected in that day. Against these conditions Miss Dix pitted herself with increasing vigilance and undaunted courage, in her single-handed crusade.

She approached the problem with a thoroughness of effort, a daring and fortitude of spirit that has rarely been equalled. She discovered that conditions in East Cambridge were no exception; in fact, many places were far worse in comparison. She resolved to do something about them. Very carefully and thoroughly she gathered all of her facts and then presented them to the legislature in no uncertain terms. Specifically and in detail she described the situations in the various towns of Massachusetts—the squalor, the filth, the cages, stalls, cellars, pens, in which the insane were chained, often naked, often beaten and humiliated. In most cases she found that the insane were thought of as beasts and treated as worse. She told the legislature that the solution did not lie in the reprimanding of the guilty individuals and communities but rather in the building of state hospitals in which these people could be properly treated and cared for. Naturally, her presentation raised a storm of opposition, which only spurred her on to greater efforts and, with the aid of Samuel Howe, Horace Mann, and others, a bill was passed which allowed for the enlargement of Worcester State Hospital.

It is impossible to list all of Miss Dix's activities, even all of her triumphs. After her success she moved out into larger circles. She made a similar survey in Rhode Island, revealing the same circumstances. Rhode Island was as yet without a mental hospital and she proceeded to see that one was established, securing a contribution of $40,000 from Cyrus Butler, a feat many thought impossible. So it continued, from state to state; she moved to another as soon as her task in one was complete, traveling more than ten thousand miles in three years, in a day when travel was very difficult and she was still sickly and frail. The greatest of her difficulties was the opposition of the public, the narrow-minded politicians and the tax-payers. She was of a truly heroic mold, the type of person who thrived on struggle, indefatigable in her efforts, of undiscourageable will, with keenness of vision, unaware of the meaning of the word "impossible."

One of her greatest dreams was defeated, however. Congress had been making many generous grants of land for various purposes and she conceived the idea of asking them to grant 5,000,000 acres to each of the thirty states, the proceeds to be used for the benefit of the indigent insane, which she described in her memorial to Congress as "wards of the nation." The bill carried Congress but was defeated by the president's veto. The defeat was so discouraging and she was so exhausted from her efforts that she sailed to England for a much needed rest. However, while on her so-called vacation, she became interested in the hospitals and charitable institutions and was soon involved in the same sort of work in Europe that she had done in America. The result of her efforts in Scotland completely revolutionized their system of caring for the insane, so she continued her work, establishing hospitals, reforming others; she did not hesitate to challenge the Pope himself with mistreatment of the insane which she found in Rome itself, and she received in reply the promise of a new hospital to be erected at once.

She returned to the United States just at the outbreak of the Civil War. She volunteered to the administration at once and was made Superintendent of Women Nurses, but, once the war was over, she returned to her work for the mentally ill. Although now sixty-five, she carried on her program of reform and mercy, gathering information, agitating for legislation, founding institutions for fifteen more years, not retiring from active work until she was eighty years of age.

There were two other women of similar spirit, both contemporaries of Miss Dix, although both were twenty years her junior, Florence Nightingale and Clara Barton. The name of the first is forever associated with nursing and that of the second with the American Red Cross. Florence Nightingale was the child of a privileged family but a girl who felt God had called her to a special service. When she was about twenty-one years of age, she became interested in hospitals and convinced they needed reforming. For twelve years she studied hospitals and nursing methods in Germany and France. It was the Crimean War that brought her into prominence. The story of her efforts in overcoming almost insurmountable obstacles is one of the great records of humanitarian achievement. It was because of her care for the individual soldier that she received the title, "Angel of the Crimea," and, also, "The Lady with the Lamp." It was said there was no case too hopeless nor any contagion too terrible to daunt her. One soldier wrote of her work, "She would speak to one and another, and nod and smile to many more, but she could not do it all, you know, for we lay there by hundreds; but we could kiss her shadow as it fell, and lay our heads on the pillow again, content." [8] Her health was permanently impaired by her work in the Crimea and she spent many years as a semi-invalid, but, even so, she continued her efforts. Her "Notes on Nursing" is recognized as a classic. While there were nurses before Florence Nightingale, nursing today is what it is, to a large extent, because of her efforts, and she is usually considered the founder of modern nursing.

Clara Barton was another who took as her motto the passage, "Inasmuch as ye have done it unto one of the least of these my brethren ye have done it unto me." As a girl, she was extremely shy, almost to the point of abnormality. In fact, she said that the only memory she had of her own childhood was one of fear. Her first release from her own timidity came when her brother had an accident and was ill for two years. She forgot about herself in caring for him. It was said that she could do *anything* for others who were suffering. She was working in the patent office in Washington when the Civil War broke out. Some of the casualties brought to Washington were from her own community. She went to the hospital to help them and found them with very little care. She began to go down the river to meet the steamers that were bringing the wounded back and soon found herself going to the battlefield itself. She administered first aid, distributed stores that friends provided, helped in any way she could—often in the very front lines. Her career was an arduous and dangerous one.

Following the war Clara Barton went to Europe for a rest. Here she became acquainted with the International Red Cross. While she was in Europe the Franco-Prussian War broke out and she volunteered her services and again cared for the sick and the wounded. During the war she saw the Red Cross in action and returned to America resolved that America should also have this organization. However, it took a great deal of effort against much misunderstanding and opposition before the proper legislation could be secured. She conceived the idea that its contribution need not be limited to war but could apply to any national disaster or need. The outbreak of the Spanish American War found her again, although seventy-seven years of age, on the battlefield. For over fifty years she gave herself to the suffering and the unfortunate, and she left as her legacy to the future the organization that is now worldwide in scope and in activity on behalf of suffering humanity.

Conditions in the prisons were quite as bad as they were in the institutions for the insane. When John Howard began his work in the latter half of the eighteenth century, he found men and women housed in such filthy and unsanitary conditions that disease and plague were inevitable; he found men kept in underground dungeons with no light, often no heat and, at times, with ceilings so low that the inmate could not stand upright. Men and women, the sane and the insane, the children and hardened criminals, were crowded together in common cells and pens. Brutality, cruelty and neglect were everywhere. Howard, who knew something of the meaning of imprisonment himself, having served as a prisoner of war, set out to reform these institutions. He was a man of deep religious spirit and great compassion. In the interest of prison reform he traveled over all of Europe. Burke, in his eulogy of Howard, referred to his travels which, he said, were not made to study palaces or temples, to secure fame or recognition, "but to dive into the depths of dungeons, to plunge into the infection of hospitals, to survey the mansions of sorrow and pain, to take the gauge and dimensions of misery, depression and contempt; to remember the forgotten, to attend to the neglected, to visit the forsaken, and compare and collate the distresses of all men in all countries. . . . It was a voyage of discovery, a circumnavigation of charity. Already the benefit of his labor is felt more or less in every country." [9]

Elizabeth Fry, Quaker, mother, quiet and reserved, seems like a strange person to list as a reformer of prisons but the results of her work were far-reaching. When she first went to Newgate prison, it was not with the idea of starting a career but merely because she felt it was a place where she could be of help. She went to do what she could to make a human contact with women prisoners. Even the turnkeys traveled in twos when they went into the yard, and ministers who came to read prayers kept at a safe distance from the bars. Elizabeth Fry, however, insisted on going in alone, into the very yard where the most violent women were grouped. The women crowded around her but nothing happened. She picked up a child and said to the women, "Friends, many of you are mothers. I, too, am a mother. I am distressed for your children. Is there not something we can do for these innocent little ones?" [10] She had won the women and started a career, a career that would carry her throughout Europe and into the presence of kings and ministers of state. She met with the women regularly, read Scripture to them, prayed with them, gathered their children together into a class and taught them. She forced the government to clean up the cells, provide mattresses to sleep on, decent food to eat and women jailers instead of men. Her success at Newgate led to her efforts throughout Europe.

Such reforms do not continue without constant effort. Even in the twentieth century Thomas Mott Osborne found similar conditions in the state of New York. In one prison he found men forced to live in dungeons twenty feet below ground, with arms and legs manacled, stooped in cells in which their heads were but two feet from the ground. Osborne voluntarily entered Auburn prison as a prisoner. He was booked as Tom Brown and endured all the routine of prison life. He discovered for himself the terror, monotony and horror of "solitary"; he saw the results of fear and brutality. He did not believe that all men in prison were perverse and vicious and felt that some would respond if treated humanely and with different methods. He tried his methods in Auburn, Sing Sing and Portsmouth but he became the victim of political opponents and was forced out under a cloud of criticism. This left him with a feeling of bitterness and frustration. It was not until after his death that the value of his work was recognized; then a monument was erected in his home town of Auburn, New York, where he had served voluntarily as a prisoner.

A different type of humanitarian effort was that of William Booth. He was a combination of evangelist, philanthropist, reformer and counselor. He began as an evangelist, stating that all he wanted was the opportunity to spend his life and powers in "publishing the Savior to a lost world." As a part of this was one of the deepest concerns that ever existed in the heart of any man for the most unfortunate and depraved. While he was still serving as an apprentice, although his hours were from seven in the morning until seven in the evening, he left his work as soon as possible to spend the entire evening speaking at street or cottage meetings, visiting the sick, comforting the dying, often until as late as midnight. His heart went out after "the poorest of the poor" and, to meet the needs of these people, he went into one of the worst sections of the world, the slums of London, and here he started his organization, the Salvation Army. At first Booth's thought was not to form a new agency but to send people to the churches that already existed, but he soon found out that they would not go. They were not wanted if they did, and besides he wanted them himself. His biographer lists the other work he did in addition to his evangelistic work, such as the various enterprises for the starving, drunkards, paupers, unemployed, homeless, criminals, daughters of shame, and the sick.[11] The program of the Salvation Army has now spread to every corner of the world and has touched the lives of millions; the extent of their work for the unfortunate is unequaled by any other agency except perhaps the International Red Cross. They have made their contribution in their own way to the story of the "cure of souls." General Booth was well aware of the perversities and problems of human nature. It was said, "All the sorrows of the world knocked at his door." Nor were any turned away. He said that the first vital step in saving outcasts consists in making them feel that some decent human being cares enough for them to take an interest in whether they are to rise or sink. Harold Begbie made a study of some cases in London that the "Salvationists" had saved by individual work. He published it under the title *Twice-Born Men: A Clinic in Regeneration.*[12] All of the cases were of an extreme variety, described under such chapter headings as, "The Lowest of the Low," "Rags and Bones," and "Apparent Failure." They were cases of individual work which required such patience, courage and faith as Begbie felt only "these Salvationists" possessed.

Some mention should be made of settlement houses. The same spirit which led to the founding of hospitals and which demanded reforms in prisons and mental institutions caused Jane Addams to establish Hull House in Chicago. When she was but a small girl she visited the slum section of a large city with her father and resolved that when she "grew up," she would have a big house, not where the other big houses were, but where poor children could come and play in her yard. When she was in Rockford College she read from her Greek New Testament every Sunday morning, noting particularly those passages where Jesus showed compassion upon those in need. It is a long way from a childish statement at the age of seven to the actual realization of a home among the poor, especially considering the physical handicaps under which Jane Addams worked, but she accomplished it. Its story is told in two of the classics of American autobiography, *Twenty Years at Hull House*, and *Second Twenty Years at Hull House*. The contribution she made to the lives of the people and the inspiration of her own personality cannot be overstated.

Similar in nature was the work of Muriel Lester who established Kingsley Hall in London.[13] Both women voluntarily left a life of relative comfort to live among the poor; both saw the influence of social conditions and sought to improve the community, provide recreation, fellowship and more sanitary living conditions. Both tried to meet the needs of individuals in any way they could, by providing classes, individual counsel—whatever the case might need or warrant. Both faced great obstacles, unfair opposition, staggering work. Both were inspired by a deep religious motive.

One cannot estimate the influence of such personalities, not only through the institutions they established or the reforms they secured, but through the individuals they helped and, not the least, the lives they inspired to carry on humanitarian work, although it may have been in a different field and in a very different manner.

THE SOCIAL GOSPEL

The social gospel has been called "America's most unique contribution to the great ongoing stream of Christianity." Although the term "social gospel" would indicate that it is primarily concerned with society, yet it has always been deeply concerned with the plight of individuals, and some of its strongest advocates received their initial impulse as a result of counseling with individuals who were the victims of society's misfortunes. Shailer Matthews, a pioneer in the movement, defined it as "the application of the teaching of Jesus and the total message of the Christian salvation to society, the economic life, and social institutions . . . as well as to individuals.[14] Henry C. Potter, while rector of Grace Church in New York, preached his sermons on the perils of wealth, indifference to social need, the tenement problem, the children of the slums, and other similar subjects, as a result of his parish work. Charles Parkhurst launched his crusade to explore Tammany Hall and the graft and indifference that existed in the New York Police Department because, he said, it was not enough to try to help individual victims of vice and alcoholism; it was also the church's task and duty to strike at the administration that permitted and fostered them. Washington Gladden, one of the greatest of all exponents of the social gospel, entered the social struggle as one of the responsibilities he felt were his as a Christian pastor and counselor. He says, in regard to the cause of labor, which he championed at a time when it was very unpopular to do so, ". . . at the beginning of my ministry in Columbus, the labor question in its most acute form was thrust upon me. I was not required to go in search of it: it was made my duty, as a Christian teacher, and as the moral counselor and guide of the men under my care, to grapple with it, and try and get at the rights of it." [15]

The one name that stands above all the rest as the leader of thought in the social gospel is Walter Rauschenbusch. For eleven years he served as the pastor of a little Baptist church on the edge of Hell's Kitchen in New York. Here, working with the people of his congregation, many of whom were "out of work, out of clothes, out of shoes, and out of hope," he received the social passion which stayed with him all of his life. His first ambition was the orthodox one, to save souls, but he soon discovered that conditions in the city were so bad that it was not a safe place for saved souls. He saw in his own congregation the effects of poverty and unemployment, the tragedy of malnutrition and the terrible waste of life due to disease and crime in the tenement district. He felt that the church must not permit people to live in such poorly ventilated, over-crowded shacks; they must have homes and playgrounds and an opportunity to work.[16] Dr. Fosdick said of him, "He knew in detail the plight of human lives, and he cared. He valued above all else human personalities; and was outraged at their wrongs. When he spoke, therefore, about society and its crying need of reformation, it was the individual he was thinking of and the impact of society on persons that he was trying to affect." [17]

Rauschenbusch once told his class in the seminary how many times a mother in one of the tenements in his early parish had to lift her baby carriage up a curb, in going either north, south, east or west, before she could find a square yard of grass for her child to play upon, His attitude toward people is revealed in a reported conversation in which he said, "When traveling on railway trains alone I used to meditate on the life problems of the people I saw. I then would shut out of my mind everything else but the needs of these people." [18] He gave himself without reserve to the needs of his people. It was said he "could not refuse" the cry of the needy. In fact, it was because he left his sick bed too soon to answer a call for help that he suffered a relapse which resulted in the deafness which was such a burden to him all the rest of his life. As a result of his almost total deafness, he was shut off from much natural intercourse and companionship that he craved and it left him at times quite lonely and depressed.

Rauschenbusch was searching for an idea that was big enough to include both the individual and social aspects of religion. He found it in his conception of the Kingdom of God. For him it was all-inclusive and he gave himself to it completely. He resolved to live literally by the teaching and spirit of Jesus. As much as any man is capable, he lived up to his ideals as preacher and pastor, professor and author, husband and father and friend. A workman in his New York parish said, "We have found in him more that is Christlike than in any human being we have ever met." [19]

It was, of course, after he left the pastorate and became a professor at Rochester Theological Seminary that he formulated and expressed his theories of the social gospel in his lectures and a series of books which changed the direction of American Christianity. While serving as professor he did not lose his interest in individuals. He participated in a sort of clinic which had a division to aid the unemployed, another for those needing personal help and another for those who had religious doubts under the direction of Rauschenbusch. A physician was available without expense and clothes were available for those who might need them.[20] His former secretary tells of the influence of the many letters he wrote to children in hospitals, to pastors and Sunday School teachers, to men who were tired and discouraged.

It was said of Walter Rauschenbusch that "he knew the human heart as few men ever do." He was interested in human nature. Among his unpublished papers are psychological studies of his first two children before they were a year old. But, most of all, it was a knowledge gained from intimate contact and from sharing the struggles of the underprivileged and unfortunate, together with years of prayerful meditation as to how these problems might be alleviated, that gave him his understanding. He put his knowledge to good use, for few men have had a more farreaching influence in the life of American Christianity than Walter Rauschenbusch. D. R. Sharpe says, ". . . he introduced a new element, that of compassion for the common people." [21]

Another social prophet who found his interest in the social gospel as a result of his work with individuals was Graham Taylor. Like Rauschenbusch, he had a great concern for individuals and, also like Rauschenbusch, out of his efforts to guide, comfort, and counsel individuals, he saw the necessity of facing social conditions which were making individuals what they were. In his first parish he came in contact with the results of poverty, poor housing, overcrowding, unemployment, and he saw their results in the moral and spiritual life of the people. He was faithful in his pastoral duties to the rich and poor alike; he visited the sick, cared for the unfortunate and tried to mold his people into a brotherhood. Seven years of such efforts changed his major emphasis from one of proper doctrine, with which he began his pastorate, to one centering in human needs and true neighborliness. From this rural pastorate he went to the Fourth Congregational Church of Hartford, a city church in a rundown condition. Here he applied the same neighborly principles he had used in the rural parish. Since the people did not come to the church, he went to the people. "He visited the jails and the state prison and talked to men through cell bars. He went from house to house, office to office, and tenement to tenement, meeting men and women where they worked or lived, making friends with them just as he had done with the tenant farmers of Dutchess County. And the results were the same: the lonely and the poor, the outcast and troubled, responded. They began to come to his church to hear more of what he had to say. . . . Here, too, he opened an office to which the friendless and the troubled came and talked out their difficulties with him." [22]

When Taylor was called to the chair of practical theology at Hartford Theological Seminary he accepted, on the condition that he could remain with the church and use it as a clinic where the students could come in contact with actual human need. He donated his own salary to the church to enable them to secure a co-pastor. Later he went to the Chicago Theological Seminary where he held the first chair of Christian Sociology in the United States. In his inauguration address he told the students that their chief text-books would be people, the men and women of the shops, the factories, the street. He said he would establish a clinic similar to those used by medical students, where they would study the cause and cure of poverty, intemperance and crime, and the relationship of heredity and environment and their influence on the making of character. When the school was unable to raise the funds for this clinic which he wanted, he did so himself by renting an old house out of his own salary in a congested part of the city. It was cleaned up and christened "Chicago Commons," a name which later gained such deserved fame after the project had proven a success. Here his students met with him and his staff and compared notes on their week's activities. One such evening is described. "One recounts what he has seen and heard visiting jails that day, another his experiences in a hospital, a third his interviews with employers and labor leaders, a fourth his observation in the courts and at probation agencies, a fifth his studies of child life in the neighborhood, a sixth his survey of health and sanitary conditions, a seventh a report of the churches of the district, and an eighth his impressions of social conditions in the ward. Discussion follows each student's presentation of his facts gathered at first hand, questions are raised, the next steps planned, and Professor Taylor draws the meeting to a close by showing the relation of their work to the upbuilding of the kingdom of God on earth." [23]

There is a close relationship between the social gospel and the pastoral counseling movement. The disciples of the social gospel developed the sociological study which is closely akin to the psychological study of religion. Both are concerned about the welfare of the individual. It is now realized that neither one can achieve its goal without the other. Leslie Weatherhead, who has achieved fame for his use of psychological methods in pastoral work, recently stated that the church must show more concern about mental and physical health. He goes on to say that in order to do this, it must also eradicate the slums and the conditions under which men and women live and work which destroy mental and physical health.[24] At the same time all have recognized that even the providing of ideal surroundings has never eliminated all personal problems. But the two are inseparably related. These men recognized this and, through their efforts, prepared the way for such men as Fosdick, McConnell, Holmes and other advocates of social righteousness and crusaders for the good community of a later day.

Chapter X

FAITH HEALING, CHRISTIAN SCIENCE
AND THE CULTS

The subject of faith healing has had an important bearing on the development of pastoral counseling. It is a long, varied and involved subject, as has been ably shown by Cutten in his *Three Thousand Years of Mental Healing.*[1] It is not at all confined to Christian groups but seems to have been a part of almost every religious expression. Among the primitive groups it was the only form of medical practice in which the office of the priest, physician, and magician were fulfilled by the same person. Charms, amulets, talismen and healing rites and customs of all sorts were practiced. Healings were commonly recorded by the religious leaders of the ancient Egyptians, by Mohammedan and Buddhist monks. In fact, it is not confined to religion as such at all. The "King's touch" was commonly reported in medieval Europe, supposedly beginning with Edward the Confessor in England and St. Louis in France. Many reports of cures by the laying on of the king's hands are available, but it was supposed to be especially effective with epilepsy and scrofula. Not only theologians but physicians testified to the efficacy of the king's touch. Charles II was supposed to have touched one hundred thousand persons, and James, on one occasion, touched eight hundred persons in Chester Cathedral. In fact, when William III refused to carry out the practice he was severely criticized for cruelty.[2]

Roman Catholic Christianity has had many expressions of faith healing, centered around the saints, relics and shrines. It was believed that the Church had a supernatural power all her

own that centered in these personalities and in these places.
Very often a saint was attributed with this power and exercised
it by direct contact with the people. After his death it was felt
to continue in some relic or some shrine with which he had
been associated. These relics were sometimes of the crudest
and strangest sort, toes of St. Peter, finger nails and toe nails
were common, hair, nails of the cross, pieces of wood supposedly from the cross, blood, tears, milk from the virgin Mary,
etc., etc., of every type and description. It was all extended by
the crusaders who brought back many relics from the Holy
Land. Pilgrimages and visits to these places were very extensive
and many cures were reported. In many churches and cathedrals in Europe crutches have been left as a testimony to those
who have been healed there. During the Middle Ages there
developed quite a specialization among the saints and shrines.
Certain ones were believed to be effective with one disease or
for certain areas of the body while others had more success in
other areas. Cutten gives a long list, a few of which are as follows, St. Agatha against sore breasts, St. Apollonia against
toothache, St. Avertin against lunacy, St. Clara against sore
eyes, St. Erasmus against the colic, St. Herbert against hydro-
phobia, and so on for more than thirty-eight different saints
and diseases.[3] The relics of St. Ralia at Palermo were credited
with effecting cures and warding off epidemics for many years.
When an eminent osteologist, Professor Buckland, revealed the
fact that they were the bones of a goat it apparently had little
effect on their healing power.[4]

The two most famous shrines have been Lourdes in France
and St. Anne de Beaupré in the province of Quebec. Both of
these shrines are visited by literally thousands of people every
year. Lourdes is reported to receive three hundred thousand
visitors annually, the majority of whom are Catholic but not
a few are Protestant or with no religious affiliation. The source
of the healing power of Lourdes supposedly goes back to a
vision of the Virgin received there and to the healing power of

a spring in which the patients may bathe. Of all the shrines it has been the most closely examined and investigated by medical men, and, while many are not cured, there is ample evidence that many cures do take place. Such authorities as Janet and Alexis Carrell testify to this fact. Charcot, while at the Salpêtriere, sent many patients to Lourdes annually. While he did not agree with the patients as to the source of the healing he felt that it could be utilized in his practice. St. Anne de Beaupré has had similar results in America. Its healing power is said to come from the wrist bones of the saint.

There were several developments that took place outside the church which came to have somewhat of an influence on the church and the ministry, such as phrenology, mesmerism and hypnotism. Phrenology was developed by Franz Joseph Gall, an anatomist, who was primarily concerned with the head and brain. As a school boy he believed he had observed a close relationship between the people's characteristics and the shapes of their heads. Later he carried his investigations into jails and insane asylums. As a result of his investigations he formulated his theory that characteristics of personality can be found in the size and shape of the skull. It was Spurzheim who adopted the term phrenology. He did much to dignify the movement as he dealt more with the common and respectable traits of men than with those associated with jails and asylums. Phrenology had a tremendous popular appeal.[5] Henry Ward Beecher heard Spurzheim speak when he was in Junior College. He was very much attracted by the theory and carried on a life time study of its principles. He once said that every minister of the gospel could not be without a practical knowledge of men and there was nothing that would aid him more in securing that knowledge than phrenology.[6] However, while there were others who accepted the theories of phrenology, its influence on the ministry cannot be said to be large. In spite of the fact that modern anatomy and psychology have completely undermined the basic assumptions of phrenology, there are still people who consult so-called practitioners who claim the ability to read character and personality from the "bumps" on the head.

Of far more significance for their influence on religious groups was the development of mesmerism and hypnotism. The state of hypnotism is probably as old as man in one form or another. A man by the name of von Helmont in the sixteenth century presented the idea of animal magnetism by teaching that a magnetic fluid radiates from all men and, by force of will, may be used to influence the minds and bodies of others. Mesmer, a physician in Vienna, had a view similar to von Helmont's but he tried to explain the effect of the stars upon human beings. He felt that there must be some principle that permeates the universe that is probably identified with electricity or magnetism. This idea led him to experiment with the effect of magnets on persons and, in stroking their bodies with magnets, he discovered he could produce what would now be called hypnosis. As a physician, he used this method in healing certain diseases and published his findings in a book in 1766. Some years later he became associated with a Catholic priest named Gassner who had considerable success as a faith healer but who did not use magnets. Mesmer then realized that his magnets were unnecessary; he accordingly altered both his method and his theory. He then felt there must be some occult force residing in his own person that was capable of influencing others. He called this force animal magnetism. In Paris he constructed his famous baquet, a great oak chest with appendages of iron which Mesmer had supposedly magnetised himself. The patients sat in a circle about it, their hands joined or connected by cords. Mesmer would then appear and pass about the circle, touching some, passing his hand over others or just fixing his gaze upon them. Many cures were reported. This received wide publicity and was a subject of much interest in both lay and scientific circles. It was an English physician by the name of Braid who was the founder of hypnotism as a science and who was the first to use the name. Mesmerism, while no doubt creating the state of hypnosis, postulated a different theory. It was believed there was an influence or a fluid which passed from the operator to the object. Mesmer never dropped the term magnetism even when he discovered that magnets had nothing to do with it. Braid was not a mesmerist; he viewed the whole matter from the basis of a scientific physiologist and saw that it was the patient's own mind which was controlling his body. To his own surprise he discovered he could produce an artificial sleep in the members of his own family by having them stare rigidly at some bright object above the line of vision, but this is getting ahead of the story. While Braid and later Bernheim, Charcot and others were investigating hypnotism on a scientific basis, mesmerism traveled to America and found a place with transcendentalism of Emerson and many other ideas that were attracting attention in New England.

The man who utilized some of these ideas, whose works were the subject of endless controversy and whose influence through two or three of his patients reached far beyond anything he ever dreamed or anticipated was Phineas Parkhurst Quimby. Quimby had been very ill with consumption, the victim of much medication, but had recovered through an emotional crisis. He studied mesmerism and traveled with Lucius Burkmer over whom he had a strong influence. When Burkmer was hypnotized he was supposed to be able to see into the bodies of Quimby's patients and report their condition. Many cures resulted. Quimby, however, though uneducated, was not without intelligence and was not satisfied with merely the occult. He came to the conclusion that what Burkmer saw was what the patient thought and he made the sweeping generalization that what caused the cure was the patient's confidence and not medicine. This led to his defining of sickness as belief. He identified sickness as wrong belief and health as right belief. He became quite well known and, in some cases, was highly successful. G. G. Atkins says of him, "He became a skillful diagnostician of states of mind and a healer of such diseases as could be so treated. But he knew, scientifically, no more of what lay behind it all than a ploughman may know of what lies beneath the furrows he turns." [7] He called his system a science since he felt it operated by certain laws and he tried to reduce it to a system. He saw a parallel to his efforts in the gospel narratives of the healing miracles so he claimed Christ as the founder of the science. In fact, he actually used the term "Christian Science." But it was one of Quimby's patients who popularized it, capitalized on it and expanded it into a movement that gained world-wide attention. It was Mrs. Patterson, better known as Mary Baker Eddy, the sick, nervous, unhappy wife of an unsuccessful dentist who came to consult him at the height of his success. She was the one who was first healed by him and who then utilized the material he developed in carrying out her own unusual career and in developing her own church which has had such a tremendous following and such a wide influence.

The story of Mary Baker Eddy has been frequently told and the events of her life are too well known to need much repetition here. [8] Perhaps no character in history has been pictured in more contrasting extremes. She is described as a precocious, moody, neurotic child, subject to fits and seizures, and very severe attacks of hysteria. These attacks, sometimes of a very violent nature, continued into her adult life. When a girl she joined the Congregational Church at Tilton but, as time went on, she became interested in mesmerism, spiritualism, supposedly heard "calls" from the other world, frequently fell into trances, even when on a social call, and was supposedly spoken to by spirits. She had much difficulty getting along with people, according to most of these sources. After her second divorce she lived with relatives, but this did not prove satisfactory and they apparently turned her out. Dakin, one of her biographers, described her condition at the age of forty as one who was alone, unloved by her own relatives, sick and discouraged, with no purpose and no means of support.

It was in this condition that she sought out P. P. Quimby whose reputation was at its height. When she arrived at Quimby's office she was so weak she had to be assisted up the stairs. His power over her was manifested at once. Even in the act of shaking hands she sensed something dynamic and vital. She was his most ardent admirer and disciple even to the point of embarrassment to him. She haunted his offices, studied his manuscripts, wrote poems of his greatness. She was apparently completely cured and her gratitude knew no bounds.

Quimby died in 1866. Somewhat later Mrs. Eddy suffered a severe fall on the ice. She was attended by a physician, Dr. Cushing, and she also sought the help of Julius Dresser, one of Quimby's pupils. There has been much controversy as to what happened and different reports have been made. This Dr. Alvin Cushing said he attended her for two weeks and left her practically recovered. Mrs. Eddy came to the conclusion that she had healed herself. In terms of the final result it is her own interpretation that is important. She felt that she had recovered from an injury that neither medicine nor surgery could reach. She later said that this was the event that led her to the discovery not only of how to be well herself but how to make others well also. She said it was in February, 1866, that she discovered the Science of Divine Metaphysical Healing which she afterwards named Christian Science, although the date of the founding of Christian Science has been the subject of much controversy. For many years previously she said she had been attempting to trace all physical effects to a mental cause, but it was in 1866 that she came to her feeling of certainty. Now that Quimby was dead, she was left on her own resources and was free to develop what she had gained from him along her own lines.

However, she did not give credit to Quimby, but claimed it as her own revelation. After her healing she said that she withdrew from society for about three years to think through her mission and to search the Scriptures. She did admit using the Scriptures, in fact called it her textbook, and said that while it answered her questions as to how she was healed it contained no direct interpretation of her principle of healing—to secure this it was necessary to have her Key which will be mentioned later. She felt and stated that she was the first one to understand the Scriptures, that the Heavenly Father had revealed them to her and she was the first one to present their true spiritual meaning.

She announced her system in 1867, claiming it to be the first purely metaphysical system of healing since the days of the apostles. It was not until 1875 that an attempt at organization was made. She continued as a speaker, teacher and healer, ever gaining a larger following. Many miraculous cures were reported of all sorts and degrees of illness. She described one experience when she was invited to speak in a certain town in Rhode Island. Upon her arrival she found that the next-door neighbor of her hostess was dying and that the physicians had given her up; in fact, her clothes had been prepared for the burial. Mrs. Eddy was granted permission to see the patient and, after she had stood by her bedside for about fifteen minutes, the woman rose from the bed fully cured. Many such stories are included in her writings. It was not always necessary for the patient to have her personal ministration. Many claimed to have been healed merely by hearing her speak. As her following increased she secured pupils who received her course of instruction for one hundred dollars and who returned to her a portion of the income from their practice. Later she felt that God "impelled" her to increase the price to three hundred dollars which she admitted seemed like a startling sum for two weeks of instruction, but God led her by a "strange providence" to accept the fee and had shown her in many ways the wisdom of her choice.

It was in Lynn, Massachusetts, 1875, that the first society known as Christian Science was organized. It was also this year that marked the appearance of *Science and Health* after considerable difficulty in getting a publisher. Mrs. Eddy, because of her meager education, had much difficulty with her spelling and punctuation. By her own admission, after her discovery of Christian Science, most of the knowledge she had gained from school books "vanished like a dream." She was helped by the Reverend Wiggins, a retired Unitarian minister, who claimed to have rewritten great portions of it. The whole question of the relationship of *Science and Health* with the Quimby Manuscripts has been the subject of endless debate and controversy and much litigation. The book has been frequently revised and many of its earlier contradictions and crudities removed. The first society was not too successful and the first incorporated Church of Christ Scientist was chartered in 1879 in Boston with twenty-six members. Boston then became the center of the movement. It was here that Mrs. Eddy maintained the Mother Church and here she founded her Metaphysical college in 1883. There was a great deal of strife—divisions, jealousies and much litigation—but the society continued to grow.

The philosophy which she developed has been described by G. G. Atkins as a "strange mingling of the true, the assumed and the false." [9] It is based on the assumption that mind is all and all is mind. God is all powerful, God is good, and God is mind. Since God, who is spirit is everything, there is no such thing as matter. Matter is mortal error, unreal, temporal and to be denied. Sickness and all disease, even death is an error of mortal mind. Its assumptions were backed up by selected illustrations and testimonies of which the Christian Scientists had plenty and all that challenged them was ignored. Mrs. Eddy even included the "collective error" of mortal mind which was very powerful in its influence. For this reason arsenic could have harmful effects even on a Christian Scientist because of the collective error that it was a poison. Thus there were two perfect alibis. If a cure failed, either the patient lacked faith or he was the victim of the errors of the minds of others.

By a strange inconsistency the Scientists accepted the diagnosis of the medical men of a condition which did not exist. Also Mrs. Eddy advised her practitioners that until the advancing age admits the supremacy of Mind, it was better to leave the setting of a broken bone to the surgeon. Later she decreed that they were not to treat contagious diseases but claimed also that these were limitations that were to be overcome.

The movement grew with great rapidity and soon developed an enormous following. There are various factors that explain its growth. Again, to quote Atkins, the theology, the medical science, the philosophy and psychology of New England of this period by their very limitations prepared the way for such expressions.[10] Also Mrs. Eddy was a type; she spoke for many dissatisfied, nervous, neurotic, self-centered people who needed a new sense of faith and courage. As one man said, "Any system that will enable people to ignore their troubles will have a large following." Furthermore, there was sufficient truth in her doctrine to produce results in many cases and to provide dramatic testimonies that had a great influence. Psychology is not completely agreed as to how suggestion affects bodily functions but it is common knowledge that it is very powerful. Wrong suggestion can weaken or impair bodily functions, produce definite symptoms of actual illness; right suggestion can strengthen and eliminate many such conditions. Since a vast range of nervous and even physical ailments are functional in nature, suggestion such as Christian Science utilized, produced by faith in the movement and its founder, did produce many practical results.

The rapid growth of the movement caused increased concern in the more established churches. Since the vast majority of its members were recruited from other Protestant churches, it soon became the subject of much opposition, denunciation and ridicule. Some tried to deny any cures, only to be answered by more testimonies. Others opposed its bizarre theological conceptions and misinterpretations of the Scriptures. Others were concerned with its discount of the medical profession and the danger resulting from its refusal to utilize scientific medicine and care. It also had an indirect influence on the work of the pastor which came quite as a by-product. There were other pastors who would not accept its theological and philosophical presuppositions any more than would its harsher critics but who realized that its rapid growth indicated a limitation, an omission in the thought and program of the church. Christian Science thus brought home very forcibly the need of facing the relationship of religion and health. Also its obvious success in some cases presented a possibility of what could be done by faith and prayer but on a more sound and scientific basis. Perhaps, more than any other movement, scientific or religious, it forced the Protestant pastor to face the question of human nature which he might otherwise have ignored, especially the relation of faith and religious attitudes to emotional wellbeing and to physical health.

We have dealt extensively with the Christian Science movement because it has had such a wide influence. There were many others who claimed to have the power to heal or for whom it was claimed by others. St. Francis, John Wesley, George Fox, all were reported to have effected cures. Martin Luther was said to have cured his friend by prayer. Joseph Smith, founder of the Mormons, reportedly acted as a healer although he admitted failure in a cholera epidemic. His conclusion was that God had decreed destruction on the people and it was futile to attempt to stay his hand. There were many men who gained a following through their healing power although none of them reached the proportions of Christian Science. Pastor Blumhardt of Wurtemberg was reported to have made many miraculous cures through prayer. Francis

Schlatter, a Roman Catholic of Alsace, later came to America where he achieved a wide reputation as a healer. He wandered about the country and was sought out by immense crowds. From two to five thousand people would form long lines just to be permitted to hold his hand while he prayed. Healing power was not limited to any country or denominational group. Father John of Cranstadt was of the Orthodox Church of the East and his fame as a healer became so great in Russia that he had to leave the church by a side door after celebrating communion. John Alexander Dowie, who served as a Congregational minister, founded his own sect, the Christian Catholic Apostolic Church of Zion. He believed that all bodily ailment was the work of the devil and that Christ came to destroy the works of the devil. He believed in divine healing in direct answer to prayer and claimed to pray and lay his hands on seventy thousand annually. He established his headquarters at Zion City, near Chicago, where he built a tabernacle and lined the walls with trophies of his healing. The movement was much involved with the law, as well as with divisions and controversies among the members themselves, and, with the death of Dowie, lost most of its vitality.[11]

Another outgrowth of the work of Quimby was the development of what became known as New Thought under the leadership of Dresser who, like Mary Baker Eddy, had been his patient. The first New Thought society was organized in Boston in 1894 and the first New Thought convention was held in 1899. In 1917, a creed was formulated which emphasized a series of affirmations such as, "We affirm the good . . . we affirm health . . . we affirm the divine supply" . . . etc.[12] New Thought followers did not ask members to leave other churches but rather to stay in them and be better members than they had before. They produced considerable literature on health and healing, character and the spiritual fulness of life, and the application of New Thought principles to the practical affairs of life. Perhaps the most notable of these books has been Trines' *In Tune with the Infinite*. New Thought did not deny matter or suffering, as, for example, did Christian Science, but the members claimed there were healing forces which were available and which would do their healing work if man trusted them and yielded himself to them. This philosophy consisted of an emphasis on the bright side of every situation; it stressed the realities of health, beauty, and success. Its key words were Harmony, Realization, Affirmation and Poise.

A similar group is the Unity Truth Society, with headquarters in Kansas City. They publish a weekly magazine, "Weekly Unity." Each week there is a meditation for each day such as, "I am a happy healthy child of the living God who will help me in all I do," or, "I fearlessly depend upon God as the unfailing source of all I need." The influence of such suggestion and affirmation upon those who practice it faithfully is at once evident. Also each issue contains a section, "The Society of Silent Unity; the Healing Department of Unity." This consists of a group of consecrated persons who will pray with the individual who writes them requesting their prayers. They have published a little booklet entitled *Health Is Catching*,[13] which consists of letters of testimony by those who have been cured by Silent Unity. The table of contents lists arthritis, asthma, broken bones, cancer, diabetes, eczema, epilepsy, goiter, grief, and many others, as well as help in the rental of property and the improvement of subnormal children. They maintain a Unity School of Christianity where instructors are trained who maintain classes in local communities.

There have been many other individuals and groups where healing has had a major or a minor part, such as the Nazarene movement under the leadership of Henry D. Wilson, or the Four Square Gospel and the somewhat checkered career of Aimee Semple McPherson, or the various expressions found in the Pentecostal Cults. Many of these groups hold healing missions throughout the country to which the public is invited to come. Some use the laying on of hands, some follow James 5:14

and anoint with oil; almost all depend strongly on prayer and faith. Their emphasis is on a literal approach to the Bible and the gifts of the spirit. The cults feel that since the early church practised healing, the church today should also. Most of these services resemble the average church service, or rather a revival service type of expression. The hymns, prayers, the personality of the leader all tend to produce a crowd psychology, to increase emotionalism. The address of the speaker and the testimonials of others are such as to increase expectancy and faith. Such groups have for some time been a part of the Christian movement; they are especially prevalent during times of national crisis and upheaval. New groups are constantly springing into being and others disappear. A study of the United States Religious Census for 1936 reveals that there were at that time two churches which made healing their primary emphasis and thirty-five groups which were listed as emphasizing healing in their doctrines.[14]

Another movement which had its origin outside the church but which had some following in religious circles was that of the Frenchman, Coué. He had considerable success in his native country and also gained a rather extensive following in the United States. Mr. Coué's method was to have the individual repeat a formula every morning and every evening, "Every day in every way I am getting better and better." He was credited with unusual success at Nancy, was sought by great crowds and his theory achieved worldwide publicity. Among those attracted by it were some ministers who felt that in it could be found a new method that would be of great usefulness by the clergy and the church. As one of them expressed it, "It offers a means by which the Church can escape from its present lethargy and impotence and become once more a source of energy, inspiration and heroic life." [15] They recognized that Coué's method was plainly secular but proposed to develop, side by side with it, a Christian practice of auto-suggestion. They contended that there was no active power in auto-suggestion that was not available in the teaching of Jesus, but a knowledge of auto-suggestion, if applied to Jesus' teaching, made it much richer and more effective than had usually been recognized.[16] In a book *Christianity and Autosuggestion*, written jointly by a practitioner of auto-suggestion, C. Henry Brooks, and a minister, the Reverend Ernest Charles, the authors present the idea that auto-suggestion is not an isolated scientific method but is inherent in Jesus' teaching on faith and is but a statement in psychological terms of the religious truth that Jesus preached and practiced. They compare Coué's curing of a blacksmith who had a paralyzed arm with Jesus' curing of the man with the withered hand, although they admit that Coué's cure was slow and laborious in comparison with that of Jesus. They do not oppose the use of medical aid and feel it should be used if needed. They feel that there should be no opposition between medical care and treatment by auto-suggestion and prayer.

There are other groups that can be mentioned—the whole realm of the occult and esoteric. The fad of the ouija board, the ever-present astrologers, palmists, and other such groups, usually find something of a following and are consulted about all sorts of matters from family problems to where to find a lost pocket-book. The number of people who frequent these individuals would indicate the mass of people in any generation who need guidance and counsel and who are hungry for something that will give them confidence and faith.

These groups have met with a varied response from the ministry. Opposition was to be expected; they were met with all degrees of denunciation, ridicule, and condemnation. Many ignored them. There were others who felt there was something to learn from them. They recognized the fact that the huge following some of these groups secured indicated an omission in the traditional emphasis of the church and a weakness in its program and method. While not accepting their theories, they felt that the cults indicated the necessity of facing the question of how spiritual power could be made available for daily life.[17] They felt that their concern for the unfortunate and their recognition of the relationship of religion and health, both mental and physical, was something that the church could well emulate, although they could not accept either their philosophy or their methods. Furthermore, the results which such groups did produce would indicate that there is a vast area that needs careful and thorough investigation and research. Fritz Kunkel, the psychotherapist, speaking of such groups, says that none of them really achieved the position they claimed but all of them have proved that there are "hidden energies in the deeper layers of the human mind" which can be utilized if properly understood and controlled.[18]

PART IV

FROM WORLD WAR I TO WORLD WAR II

Chapter XI

ADVANCES IN PSYCHOLOGY, CASE WORK, AND PSYCHOSOMATIC MEDICINE

One of the most characteristic expressions of our modern era has been an interest in things psychological. It can truly be called a psychological age. Common conversation has been filled with such terms as "repression," "sublimation," "the subconscious," "inferiority complex"; often without too much understanding as to their true meaning. There has been a veritable flood of psychological literature of all degrees of quality and usefulness. It has been further popularized by many novels, movies, magazine articles, the radio and the newspaper. The importance of the findings of psychology has been recognized in the fields of education, medicine, religion, law, industry, advertising, penology, social work and many other areas. Novelists, historians, poets, playwrights, biographers have turned to a psychological interpretation of their subject matter. Psychologists, psychiatrists and general counselors, have been added to the staffs, or utilized in the programs of schools, colleges, juvenile courts, corrective institutions, welfare organizations, churches, industrial institutions and business establishments. The frequent reminder that approximately one half of all hospital beds in the United States are occupied by mental patients and that one out of twenty-two persons in the United States experiences some sort of mental illness, has served to remind the people of the seriousness of the problem.

Psychiatry as a specialty in medicine became popular during World War I. It was with some difficulty that it had received recognition previous to this time but, through the study and treatment of so-called shell shock, it received a great impetus. The development of group testing was also greatly advanced in this war, through the use of tests that were developed for the army. That World War II will have similar effects is no doubt true but it is too early to tell just to what extent. The social and economic conditions that existed between the two wars, resulting in nervousness, restlessness, fatigue, strain and worry, did much to create an interest in anyone or anything that could offer some relief. The mushroom growth of cities, belt-line production resulting in monotony and tension on the job, the depression with its fear of unemployment and uncertainty of the future, the over-stimulation of commercialized amusements and the speed and strain of a mechanized society all added to this picture. One psychologist said, "There have been few periods in history . . . more laden with doubt and disillusionment than the twentieth century. . . . There never was a time in which more people were in a state of confusion, their lives unadjusted, the future uncertain." [1] Karen Horney wrote a book entitled *The Neurotic Personality of Our Time* and closed with the sentence, "We might call him a step-child of our culture." [2]

Academic psychology, too, continued to increase. True, it was divided into several competing schools and camps not dissimilar to the denominations of Protestantism, but each college and university had a department of psychology. Other schools appeared to defend their positions alongside of structuralism, behaviorism, functionalism and others mentioned in an earlier chapter. McDougall at Harvard, and later at Duke, presented his school of purposivism or hormic psychology. Woodworth at Columbia advocated what was termed Dynamic Psychology, while Kohler and Koffka made their famous observations of the apes and presented the world with the new Gestalt psychology, or the psychology of configuration. Of course, many took the middle of the road or eclectic position. It would take us too far afield to trace the various positions and doctrines of these various groups. Suffice it to say that psychology had established itself in the scientific world and in the popular mind. While it was, and still is, far from complete, full of many contradictions, divisions, with much yet to be established, yet no area of life could ignore its findings or fail to recognize its significance. We shall consider the areas which were especially affected and which had a close relationship to the ministry, both because of their influence and the close relationship of their efforts: they are social case work and psychosomatic medicine.

SOCIAL CASE WORK

The development of social case work did not receive the attention that the field of psychology did, but it was not without significance. Social work grew out of the philosophy and the practice of the Christian church in the first place. During the middle ages, following the decline of feudalism and in such tragic periods as the invasion of the Black Death, it was the church which cared for the poor, distributed alms, cared for transients, the sick, the aged and the orphaned. The first attempts to organize society for the benefit of the poor was in Hamburg, in the early part of the eighteenth century. The town of Elberfeld accepted and improved upon the plan. In England the first "Society for Bettering the Condition and Increasing the Comforts of the Poor" was founded in 1796, by Thomas Bernard and assisted by the Bishop of Durham. Other plans and projects for the caring of the socially unfortunate were soon inaugurated. Some prominent churchmen were active in these movements, among them Charles Kingsley and Cardinal Newman. The Quakers were truly pioneers in all of these developments, being active in poor relief, public health, care of the insane, prison reform and other areas.[3] As early as 1826, Joseph Tucker was appointed by the Unitarians to a "ministry at large" to the unchurched classes of Boston, being one of the first, if not the first, church social worker in America.

The term, social work, is a twentieth-century term. It had previously been known as poor relief, charity and philanthropy. Josephine Strode, in her *Introduction to Social Case Work*,[4] traces its development as it is revealed through definitions. She traces these definitions from the concept of house-to-house visitation of 1874 to the modern scientific basis of case recording, psychological understanding and utilization of a variety of agencies. Very prominent and influential in this development has been the work of Mary Richmond. In 1897, she presented a paper on "The Need of a Training School in Applied Philanthropy." The following year a summer institute was established and, in 1904, the New York School of Philanthropy was organized, which later became the New York School of Social Work. In 1907, she read a paper entitled, "Friendly Visiting," which was a significant development in the field of scientific charity.

The further development can be marked by three important books that appeared. Mary Richmonds' *Social Diagnosis*,[5] which appeared in 1917, marked a milestone in the development of social case-work practice, for it indicated that a scientific method had been slowly developing. It marked the sociological approach to case work when the emphasis was upon diagnosing the client's need and an attempt to supply it. Five years later her *What Is Social Case Work?* [6] stressed the psychological aspects of case work instead of the sociological emphasis that had predominated in her earlier volume. In 1930, Virginia Robinson published *A Changing Psychology in Social Case Work*,[7] which defined case work further as an individual therapy through a treatment relationship rather than through social welfare.

Case work was profoundly influenced by the findings of psychology and the mental hygiene movement and developed what is now known as Psychiatric Social Work. In 1918 the first course in psychiatric case work was offered at Smith College in coöperation with the Boston psychopathic hospital. Soon similar courses were offered in other schools.

Social work received its great impetus as a result of the social and economic conditions during the depression following the crash of 1929 and by the mandate of the Social Security Act of 1933. The government had had bureaus in the interest of social welfare but nothing in any way comparable to that which followed the signing of the above mentioned act. This act made available $500,000,000 for relief work. In April, 1938, there were over 6,400,000 households and some twenty million people receiving public aid at a total cost for that one month of $241,031,000.

As a result of such developments social case work created a very wide range of contacts and interests. Social workers are connected with hospitals and clinics, churches and schools, institutions for dependents and delinquents, social settlements, industry and welfare organizations. They deal with such problems and subjects as child welfare, delinquency, probation, recreation, health, family relief and rehabilitation, housing, community life, mental hygiene, immigration and social service. They have developed skills and techniques based on the developments and findings in the fields of sociology, education, medicine, psychology, psychiatry and other allied fields. They have consistently improved and refined their techniques of interviewing and case recording and have developed a philosophy and a professional code of ethics.

It is strange that more attention has not been given to the methods of the case worker by those interested in pastoral counseling. In many ways their methods and experiences have much more in common with the work of the minister than does that of the psychologist or psychiatrist. They both study the individual in relation to his whole social situation, they both deal with the more normal cases. Some of their books on interviewing such as Young's *Interviewing in Social Work* [8] or Garrett, *Interviewing: Its Principles and Methods* have much that would be of value to the pastor. There have been a few such as Holman who have utilized them but in the main they have been neglected for the writings of the psychologist and psychiatrist. The one, perhaps, most widely read by the clergy has been Karl de Schweinitz' little classic *The Art of Helping People Out of Trouble*. De Schweinitz gives a large place to religion saying, "However religion expresses itself, it is the most vital thing in the life of the indvidual in whom it exists, the primary source of inspiration and anchorage, the influence that sustains and steadies him in every adjustment that he must make." [9]

Not all social workers shared de Schweinitz' enthusiasm for religion, in fact many were quite indifferent; as with the psychologists, this varied with the individual. Others advocated coöperation with the church and utilized the services of the minister or priest when it was possible. There were some of the larger churches who began to employ full or part-time social workers on their staffs. A National Conference of Church Social Workers met in conjunction with the National Conference of Social Work in 1944. More and more the subjects such as "Religion as a Resource in Social Work," which was the basis of a round-table discussion at one meeting, have been finding their place in the program of social workers. [10]

PSYCHOSOMATIC MEDICINE

One of the most important developments of recent years has been the increased attention given to what has been termed psychosomatic medicine. The term comes from two Greek words, "psyche" and "soma" which mean mind and body and are joined to indicate the interrelationship that exists between the two. As in all of the other movements and developments we have discussed we find that this has a long history. Even Socrates said that one reason the physicians of Hellas were so ineffective was because they were so ignorant of the "whole." Plato said, "The office of the physician extends equally to the purification of mind and body; to neglect one is to expose the other to evident peril. It is not only the body that by its sound constitution strengthens the soul but the well-regulated soul by its authoritative power maintains the body in perfect health." [11]

The common sense of mankind has always recognized a relationship between mind and body and has realized that a sick mind can cause a sick body. It is evident in such a common expression as "worried sick." In one sense the understanding family physician has always practiced psychosomatic medicine, that is, he has always treated his patient as a whole, but in recent years very extensive and definite scientific studies of the emotions as factors in illness have been made.

The great physicians have long recognized this fact and taken it into account. Dr. William Osler said, "What happens to a patient with tuberculosis depends more on what he has in his head than what he has in his chest." [12] S. Weir Mitchell saw that an attitude of faith, an interest in things, a sense of humor could do something for a patient that nothing else could do.[13] Dr. Adolf Meyer insisted that it was the patient and not the disease that had to be cured and to do so all the aspects of the individual as a whole—hereditary, environmental, constitutional, physical, social and economic—must be considered. Richard C. Cabot, pondering the problems of how to care for the tuberculous, how to restore balance and happiness to neurasthenics and how to help a girl facing motherhood without a husband, wrote his book *What Men Live By*.[14] This book is now recognized as a classic and its four major emphases, Work, Play, Love and Worship, are well known, although Dr. Cabot admitted that to include worship was to shock many of the scientifically minded.

There are innumerable instances that could be cited where individuals recognized the importance of emotional and psychological factors in certain diseases, especially those of a gastrointestinal nature which was one of the first to be recognized.[15]

That would add little to our purpose in such a study as this. It was Walter B. Cannon of the Harvard Medical School who did so much to put the whole subject on a scientific basis and to draw popular attention to it. Cannon, after long and careful experimentation, published his findings in a volume entitled *Bodily Changes in Pain, Hunger, Fear and Rage.*[16] In this volume he showed conclusively that, during strong emotion, adrenal secretion is increased, blood sugar is increased, anger and fear can greatly affect proper digestion, in short, that whatever heightens the emotions modifies the very chemical structure of the body. In 1935 Flanders Dunbar published the first edition of her monumental work, *Emotions and Bodily Changes.*[17] This was a survey of all available literature on psychosomatic relationships since 1910; later it was revised and brought down to 1945. In this later edition she quotes exactly 2,400 different titles. She divides her study into the chapters dealing with various organs and organ systems and even includes a section on the bones as well as the usual discussion of the endocrines, gastro-intestinal system etc. In the introduction she points out how extremely complicated and complex the whole subject is and how limited our knowledge still is. She feels that the scientific study of emotions and their resulting effects on the body mark a new era in medicine, and also that we have scarcely begun to use the knowledge that we have.[18]

A very practical study was made by G. Canby Robinson in coöperation with the staff of the Johns Hopkins Hospital. As a young physician he took an interest in the personal problems of patients as they protruded above the routine medical care. He came to the conclusion that an understanding of the way in which personal problems, involving the "patient as a person," bear on a given illness were as important as the medical history and physical diagnosis if effective treatment was to be planned and applied. Consequently he made his study of a group of unselected patients at the hospital which he later published under the title *The Patient as a Person.*[19] He reached the conclusion that disease is only one element in illness and not the only cause of disturbances in the activities and functions of the body. He said, "Disease does not necessarily cause illness and illness may exist without disease." [20] Both the cause and the recovery of disease must be seen from this point of view. He stressed the fact that the recovery of many patients could be hastened by clearing away mental habits and by relieving them of worry that was wearing down courage. It was his conclusion that in 36 percent of the cases he studied the illness was caused by emotional disturbance. Eighty percent of the patients studied had adverse social conditions in their lives, while with 66 percent these conditions had a definite relation to their illness. He pointed out the further fact that such conditions often confused the diagnosis and many physicians merely considered them but hindrances or annoying complications rather than matters for serious study. The depth and duration of the emotional disturbance was seen to be of primary importance.

There have been many other studies and experiments made. More and more the significance of this phenomenon has become accepted. A statement by Edward A. Strecker has been very widely quoted both by medical men, psychologists and in religious volumes. He said, "Fully 50 percent of the problems of the acute stages of illness, and 75 percent of the difficulties of convalescence have their primary origin, not in the body, but in the mind of the patient." [21] Gray in *The Advancing Front of Medicine* [22] cites many interesting examples of which one will be selected as typical. He tells of a man whose blood pressure was 280; he was afflicted with a lung disorder and traces of albumin were evident in the urine. Rest and medication provided no relief. A chance remark revealed the fact that he had done a great wrong to his wife. A meeting was arranged between the estranged husband and wife, and a reconciliation was made possible. As a result his blood pressure fell to 150, his lung symptoms abated and the albumin disappeared, nor was there any recurrence after several years. Similar illustrations

as to how emotions have influenced the health could be referred
to in relation to eczema, asthma, backache, headache, ulcers
and other gastro-intestinal disturbances, and many others. Some
would say the list, where the progress of the disease at least is
influenced, is endless. Dr. Cabot even related a case where a
fractured leg failed to knit due to a patient's anxiety over his
family while he was in the hospital. His anxiety affected his appetite, this impaired nutrition and, as a consequence, the frac-
ture failed to knit. Assured that his family were being well
cared for, his anxiety ceased, his appetite returned and his
broken bones began to knit.[23]

There is much difference of opinion as to the validity and
usefulness of such findings. The medical profession, like the
clergy, are traditionally conservative about accepting new
ideas. Indifference, skepticism and opposition were commonly
expressed. Dunbar states there are three groups—those who
say that illness is all organic, those who say it is all psychic and
those who recognize it as a combination or an interrelationship
of the two. More and more, however, it has become a question
of the degree of influence that is ascribed to emotions. That the
emotions, such as fear, anxiety, hatred, do have an effect upon
the body and one's physical health and well being is now an
established fact. The recognition of this fact has had a profound
effect upon the practice of medicine and also upon medicine's
attitude toward religion. Since the latter part of the nineteenth
century many medical workers have had a materialistic philosophy which had little place for other values and often resulted in an open cleavage between the two groups. This new
emphasis served to make them aware, from a scientific basis, of
the values of the religious life and practice. Gray expressed it,
"The man who is frightened by some impending danger or
threat, is being poisoned by the secretions released into his
blood stream by an excited nervous system. But suppose despite
the events he is not frightened. Suppose he has faith in his destiny, confidence that the universe is friendly, suppose he is bet-

ting that God is and that the supreme power is interested in his welfare—then the chemicals which go with fear and uncertainty and resentment are not released by his nerves and his blood is not saturated with these overactive secretions. Thus religious faith, even a superstitious and animistic faith, may exert a bio-chemical influence, moderating the internal environment and thereby aiding the body to maintain a well-balanced equlibrium in the face of untoward external events." [24]

Gray also reports a study made by Dr. L. T. Swain and G. G. Harris of rheumatoid arthritics. In an astonishing number of cases they found that they were "fearfully facing life's responsibilities," and that "the solution begins in the honest facing of themselves with the doctor, and with his aid ends in the development of a vital faith. A deep religious faith is the most effective faith, provided the doctor himself has such a vital faith to give. Five years of observation has convinced us that just facing these negative attitudes is not enough to overcome them, but, with the development of a faith, fear goes, improved health follows, and, most important of all for the future welfare of the patient, personality changes take place. . . . All our combined medical and orthopedic skill is vitally essential for recovery, but because of the psychogenic factors found in most rheumatoid arthritics we will fail to prevent recurring attacks unless we develop, in the patient himself, a power to control his negative emotional reactions. From these observations we are convinced that the control of the psychogenic factors in chronic rheumatoid arthritics lies in the development of a vital faith, which will meet these needs, with its positive philosophy for living." [25]

Dr. Alexis Carrell said, "Such facts are of profound significance. They show the reality of certain relations of still unknown nature, between psychological and organic processes. They prove the objective importance of the spiritual activities, which hygienists, physicians, educators and sociologists have almost neglected to study. They open to man a new world." [26]

This has been especially true of the psycho-therapists such as Jung, Hadfield, Kunkel, Bond and Masters. Dr. Hadfield made a statement a few years ago that has been widely quoted, "I am convinced that the Christian religion is one of the most valuable and potent influences that we possess for producing that harmony and peace of mind and that confidence of soul which are needed to bring health and power to a large proportion of nervous patients. In some cases I have attempted to cure nervous patients with suggestions of quietness and confidence, but without success until I have linked these suggestions on to that faith in the power of God which is the substance of the Christian's confidence and hopes. Then the patient has become strong." [27] Fritz Kunkel expressed similar ideas in his recent volume, *In Search of Maturity*,[28] and suggested that the psychologist, the physician and the minister need each other and must work together. Such statements, while not receiving one hundred percent acceptance by all psychotherapists, have been increasingly common of recent years.

The results of such discoveries have not only given religion a new significance in the eyes of certain scientists but have awakened many ministers to the tremendous possibilities and the farreaching implications inherent in the meaning and practice of religion. Religion, it has been seen, has a definite and concrete place in the mental and physical health of an individual, not in some esoteric fashion, but due to the observed and demonstrated fact that the whole person is involved in either illness or health. This idea has presented a new opportunity for the relationship of the professions; it has given a new meaning to the work of the pastor in his own right. The minister and the church, so closely related to the emotions and attitudes of life are seen with a deep responsibility and a great opportunity. To counteract and to replace those attitudes of anxiety and fear, resentment, and frustration, hatred and envy, irritability and despondency, hopelessness and despair, with attitudes of

confidence and courage, calmness and contentment, even in adverse situations, forgiveness, love and goodwill, faith and hope,
in short to create and develop an indomitable and victorious
spirit is the great task of the minister and of the church.

Chapter XII

SOME MODERN PASTORS
AND PASTORAL SPECIALISTS

The clergy took various attitudes toward the development of this new psychology. As was stated in the preceding chapter, some opposed it, many were not even aware of it, but there were a few who, like the pastors of an earlier generation, were deeply concerned about the problems presented to them and saw here valuable insights which offered new opportunities and possibilities in their efforts to bring counsel and guidance to their people. Dr. Harry Emerson Fosdick is commonly recognized as one of the greatest preachers of his day. His sermons, from the pulpit and on the air, have been heard by thousands. He is equally well-known as a teacher, author and lecturer, but those who know his work the best have felt that perhaps as significant as anything else he has done has been his personal service to perplexed and needy people in what he calls his "confessional conferences." Certain hours each week were set aside for this part of his ministry. Dr. Hayward in a brief biographical sketch of his career spoke of these conferences and said, "In them he uses the best of modern psychology, as well as the deeper ministry of religion, and the contribution of deep sympathy and common sense." [1] Dr. Fosdick has himself described how this started.[2] While he was serving the First Presbyterian Church of New York City, where his primary responsibility was preaching, he desired more intimate relationship with the people and announced definite hours when he would be available. He immediately found himself confronted with a host of problems, some of a very serious nature, some of a type of which he had not even known existed. Sensing the seriousness of such a responsibility, conscious of his own inadequacy in the presence of some problems "whose genesis and diagnosis I could not give, and before which I stood helpless," he sought guidance and help.

He was a friend of Dr. Thomas W. Salmon, one of America's great pioneers in the field of mental hygiene and went to him for assistance. His own words describe their relationship, "Case after case, involving problems beyond my depth, he took on, and then with infinite patience went over them with me, explaining his diagnoses and therapies, illustrating his explanations from kindred or contrasting cases out of his practice, and sometimes turning the patients back to me as a collaborator to help them correct their spiritual attitudes and secure religious resources. My indebtedness to Dr. Salmon is incalculable. He opened a new world to me. Since then, books, a large and varied clientele, and able coöperators have helped to enlarge that world, but to my 'clinical' experience with Dr. Salmon I owe the best I have been able to do in personal counseling." [3] They had planned to conduct a clinic together at Riverside Church but this was prevented by the death of Dr. Salmon. Dr. Fosdick continued to utilize the services of psychiatrists, psychologists and neurologists in his work with people.

Dr. Hayward, in the article mentioned above, feels that perhaps Dr. Fosdick's deep understanding of the distressed and discouraged also came from his own experience of passing through a severe physical and nervous breakdown when he was in seminary. Dr. Fosdick described this experience in his own words in a sermon. "Sometimes I think we preachers, overawed by the formal dignity of the pulpit, talk too anonymously and impersonally. Here I am today, an older man talking to you about the secret of spiritual power in general, when all the time what I am really seeing in my imagination's eye is that young man I was years ago, shot all to pieces, done in and shattered in a nervous breakdown, foolishly undertaking too much work and doing it unwisely, all my hopes in ashes and life towering over me, saying, You are finished; you cannot; you are done for. People ask me why in young manhood I wrote *The Meaning of Prayer*. That came out of young manhood's struggle. I desperately needed a second chance and reënforcement to carry on with it. I was sunk unless I could find at least a little of what Paul had in mind when he said,—'In Him who strengthens me I am able for anything.' " [4]

Undoubtedly this experience did play a large part for perhaps no one ever became a great counselor until he knew something of the meaning of suffering or tension from personal experience. At least, through his own experience, together with his study of human nature, he has been able to help thousands to find reënforcement and a second chance. In spite of all he had to do, he still felt it was essential to deal with people in private conferences. He received considerable publicity a few years ago when, in an address before the Greater New York Federation of Churches, he told of his own experiences in conducting what he termed a "Protestant confessional." He paid tribute to the Catholic confessional and regretted the fact that Protestantism had nothing to compare with it. He said, "I have an office where people who know they are spiritually sick and mentally disturbed can come with their problems. Why shouldn't I minister to them? Never again will I be without such a place where people can meet me alone. Week after week I meet pretty nearly as many people as a priest. They are sick souls who need ministration." [5]

Dr. Fosdick often paid tribute to the psychologists and psychiatrists, quoting them frequently in his sermons. In fact, in one sermon he said, "I am strong for psychiatry. Sometimes I think that were I not a minister I would be a psychiatrist." [6] However, he also emphasized the fact that psychiatry has its limitations and religion must go beyond mere psychiatric readjustment. "It takes more than a knowledge of psychiatry to pull a personality together, else some of the psychiatrists themselves would be better integrated than they are. It takes inner reserves of power, available for daily use, the consciousness of which brings confidence, security, and courage." [7]

In a recent statement, published some twenty years after he first issued an invitation to meet with those who had personal problems, he stated, "As I look back on my ministry now, I wish that I could have extended my personal counseling farther, organized it better, and handled it more competently. At times a crowded schedule has reduced it to a minimum. I have never been able to give myself to it as once I dreamed I might, but a steady stream of troubled minds and disturbed emotions seeking help has willy-nilly kept me at it, and nothing in my ministry gives me more satisfaction now than the memory of some of the rseults." [8]

In England, none is better known for his work with individuals than is Dr. Leslie Weatherhead, formerly of Leeds, now of the City Temple in London. His work with hundreds of people in what he calls his "psychological clinic" has been widely heralded by many writers, and his numerous writings on psychological subjects have been referred to both in England and in the United States. He says that his interest in the subject goes back to an experience that occurred during World War I.[9] He was standing in a ward in a war hospital when a doctor who practiced psychotherapy turned to him and said, "You padres ought to be doing most of this." Dr. Weatherhead said, "Ever since that date my chief hobby-study has been psychology, with a special interest in the possibilities of using it in the practice of my profession." After five years of careful study in India and England he began to test it out in a practical way and to develop a technique suitable to the minister that would not trespass on the fields of either the doctor or the psychotherapist. He specifically warned that every minister should not attempt this function unless, he, too, was willing to give the five or six years "hobby-study" necessary. His work in his "psychological clinic" is done in full coöperation with the medical profession and he refuses to take a case where there are physical or serious mental symptoms unless he can work in coöperation with some medical men.[10] Many times men of the medical profession have sent their patients to him. He tells of one case of a young girl who had been lame for two years but her physician said, on sending her to him, that there was nothing whatever the matter with her legs. He found that under hypnosis she was able to walk. It was a long and involved case but the result was that the source of her difficulty, which resulted in her lameness, was discovered, she regained her ability to walk and her walking stick remains in his office.[11]

Dr. Weatherhead goes much farther than the average pastoral counselor in using the methods of the psychiatrist or analyst, such as hypnosis in the case above, or word association, dream-analysis, and suggestion. He cites another case of a woman who had been to two Harley street specialists and received no help. She was exceedingly depressed and was unable to sleep. She was obsessed with the fear of insanity and a dread of suicide. The source of her difficulty was found to be in the feeling that she had done something for which she could never be forgiven. Dr. Weatherhead spent an hour a day for a period of a month, treating her by attempting to get her to accept ideas; first, the idea that God was forgiving, then that he had a purpose for her, and then that his grace would prove sufficient for her to go back and face life confidently and courageously. On one occasion, during the treatment, he had her relax completely on a couch while he repeated one hundred times, "In Him who strengthens you, you are able for anything." The treatment was highly successful, but this is not a method the average minister would have the time, the ability or the training to use.[12] Dr. Weatherhead's work has been one of the real pioneer efforts in this field. His work during the recent war, especially during the terrible days of the blitz over London, was particularly outstanding.

There are others who could be mentioned such as W. A.

Cameron, in Toronto, who conducted what he termed a "clinic" in his church as well as much counseling through the mail by virtue of a "confessional page" in a newspaper.[13] John Sutherland Bonnell, of Fifth Avenue Presbyterian Church in New York City, has had noteworthy success. For forty-six years his father was Superintendent of a mental hospital. When just a boy he went on the rounds of the hospital with his father, who would discuss the patients with him, tell him of the nature of their problems and the best methods of dealing with them. He made friends with many of them and later served as an attendant in the wards. Here he said was his apprenticeship to the ministry.[14] There are other modern pastors who have utilized the findings of modern psychology and case work and have been very effective in their work with individuals. Such men as Albert E. Day, Roy Burkhart, Samuel Shoemaker, George Buttrick, are but a few who represent many, whose names are not so well known, who are utilizing the best of modern science to enable them more adequately to carry on their work with individuals.

Another form of experiment in connection with the program of a church has been what has been called a "Life Adjustment Center." The first of these was organized in Washington, D.C., in December, 1928, by Rev. Moses R. Lovell, who was pastor of the Mount Pleasant Congregational Church of that city. Mr. Lovell had been deeply concerned about the question of how the church could be of more direct and vital help to those who were finding the circumstances of life difficult. He finally conceived the idea of offering the services of a free clinic to those who needed help. He said, "We wanted to add science to religion in dealing with life's problems, and we wanted to open our doors widely to all types of human problems—in fact, make this truly a life adjustment center where people might come with all kinds of problems and find relief and help." He secured a volunteer staff, consisting of a doctor, a psychiatrist, a social worker, a general counselor, a director of religious education.

The first night about thirty people applied for assistance in the clinic which opened at seven o'clock and continued until nearly midnight. In the course of the first year so many presented problems of vocational difficulties and of unemployment that an economist was added to the staff, but the majority of the problems were in the field of mental hygiene. Mr. Lovell, in summarizing the first year of the clinic, reported that ninety-six percent of all those applying for aid would be included in what is commonly called the middle class group of people.[15]

Dr. Charles T. Holman, in his chapter in *The Church at Work in the Modern World*, lists several types of program that churches are maintaining. In one church of about five hundred members, the minister, who is well trained in psychology, sets aside certain hours when he is available for religious counseling and supplements this with much home visitation. He also has organized a board of consultants, consisting of a nutrition expert, a social case-worker, a child guidance expert, a psychiatrist, and a doctor. He has organized study groups on the home, child care, health, and such subjects. A large church in the East was confronted with the problems created by problem children in the church school and, feeling a sense of responsibility for them, added a consulting psychiatrist to the church staff to serve on a part-time basis. Counseling was then done not only with the children but also with their parents, teachers and club leaders, and an attempt was made to utilize all community agencies. He describes another church that carried on a most elaborate program in its church school. It was a unique situation in the fact that all of the teachers were paid and trained. Each child in the school was given psychological and personality tests which formed the basis of an elaborate counseling program that included the children, their parents and teachers, as well as other adults. Supplementary to the program of counseling there was maintained a series of lectures on child guidance and applied psychology in everyday life. Another church, which had as its purpose to make the entire church sensitive to the need and opportunity for individual guidance, had a counseling committee composed of the ministers on the staff, the representatives of the church school and other organizations, and also experts in the vocational, educational, marital and psychological fields. Another maintains a regular clinic with offices that are open daily and a special clinic open every Monday evening. This is financed by the community chest which provides for a small salaried staff and for many volunteer workers; the offices, reception and counseling rooms are furnished by the church.[16]

Other programs have been maintained; many churches have added counselors, pastoral consultants, or social workers to their staffs, often to spend part time in connection with a private practice. Two churches in Southern California, a Methodist and a Congregational, have availed themselves of the services of Dr. Fritz Kunkel, a noted psychotherapist and author. He not only meets with individuals but lectures to youth groups and adults on the relationship of depth psychology and religion. The Marble Collegiate Church of New York City has conducted a church clinic in which the pastor, Norman Vincent Peale, and a psychiatrist, Dr. Smiley Blanton, have collaborated. Hazen G. Werner conducted a Person Trouble Clinic in Detroit in collaboration with a psychiatrist, a family visitor, and in coöperation with the Public Health Department and the Police Department. As a rule they follow certain generally recognized principles—that the church clinic deals with those difficulties that are of a functional or nervous nature; they utilize the best medical and psychiatric counsel available and do not attempt to handle a case that needs medical or surgical attention, except on the advice of a physician. Anton Boisen criticizes the church clinic on the grounds that it usually merely makes available the methods of orthodox psychiatrists and does not attempt to explore the religious significance of the situation, or to provide the distinctive contribution the religious counselor should make. In the main, such programs have, of necessity, been confined mainly to the cities and there to the larger churches. It is too early, yet, to predict what their future will be.

There were other men who were interested in the application of scientific methods and principles as applied to religious work with individuals, and who began to train themselves to work as specialists in the field. They were ordained ministers but they did not serve in a local church but in some institution such as a mental hospital, general hospital or a prison or training school. The first to serve as a full-time chaplain in a mental hospital was Anton T. Boisen who has been one of the foremost pioneers in this whole field. His experience is a unique one and is told in his own words in the Introduction to his book, *The Exploration of the Inner World*. He had specialized in the psychology of religion at Union Theological Seminary and had spent several years making social and religious surveys for the Inter-Church World Movement. In 1920, while riding on a train in North Dakota, he inquired of a fellow passenger about a large group of buildings they were passing, and was informed that they were the state insane asylum. He thought no more about it, not realizing that within a year he would find himself "plunged as a patient within the confines of just such an institution." [17] The nature of his disturbance does not concern us here except that he describes it as coming on very suddenly and being extremely severe. The significant aspect of the whole matter was the way he reacted to the experience and the things it led to. Naturally, he spent much time puzzling over his own case, but he also studied the problems of his fellow patients and came to the conclusion that many of them were in the hospital because of spiritual or religious difficulties.

He received little satisfaction from the doctors, who did not give him the time or the understanding that he needed. He was pleased to learn that religious services were held on Sunday

afternoons but discovered that the ministers who were brought
in to conduct them sensed nothing of the problems of the patients. He refers to one kindly old minister who gave a series
of sermons on missions in China, Africa, and Japan, and another
who used the text, "If thine eye offend thee, pluck it out," until
he was afraid some of his fellow patients might be inclined to
take him literally.

Following an unsuccessful attempt to explain himself to his
friends, he turned his attention to the others in his ward. He
noticed that most of them did nothing but look into the distance,
so he suggested games, woodworking and photography, and
wrote a pageant for them. Following his release from the hospital, he had to face the question as to what he could do with
himself, although he was clear in his own mind as to what he
wanted to do. He expressed it in a letter dated February 14,
1921, a part of which is included in the book mentioned above.
"This catastrophe has, of course, destroyed my hopes and my
plans. I came back east in July with the intention of taking a
pastorate. From this, I take it, I am now turned aside. My present purpose is to take as my problem the one with which I am
now confronted, the service of these unfortunates with whom
I am now surrounded. I feel that many forms of insanity are
religious rather than medical problems and that they cannot be
successfully treated until they are so recognized." [18] He met
immediate opposition on the part of the doctors, as well as of
his friends. Of course many thought he should do nothing but
simple manual labor. He, too, recognized the possible dangers
of his ambition but felt it was worth the risk and he was not
afraid. He was convinced that he had been exploring a new
territory in which there were great possibilities and he wanted
the chance to develop them.

After consultation with Elwood Worcester, he enrolled in
Andover-Newton Theological Seminary and the graduate
school of Harvard, taking work under such noted men as Dr.
Macfie Campbell, Richard C. Cabot and William McDougall.

He wanted a job as chaplain but found there were no such positions. He offered his services as an attendant but that was refused because he wanted access to the case records. He spent a year at the Boston Psychopathic Hospital, dividing his time between the psychological department and the social service department.

In 1925, he finally achieved his ambition and became the chaplain of Worcester State Hospital, in Massachusetts, the first to attempt to bring any real specialized religious training to the mentally ill. In 1932, he went to Elgin State Hospital, in Illinois, and served there until his retirement. His work is now recognized and its value proven. It is often referred to by doctors and psychologists in various journals. An article in "Mental Hygiene" speaks of the work of Boisen and other chaplains, "not as a tribute to religion, but as a therapeutic measure." [19]

Much credit should be given to Dr. William A. Bryan, superintendent of the hospital at Worcester, who was willing to take the risk and let the experiment take place. One of the greatest of Boisen's experiments was the introduction of theological students as attendants in the wards. He also completely reformed the program of worship which had heretofore been carried on by visiting ministers, who had placed the main emphasis on the sermon and had given little chance for participation by the patients. He studied the whole thing from the standpoint of the needs of the patients. Not finding a hymnal he felt suitable, he edited one that would have therapeutic value, as well as literary merit, and would express a theology that was not contrary to modern knowledge. He organized a choir which, as well as being a real aid to the service of worship, has been of significant value to those participating in it. The sermon he limited to ten or fifteen minutes and in it he dealt specifically with the problems of the hearers, such as, "their adjustment to the locked door, the requirement of work, to opportunities of play and recreation. We also try to help them to understand the distinc-

tion between delusion and belief, between inspiration and hal-
lucination, the danger of seeking alibis or blaming other persons or losing one's way in the land of day-dreams. The
troublesome conscience, guilt and forgiveness, elation and despair, anger and fear are other subjects which bring a good
response, at least, when they are treated in a graphic and interesting way. And this congregation of patients does respond;
the way they take part in the service has been for me a source
of inspiration." [20]

There have since been others who have worked with the
mentally ill. Most prominent of whom has been Carroll Wise,
because of his writing and speaking. In 1943 the National Committee for Mental Hygiene, in coöperation with the Federal
Council of Churches, made a survey of three hundred and fourteen mental hospitals in the United States. One hundred and
eighty-four of these hospitals replied, revealing the fact that
only thirteen had full-time Protestant chaplains, while fifty-
three had part-time chaplains. Of the fifty-three part-time chaplains only thirty-seven devoted more than one hour a week
to this work. The remaining sixteen, although recognized as
chaplains, merely conducted public worship once a week. All
chaplains reported the conducting of public worship as one of
their activities and the majority listed personal work, although
this personal work was not defined. Only two chaplains reported work with patients' families, and only one reported
teaching religious education classes. Several were responsible
for recreational activities, some edited a paper, and twelve
maintained a choir. Three chaplains supervised the training of
ministerial students, four gave courses for nurses and only
twelve attended staff meetings of the hospital. The average attendance at Protestant worship was twelve percent of the bed
capacity. The findings of the survey would indicate that properly conducted religious activities mean much to the health
and morale of the mental patient, and that they mean even

more if they are led by a resident chaplain, trained to have an understanding of the problems of mental illness, to whom the patient may go for spiritual counsel.[21]

Other institutions in which specialists are now working as chaplains are the general hospitals. As we have already seen, it has always been a recognized part of the task of the clergy to visit and minister to the sick. Since many of our hospitals were founded by church groups, they often provided for the services of a chaplain. It is comparatively recently that a definite study has been made of the distinctive function and of the possibilities of such a contribution. The work of Rev. Russell L. Dicks, together with Dr. Richard C. Cabot, at the Massachusetts General Hospital, has been of outstanding significance and wide influence. Mr. Dicks entered this field of work with a background of personal experience of hospitalization which involved a series of operations. He describes the difficulties of the experience, the struggle with pain, the personal doubts, apprehensions and fears, the horror of the anaesthetic, the confusion of hospital routine, and the different attitudes of the various doctors and nurses, and the effect it all had on him.[22] Soon after his illness, Dr. George Buttrick said to him, "Russell, some day you will thank God for this." Mr. Dicks said that at the time he did not believe it, but experience has proven it to be true.[23]

He went to the Massachusetts General Hospital in 1933, expecting to stay three months, as a supervisor of theological students who were there under the auspices of the Council for Clinical Training. He stayed four and a half years. It was during this time that he worked in collaboration with Dr. Cabot, who has given so much encouragement and wise counsel and guidance to all such efforts of the ministry. It was here that Russell Dicks began to study the whole problem of illness and hospitalization, the contribution religion had to make, the techniques available to the minister. He described his thoughts in these words, "The question which bothered me was how to deal with the situations I faced in the sickroom, how to aid the persons I saw suffering. Could religion help at all? I realized I was no more carrying on an effective ministry for the patients I saw than had been offered me when I was a patient. The psychiatric case-history methods used in mental hospitals were not adaptable to persons in a general hospital. The case-work method used by the social worker did not fit the minister's work. I decided we did not know what our work or our methods were in the sickroom." [24]

Consequently, he began to keep records in order to do his work more effectively, but first he had to determine what kind of records to keep. He began to face such questions as, just what happens when I see a patient? How does my visit affect them? What are the results of our conversation? He began to study the conversations and found that they were usually of real significance. With some it was a problem of discouragement; with some, fear; with others, guilt or loneliness. Special cases constantly presented themselves, such as one who faced a serious operation or one who knew she was to die. He studied the question of prayer and began to keep records of his prayers and to study their content and effect. Then he began to study these notes with groups of theological students and, later, with ministers in their regular parish work. Their discussions proved of real value and he discovered that ministers in their active work were just as much interested, and often just as confused, as to how these problems could be best served, as were the students.

Out of his own experiences, his questing for the best means to help the patients, and the knowledge gained in these discussions, with the advice and counsel of Dr. Cabot, he came to the conclusions he has published in several books, the first and most notable of which is the work with Dr. Cabot, *The Art of Ministering to the Sick*. They emphasized the value of listening, and gave suggestions as to the development of this art, the value of a minister's keeping and studying records as much as, or more than, a doctor, the use of prayer and the scripture. They studied the effects of hospitalization and the peculiar problems it presents to the patient which are not met by any-one unless they are met by the chaplain or the minister. They found of special importance the effect of the minister himself, his attitude, his tone of voice, his understanding of the doctor and the institution, his understanding of the nature of illness, his use of sympathy, but most of all his own poise, courage and faith. Mr. Dicks definitely does not think a minister should attempt to use psychiatric or psychoanalytic techniques. The chaplain or minister should do nothing that any other available specialist can do. His function is to deal with the patient as a whole, to help him overcome depression, bitterness and fear by arousing the greater energies, the great certainties and faiths of the Christian religion. He stressed the fact that the minister must go beyond the realm of medicine. "As clergymen, we are not content with relieving suffering as the physician and social worker are. To be sure we are concerned that suffering shall be relieved . . . but with all this we are not content. It is not enough to be free from want and to have health. As clergymen we are concerned with what you do with health when you have it. It is the pastor's task to work to relieve suffering and fear and loneliness, but it is also his task to assist people to gain faith and hope and that fellowship with God which encom-passes eternity itself. This may be accomplished even though suffering is not relieved. It is accomplished sometimes not only in spite of suffering but because of suffering. One of the most spiritually mature people I have met is a woman who has never walked a step in her life." [25]

Although the percentage of hospitals that are providing for an adequate religious ministry is still small, the number of men trained to fulfill this capacity is increasing, and there is a grow-ing recognition of its value. A popular magazine carried an article entitled, "Clergymen in White," [26] which told of the work of Otis Rice, Religious Director of St. Luke's Hospital in

New York. His work has been similar to that of Dicks, and the article tells of his work, which was sometimes to help a vigorous, bustling business executive adjust to a long period of hospitalization and convalescence, to restore a sense of self-confidence to a woman morbidly over-sensitive, and often to serve primarily as a friend, one who is interested in the person as an individual, who will deliver messages to relatives, or listen to complaints or grievances, or, if desired, administer communion, listen to confessions, or offer counsel in personal matters. The hospital provides a staff of assistants and students to work with him. A chapel is provided for religious services and ear-phones are in the rooms through which the services are broadcast. This is, of course, a more elaborate program than most hospitals can provide.

There has been a rapid increase in interest in this area of work in recent years. The Episcopalian and Lutheran churches have shown the greatest interest in this type of work. They have pioneered in methods and have far more persons participating than any of the less "liturgical" churches. The American Protestant Hospital Association has made some significant surveys that indicate the trends. A "Study of Religious Work in the Protestant Hospitals" revealed the fact that there were five methods that were being employed in 1941. Fifteen percent of the hospitals had a superintendent who was also the religious worker. Eight percent had full-time chaplains. Twenty-two percent had part-time chaplains and eleven percent had directors of religious work; they were not ordained ministers but were in charge of religious work. Forty-four percent had no religious officer at all and depended entirely upon the ministers who wished to call on their own parishioners.[27] Another survey studied all the available devotional literature for use in the hospitals. The different types and methods of using this literature for the benefit of the patient were discussed and evaluated.[28]

A very valuable report was made following another survey.

This was a "Report on the Clergy-Physician Relationship in Protestant Hospitals." [29] A very thorough study was made of the attitudes and ideas of both physicians and clergymen as to how closer coöperation and understanding could be brought about. One of the most significant efforts of all was a set of "Standards for the Work of the Chaplain in the General Hospital." [30] These standards are listed under eight heads: (1) The chaplain shall be responsible to the administration of the hospital. (2) He shall coöperate with the other personnel of the hospital. (3) He shall have a rational plan for selecting his patients; that is, he does not just make general calls but concentrates his time where he is needed the most. (4) He keeps records. (5) He conducts worship, interdenominational in character, but especially suited to the needs of the patients. (6) He must be adequately trained. (7) The chaplain should be appointed by both the hospital and the proper church authorities so that the best man available is secured. (8) His main responsibility is to serve as a spiritual leader in whatever way he can.

A similar work is being attempted in prisons and training schools, although as yet, no studies have appeared to make the findings of the work available. It was just a little over a century ago, about 1830, in the northeastern part of the country, that the churches first began to supply prisons with Bibles and to appoint chaplains to hold Sunday services and occasional classes. However, it was without any conception of the particular emotional and psychological effects that the prisoners' particular problems presented.[31] Sutherland, in his *Principles of Criminology*, states, "Prior to 1835, few prisons had regular resident chaplains and these were poorly paid and were, in general, inefficient." [32] This is no indictment, for it is only of very recent date that prisons have attempted to use psychiatrists or case workers or to give psychological or psychiatric tests. The fact of the matter is, the first educational attempts in prisons or reform schools grew out of the ministers' efforts to teach the inmates the Bible. Sutherland states that the first organized educational work in such institutions in America was done in the New York House of Refuge, when provision was made for the children to receive two hours of instruction a day, one hour of which was to consist of learning to read the New Testament. Later the time was increased and other subjects added. It was as early as 1826 that the chaplain at Auburn organized the prisoners into classes to teach them to read and write, although they were not permitted to meet in groups. The chaplain would stand in the corridor with a lantern, trying to teach the convicts who were often seated in the darkness of their cells. It was not until the middle of the century that efforts were really made to introduce even elementary education into the prisons.[33]

It is only of very recent date that attention has been given to the mental health and stability of the prisoners. Ralph S. Banay, psychiatrist at Sing Sing, writes in "Mental Hygiene," "Prisons, housing large groups of individuals, a great proportion of whom suffer from some kind of mental distress or present some kind of mental problem—such as emotional instability, moral deficiency, or an incapacity for the finer emotions—still in their present form are not equipped to handle these problems adequately." [34] Of course, the problems are tremendous; most of the cases are of long standing and many are increased or created by the nature of prison life. The field is still in its infancy and, while definite therapeutic values as yet have not been large, it is hoped that in the future, as society comes to realize their significance, new advances may be shown. It is also hoped that the ministry, both those serving as chaplains within the prisons and those in the pastorate, who deal with the men returned to society and with boys in their first experiments with juvenile crime and anti-social behavior, will be able to make some contribution. It is significant, perhaps, that the most rapid increase in the establishment of training centers for theological students has been within federal prisons and, since 1936, clinical training has been a necessary qualification to become a Protestant chaplain in a federal prison.[35]

CHILDREN, ADOLESCENTS AND THE HOME

It is now commonly recognized that the most important areas of life are childhood and youth. Of recent years these areas have been receiving increasing attention. The strategy of the church for centuries previous, however, has been in terms of adult life. Especially in religious matters the child or adolescent was thought of as a small-sized edition of his elders and what was good for them was good for him. Frank of Halle, in the eighteenth century, is quoted as having said, regarding children, "Play must be forbidden in any and all of its forms. . . . They shall be led to see that play shall distract their minds from God, the Eternal Good, and will work nothing but harm to their spiritual lives." Cotton Mather, in Colonial America, left an account of a conversation with his four-year-old daughter, in which he warned her that he must die soon and she must remember the sinful condition of her nature and must pray in secret places every day that God would give her a new heart.[36] These are perhaps extreme illustrations but are nonetheless characteristic. The whole revival system which was so prevalent and widespread was an adult emphasis. It was directed toward the adult sinner, and the child or adolescent who was often in attendance was treated by this same pattern.

There were other groups planned for young people, such as the singing schools of the eighteenth and nineteenth centuries, the temperance and missionary societies that became very popular, and the various devotional and Bible study groups that were rather common in the wake of the revivals. The next extensive program was the development of the Young Men's Christian Association which was founded in 1844 and came to America in 1851. In 1866, the first boys' department was added, which did much to convince American men of the value of work with boys and young men. The Young Women's Christian Association came into existence in 1856.

The next great advance was the founding of Christian Endeavor by Dr. Francis E. Clark and the phenomenal growth of young people's societies. Dr. Clark was not the first to have a young people' society in a church, as he well recognized. Like Raikes, his significance was not in the fact that he was the originator but that he crystallized, standardized and publicized the idea and, due to his winsome and energetic personality, was largely responsible for its early success and rapid advance. He was simply a pastor in a local church who felt the need of a program to meet the needs of young people who had determined to become Christian. Although he had tried previous societies, which had not been long-lived, his Christian Endeavor Society was popular from the start. It set young people to work for young people and, in a very real sense, ushered in a new day in religious work.

Christian Endeavor was not popular in every corner, however. Some thought it but a passing fad and others opposed it on the grounds of being unspiritual, a parasite on the church and a danger to denominations. A series of articles and newspaper stories caught the attention of others though, and by 1887 there were over seven thousand societies reported with nearly half a million members. This phenomenal growth of societies was followed by the organization of city, state and district unions, and a convention was held in Boston at which fifty-six thousand were registered. Christian Endeavor became the official youth organization for several denominations, such as the Reformed Church in America, Disciples, Quakers and Congregational. Other denominations, such as the Methodist, Baptist and Lutheran, formed their own denominational groups —Epworth League, Baptist Young People's Union of America, and Luther League—along similar lines.

Some mention should be made of Horace Bushnell and the Religious Educational Movement. There is no overestimating the influence of Bushnell, who championed the cause of children and youth against the Calvinistic Puritanism of his day. His book, *Christian Nurture*, was one of the strongest influences in creating an understanding of childhood and youth and in turning men's thoughts toward a more adequate program of training and development. The Religious Education movement which followed stressed the necessity of dealing with each age, as such, and more and more an emphasis on personality development came into prominence. While many workers were giving the major portion of their time to this work, it was not until 1915 that any denomination set apart a leader to devote his full time to young people. Since then it has grown very rapidly. In 1918, the University of Boston set up a department of religious education and among the first courses offered were some dealing with adolescents. In 1920 a department of young people's work was established. In a comparatively short time many people in the seminaries and denominational headquarters were devoting full time to the understanding of youth and the development of a program capable of meeting their needs. Many of the larger churches put a person on the staff whose one responsibility was to deal with youth.

Parallel with these developments in the church were similar activities in the field of psychology and education which were of great importance. In 1904 G. Stanley Hall presented his monumental study of *Adolescence: Its Psychology, and Its Relations to Physiology, Anthropology, Sociology, Sex, Crime, Religion and Education*. Stimulated by his work, many others also made studies of adolescence such as Cole, Averill, Thom, Richmond, and so forth. These books were widely read in religious circles and had a definite bearing on their attitudes toward childhood and youth. The emphasis of the psychoanalysts and the psychiatrists on the significance of early childhood experiences also served to stress the importance of these early years and to foster a different approach to them. Other developments, such as the establishment of the Institute of Juvenile Research, the Judge Baker Foundation and Dr. Healy's studies of delinquency, the establishment of Child Guidance Centers, all had an influence on the thought of religious workers with youth. We have already seen how one of the major interests of those interested in the psychology of religion was the religious experience of adolescence, especially as it related to conversion. Also the books on pastoral counseling, which will be described in a later chapter, usually included a chapter on "The Pastor and Adolescents," "The Sex Problems of Youth," "The Mental Hygiene of Adolescence," "Adolescent and Religious Difficulties" or some similarly phrased title.

As a result of these developments childhood and adolescence were seen in a new light and with a new importance. Childhood was seen as the time when a whole life pattern was being formed and adolescence as a time when a new self was being born. Adolescence was not necessarily the "happiest time of life" but a time of emotional disturbance with many situations that were peculiar to itself. Childhood and adolescence, particularly the latter, were seen as periods that involved many "tension points" or problem areas that needed skilled individual counsel and guidance. It was recognized that in the manner a youth faced some of these tension points real growth could occur, or previous efforts and the possibility of future growth might be destroyed. Those specializing in the guidance and counsel of youth began to give their attention not only to matters such as conversion but to the problem of religious doubt and uncertainty, to the development of a philosophy of life, to the relationship of children to their parents, and to the whole problem of the home. The problem of the child and youth's relation to the school, the whole question of vocational choice and vocational adjustment were given much consideration. The areas of habit, misconduct, right and wrong were inevitably a part of the minister's problem, bound up as they are with such intricate personality problems as guilt and a feeling of inadequacy. In fact, the whole realm of personality adjustment received much attention, with the related problems of the emotions, sex, day-dreaming, anxiety and fear.

The most recent development in the field of youth work has been the summer camp and conference program which is of particular note here because many of these conferences have incorporated a personal counseling and guidance program. This was particularly true of the conferences sponsored by the International Council of Religious Education which inaugurated a very valuable counseling program under the guidance of Dr. Percy Hayward and Dr. Roy Burkhart. They developed guides for the counselor in the form of personality rating scales to discover the conferee's needs, a permanent, confidential record which was kept on file to help guide the camper from year to year, and a home program for the young person to carry on his personal development through the year, based on his personal interview while at the conference. The conference movement, since the first camp was established in 1914, has had a phenomenal growth, running literally into thousands of individual camps and conferences. Most of them have not used such a program of guided counseling as have the International Council or Geneva camps but most of them have provided an opportunity for young people to counsel with men and women trained in the interests and needs of youth.

Closely related with the guidance of childhood and youth is the problem of the home. In fact, the two are inseparable except, as we are thinking of the home now, we are thinking of the wider context not only of youth in the home but of all the members of the family. There has always been a close relationship between religion and the family. Jesus spoke in terms of the family, and the church through all the centuries has stressed the sacredness of the home. For generations people have gone to their minister with problems that arose in the home, problems concerning their children, problems concerning the family relationship in all of its complexity and varied nature. Such questions bulked large in the problems that were taken to the pastors mentioned in earlier chapters. With the coming of new insights, arising out of the discoveries of the new psychology and the advances made by psychological and case-work methods, many saw that the home relationship had an important bearing and presented new opportunities to the pastor who, by the nature of his position in the community and by the very fact that he presided at the wedding ceremony, served as domestic counselor. Many men have taken advantage of these findings and some have made this the major emphasis of their ministry. Dr. Beaven, who had such outstanding success in the Lake Avenue Baptist Church of Rochester, New York, before becoming the president of the Colgate-Rochester Divinity School, used to give a series of Sunday evening fireside sermons each winter. These sermons dealt with the various aspects of the home and were designed to be of help both to those planning their homes and for those whose homes were already formed. He supplemented these talks with a "Question Box" period in which individuals could ask questions without their identity being made known and he provided sufficient opportunity for personal counsel.[37]

Dr. Roy Burkhart, who left the International Council of Religious Education to become the pastor of the First Commuity Church of Columbus, Ohio, has made a real contribution in this area. Because of his particular training and experience with young people he has specialized in the preparation for marriage and has contributed several volumes, both for young people to read and for the use of those who would guide them. The titles of these books indicate the extent of his approach. *Thinking About Marriage* is a discussion course prepared for the leaders of youth groups; *From Friendship to Marriage* is a book prepared for high school people; *A Guide for a Man and Woman Looking Toward Marriage* is based on an interview guide for pre-marital counseling, and *Marriages Not Made With Hands* is an interpretation for young couples before and after marriage.[38]

A man who has had a very wide influence in the area of the family and the home was Ernest R. Groves. Dr. Groves studied for the ministry at Yale Divinity School where he received his B.D. degree, but he later entered the field of sociology where his major emphasis was on mental hygiene and the family. He produced voluminous writings on the subject, writings which have had a very wide reception in psychological, sociological and religious circles. His Rauschenbusch Lectures, published under the title, *Christianity and the Family*, have been recognized as a most valuable contribution to the field of the pastor as a domestic counselor.[39]

The church has pioneered in this area of home guidance. It has produced an extensive body of literature, much of which is of excellent quality. The Federal Council of Churches has developed a Department of the Family under the capable leadership of Leland Foster Wood, which has been doing a work of farreaching significance. A bibliography on Family Life, published by this department, lists literally hundreds of volumes and pamphlets under ten major divisions which give some conception of the extent of the literature that has been produced and also of the range and nature of the activities of this department.[40] They are (1) Family Life which includes general books and parent-child relationships, (2) Aids to Family Worship and Personal Devotion, (3) Relations of Husbands and Wives, (4) Home Management, (5) Child Guidance, (6) Books for Young People, (7) Aids for Leaders, study courses, pamphlets and plays, (8) Helps for Counseling, (9) Background Books, and (10) Periodicals dealing with family relationships.

Chapter XIII

A NEW FIELD OF RELIGIOUS LITERATURE

The renewed interest in individual pastoral work, traditionally referred to as the "cure of souls," has reached the proportions of a movement.

It has expressed itself in a new field of religious literature dealing with the value, the philosophy and the techniques of pastoral counseling. Previously this function had been handled in volumes of pastoral theology and, incidentally, in books of the psychology of religion. In most cases "the cure of souls," or the personal work of the pastor, received a section or a chapter in a larger, more comprehensive treatise. The understanding of human nature was usually based on the author's practical experience and often governed largely by his theological predispositions—very seldom were scientific findings consulted or utilized. Since World War I, due to the new interest in an application of psychological and case-work methods and insights to the practical work of the pastor, a flood of volumes has appeared dealing with this work specifically. Some forerunners appeared even before the war. One of the first was *Religion and Medicine*,[1] published in 1908, the joint work of three friends, Elwood Worcester, Samuel McComb, and Isador Coriat, who had been associated in the Emmanuel Movement. The primary purpose of this book was to describe the work they had done on behalf of "nervous sufferers" in their classes and clinics at Emmanuel Church, Boston. It deals with such subjects as the subconscious mind, suggestion and autosuggestion, the causes of nervousness, the nature and value of hypnosis, the therapeutic power of faith and prayer. In 1910,

Charles Reynolds Brown published *Religion and Health*.[2] He gave his evaluation and criticism of such movements as Christian Science, the Emmanuel Movement, the Modern Faith Cures. While it is not a book on pastoral counseling, his chapters on "The Healing Power of Suggestion," "The Gospel of Good Health," and "The Church and Disease" foreshadowed much that would be written in a few years. Professor Hocking's *Human Nature and Its Re-making*,[3] appearing in 1918, was a scholarly work which had a wide influence among those who were willing to give time and serious thought to such a study. He dealt with the instincts, the will, conscience, sin, and the relation of such subjects to Christianity.

In 1924, H. Crichton Miller, though not himself a minister, published *The New Psychology and the Preacher*.[4] It is not strictly a book on counseling, but in it he attempts to show the significance of such things as the unconscious motive, the mother-complex, conflict, compensation, and projection to religion. He also deals with such subjects as the Prophet and the Priest, Dogma and Credulity, Prayer, Religious Symbolism, Faith Healing, and Psychoanalysis.

Then came a series of books which dealt strictly with counseling. In 1929, John G. Mackenzie published his *Souls in the Making*,[5] with the sub-title, An Introduction to Pastoral Psychology. He felt very definitely that the minister was handicapped by his lack of psychological insight, and so, he discusses such problems as instincts, sentiments, unconscious conflicts, their origin, development and resolution, and concludes with a chapter on pastoral method and technique and the therapeutic and integrative value of religion. It is his thesis that while a knowledge of psychology has much to offer the minister, which he illustrates by actual cases, yet "religion alone can unify the once divided life; the adjustment to God is imperative in the fully developed and unified personality." [6] In 1930, Leslie Weatherhead published his *Psychology in Service of the Soul*.[7] Dr. Weatherhead has been one of the most prolific writers on the subject, publishing books steadily. Although they do not all deal, specifically, with this subject, most of them do have references to his experiences in the field of therapeutic work. This particular book deals with the minister's work and his use of psychology. He deals with such questions as psycho-religious healing, the interpretation of dreams, the use of hypnosis, and the value of auto-suggestion and confession. The same year W. F. Halliday published his *Psychology and Religious Experience*,[8] a somewhat general book attempting, like Mackenzie, to show the relationship of the new psychology to modern pastoral work.

The years 1931 and 1932 seem to have been the peak years in the production of such books. M. H. Lichliter, of First Congregational Church, Columbus, Ohio, gave the Matthew Simpson Lectures at De Pauw University, on the subject, *The Healing of Souls*.[9] He states in the foreword that the book is written in the homiletic mood, for he hopes to win a verdict, which is "to lift the conception of pastoral work above the level of house-to-house visits" and to suggest the wide range of human contacts in which a minister is needed. He was an active pastor and discusses, from the pastor's point of view, the problems of the sick, the mentally ill, the question of sex, of tension, of fear and anxiety, of youth and old age, and concludes with a chapter on facing death. The same year, W. A. Cameron, of Toronto, brought out *The Clinic of a Cleric*.[10] This book is based on his experience in his own church and the conducting of a newspaper "confessional page," which had a large following. His opening chapter, entitled "Clinic and Confessional," states the thesis that the church seldom meets the vital personal needs of individuals. Then he continues with discussions of such needs as occur because of fear, failure, worry, passion, temptation, handicaps, suffering, cynicism, etc.

In 1932, four standard and widely quoted books appeared. Dr. Charles T. Holman, of the University of Chicago, published *The Cure of Souls*.[11] The sub-title, A Socio-psychological Approach, and the titles of the five divisions of the book aptly describe the purpose of this book. These divisions are What Ails Sick Souls? The Case Work Method in the Cure of Souls. Psychiatry and the Cure of Souls. The Function of Religion in the Cure of Souls, and Spiritual Therapeutics. This was one of the first to introduce the findings of the social case worker, along with those of the psychologist. Another volume published this year was John Rathbone Oliver's *Pastoral Psychiatry and Mental Health*.[12] Later the word "Pastoral" was dropped from the title. This is a unique book because of the author's unusual background of training in the fields of theology, medicine and psychology. He was an Episcopal priest, a surgeon, a psychiatrist and a criminologist, serving many years as chief medical officer to the Supreme Bench of Baltimore, and a medical historian, holding this chair at Johns Hopkins. Such a wide background of varied scholarship and experience gave him unusual sources from which to draw. The book was originally given as the Hale Lectures, delivered at Western Theological Seminary. His chief purpose was to give insights of psychiatry and medicine to ministers, social workers and anyone whose work brings them in touch with mental illnesses and personality maladjustments.

Twenty-three years after the publication of *Religion and Medicine*, Elwood Worcester and Samuel McComb published *Body, Mind and Spirit*,[13] which was also based upon their experience in the Emmanuel Movement and covers many of the same fields discussed in the earlier book, but now in the light of their further experience and the development of psychoanalysis and kindred movements in the intervening time. In this new volume they are deeply influenced by the works of Freud, and express their indebtedness to his genius, although of course, they differ at many points. The book is filled with numerous illustrations from their own experience and contains some most striking records of cures, often of people with whom other psychological and medical experts have failed.

They use the methods of hypnosis, deep relaxation, suggestion during sleep, which are methods not commonly referred to by the majority of writers in this field. This same year, 1932, also saw the appearance of Karl Ruf Stolz' *Pastoral Psychology*. This became a standard work and was often used as a text-book. It was revised in 1940. Professor Stolz has contributed many other volumes to this same field. This one deals exclusively with the minister's function as a counselor and is based on the conviction that the minister has here one of his greatest responsibilities, but he is often tragically impotent when brought face to face with actual life experience. He stresses the fact that the minister is not competent to deal with the abnormal; his field is to serve those who are afflicted with minor mental ailments and those who are in need of "prayer, religious instruction, confession, comfort and conversion." [14] He divides people, generally, into four groups; first, the normal with whom the pastor's work is essentially preventive and educational; second, the personally dislocated or socially maladjusted; third, the submerged or incapacitated, who are undone and defeated by poverty, loneliness, disease, ignorance or other elements. With these two groups the minister's work is primarily corrective and re-educational. The fourth group is the group that is so mentally retarded or deranged that a minister can only be of service when working in direct coöperation with a psychiatrist.

In 1935, Weatherhead published his *Psychology and Life*,[15] similar in purpose to his earlier volume, and Dr. Roy Burkhart published *Guiding Individual Growth*.[16] Dr. Burkhart served as associate director of youth work with the International Council of Religious Education. He took an advanced degree in psychology at the University of Chicago and, after he left the International Council, went to the Community Church in Columbus, Ohio. The volume mentioned above is one of the Guides to Christian Leadership Series and was written from the point of view of the place of personal counseling in reli-

gious education. Dr. Burkhart has also given special attention
to the problem of preparing youth for marriage, and has published several volumes in this field, as well as other books on
the specific problems of youth.

In 1936, Dr. Richard C. Cabot, who has done more than any
one medical man to advance the field of religious work, and
Rev. Russell L. Dicks collaborated to produce their monumental work, *The Art of Ministering to the Sick*.[17] The name
of Dr. Cabot needed no introduction, for he was well known
as former chief of the medical staff of Massachusetts General
Hospital and the author of many volumes. Mr. Dicks was a
young chaplain, whose work we mentioned in a previous chapter. The two men, in combining the points of view of their two
specialties, produced a book that basically presented a philosophy of faith which could be shared by clergyman and
physician alike, and was so essential to the patient in whom
both were intersted. The book does much to clarify the minister's understanding of the doctor, of the institution of a hospital, and, most of all, of the real value and nature of his own
particular function. Space does not permit an adequate description of the discussions of spiritual backsliding, pain, evil, and of
"Vis Mediatrix Dei," in which "a gigantic healing power fights
on our side." They gave much attention to practical suggestions as to things a minister can do, and special stress is laid on
the value of listening, quietness, prayer, Scripture, and the
keeping of adequate records of the relationship with the patient. The book received quick popularity and has had a de-
servedly wide reading. Mr. Dicks followed this with a series
of other books which we will mention here rather than according to their date of publication. He next published *Meditations for the Sick*,[18] a volume of prayers and meditations,
written primarily with the patient in mind and to be given by
ministers in calling on their parishioners. A little book, *When
You Call on the Sick*,[19] was written as a guide to laymen as
they call on their sick friends. Then he published, in 1939, a

volume he describes as a "source book," entitled *And Ye Visited Me*.[20] This book contains the actual records of the efforts of his students with certain patients. They are presented in parallel columns, the source material, containing what was said and done in the left-hand column, and Mr. Dicks' observations and suggestions for study in the right-hand column. The cases listed are cases of doubt, discouragement, bitterness, acute fear, faith, loneliness, guilt, confession, acute guilt, distrust, affection and communion. A book, *Who Is My Patient?*[21] was written to help the nurse understand and meet the spiritual needs of her patients. Two little books, *Yourself and Health*[22] and *Thy Health Shall Spring Forth*,[23] are collections of inspirational writings, prayers and Scriptures for the use of the patient himself. In a recent book, *Pastoral Work and Personal Counseling*, he leaves the specific area of the physically ill for the first time and deals with counseling as a whole. His most recent volume is *Comfort Ye My People, A Manual for the Pastoral Ministry*.[24]

In 1937, H. S. Elliott, of Union Theological Seminary in New York, published with Mrs. Elliott what they termed a counseling manual, entitled *Solving Personal Problems*.[25] The personality difficulties they handled were those of normal people, of such a nature that "an individual might do something himself, if he had the requisite insight and skill," or which would not lie beyond the experience and training of the minister. They also include much discussion of the counseling situation, the various methods of counseling, and the coöperation with experts.

In 1938, John Sutherland Bonnell presented his *Pastoral Psychiatry*,[26] although he does not use the term psychiatry in the modern technical sense, but in its historic meaning, which is "the healing of the soul of man." His father had been for many years supervisor of a mental institution and most of Dr. Bonnell's boyhood had been spent in this environment. He draws much on this experience to show how it shaped his purpose and enriched his background for later dealing with people in the pastorate. The book deals mainly with his own methods and is full of lengthy discussions of cases with which he has dealt. Hollington's *Psychology Serving Religion* [27] surveys the main social maladjustments and character defects of the successive periods of life—infancy, childhood, adolescence and adulthood. He discusses first normal adjustment, then maladjustment, and then readjustment, attempting to show what the medical and social agencies, the church and the home and the "physician of souls" can do to bring about readjustment. W. L. Northridge, an English psychologist, published *Health for Mind and Spirit*,[28] in which he attempts to show the relationship of psychology and religion in meeting the problems of life. He stresses the abnormal and extreme, including discussions of The Major Psychoses, Sexual Abnormalities, Alcoholic and Drug Addiction, Unconscious Guilt, The Unforgivable-Sin Problem and other related subjects. A book which took a somewhat different approach was *The Soul Doctor*,[29] by Charles Reed Zahniser. In this book he attempts to put church case work and pastoral counseling into the form of fiction. It is the story of one Rev. Mortimer Allison who sought to meet the needs of Old Second Church. In his perplexity as to the reasons for the ineffectiveness of the program of his church, he became more conscious of the effectiveness of the social agencies. His conclusion was that the church should maintain its own primary purpose but that he would learn from the techniques of these social agencies. His plan was to develop a program of case work in his church. The book then continues with stories of the parishioners and the problems with which he dealt. The author states in the introduction that the stories were taken from true case histories but were modified and cast into fictional form.

The year 1939 marked the appearance of a new author, Rollo May, who presented his *Art of Counseling*,[30] which was followed the next year by *Springs of Creative Living*.[31] After graduation from Oberlin College and Union Theological Seminary, he studied under Alfred Adler in Vienna. He draws from his own experience, as well as from his familiarity with the writings of the "depth" psychologists, to discuss personality problems and to give practical suggestions to those who would attempt to solve them.

In 1942, Dr. Holman published another book, *Getting Down to Cases*,[32] in which he presented six cases in some detail. He divides them into two groups: (1) the self-condemned, or those troubled by inner conflicts, and (2) the socially condemned, or those troubled by external authority. The former are condemned by their own consciences, the latter by society. Carroll A. Wise, then chaplain of Worcester State Mental Hospital, wrote a volume entitled *Religion in Illness and Health*.[33] He feels that the problems of illness and health can only be understood by considering the organism as a whole, which includes the biological, psychological and social factors in all their relationships, which cannot be completely understood if the religion of the patient is neglected. The central function of religion is to provide a "Weltanschauung" that will lead to integration and growth. Also, Carl J. Schindler published *The Pastor as a Personal Counselor*,[34] a small volume by an active pastor. His book covers much the same ground as those with similar titles.

Two rather comprehensive volumes appeared in 1943 which surveyed the whole field. They were *The Church and Psycho-Therapy*,[35] by K. R. Stolz, and *Religion and Health*,[36] by Seward Hiltner. The first mentioned was the last by Professor Stolz, who had contributed many volumes concerning the relationship between psychology and religion. He died on March 29th, the same year the book was published. He discussed at some length the ministry of Jesus, how the church anticipated psychiatry, the relationship of medical psychology and pastoral psychology, and the historical and representative therapies of the church. He also considered the program of the church, the therapeutic value of preaching, Christian education and personality development, the vocational neuroses of the minister and the value of the ecumenical movement for personality. Seward Hiltner is executive secretary of the Department of Religion and Health for the Federal Council of Churches. His book grew out of his experience in dealing with all phases of the movement and was written as a "survey" book to provide an introduction to the various phases of the relationship of religion and health. About half of the volume presents background material and basic information concerning Religion and Mental Hygiene, Medical Missions, The Historic and Contemporary Relationship of Christianity and The Maintenance of Health and Cure of Illness. The other half of the volume deals with the methods of counseling and ministry to the sick and emotionally disturbed. In 1945, Henry Jerome Simpson published *Pastoral Care of Nervous People*.[37] For many years he conducted a clinic for Personal Adjustment in his church. He based his psychological findings almost wholly on the Adolf Meyer school of psychology.

There are other books that have been concerned with more specialized areas. Numerous books have been written on marriage and the home. One of the most noteworthy was Ernest Groves' Rauschenbusch Lectures, *Christianity and the Family*, [38] in which he dealt with both the opportunities and dangers of the religious counselor. Closely allied is the field of sex instruction and guidance, such as Weatherhead's *Mastery of Sex through Psychology and Religion*.[39] Other volumes have dealt with the pastor and the problems of children and adolescence, such as the writings of Burkhart, Ligon, and Marguerite Harmon Bro. Professor Stolz contributed a volume, *Making the Most of the Rest of Life*,[40] which faces the problems of mature and later years.

Of course there are innumerable supplementary writings which also deal with the subject in part. Only a very few can be mentioned. Hardly any religious subject can now be han-

dled without some reference to this field. Albert E. Day's Lyman Beecher Lectures, *Jesus and Human Personality*,[41] and
Dr. Buttrick's *Prayer*,[42] to cite two well-known examples, are
enriched by their knowledge of psychology and draw heavily
from this field. Neither is over-awed by the psychologists,
however, and Dr. Buttrick is quick to point out their limits and
assumptions. Raymond Calkins' *How Jesus Dealt With Men*,[43]
is homiletic in nature and discusses Jesus' approach to such
personalities as Nicodemus, Zacchaeus, the Woman of Samaria,
and others. This is one of several such volumes.

Many books were written not only with the ministry in
mind, but also to be of help to the layman, such as Holman's
Religion of a Healthy Mind,[44] Werner's *And We Are Whole
Again*,[45] and Miller's *Take a Look at Yourself*.[46] These books
not only had a value in themselves but indicated the amount of
counseling that was being done. Werner's volume, for example,
grew out of a Personal Trouble Clinic he operated in Dayton in
collaboration with a psychiatrist, a family visitor and other public agencies. A rather unique book was *Faith Is the Answer*,[47]
published jointly by a minister and a psychiatrist, Norman
Vincent Peale and Smiley Blanton. Each presented a separate
discussion, from the point of view of his own profession, of
such basic problems as fear, guilt, self-criticism and failure, love
and marriage, loneliness and sorrow—problems to which each
profession can make a contribution.

The book that has had by far the widest circulation of all
such books is Dr. Fosdick's recent book *On Being a Real Person*.[48] The book was condensed in the Readers Digest, was
widely reviewed in the secular press and immediately caught
the attention of the general public. In many cities it led the
list of "best-sellers" among non-fiction books. Its popularity
was justly deserved. It grew out of Dr. Fosdick's rich experience, his wide reading and study, and from his more than
twenty years of intimately dealing with the problems of people. It is not a book on the techniques of counseling but is a

book for the layman. In the introduction he states that as he wrote he had constantly in mind typical individuals who had consulted him. One distinguished psychiatrist is reported to have said it is "the best book on personal mental hygiene ever written." [49]

Of course, many articles have appeared in the various religious journals. "Church Management," in its summer supplement of 1942, presented an Outline Study Course in Pastoral Psychology prepared by K. R. Stolz. He divided the study into four major emphases: I. The Major Objective, II. Diagnosis, III. Motivation, and IV. Therapy. "New Life," the weekly journal of the New Life Movement, led by Albert Edward Day, has included a department of "Personal Counseling," edited by Hazen G. Werner. "The Pastor" has given more attention to this field than any other journal. They have recently added a department of Pastoral Work under the editorship of Russell Dicks, which presents the most extensive and adequate material of any publication now available. Each month this department includes feature articles on a variety of subjects related to pastoral care, a question and answer section and book reviews of the most recent volumes in the religious and psychological fields. Most valuable of all is a section of clinical material, an emphasis that has long been needed and has been too frequently overlooked in the literature on pastoral counseling. This section on clinical material includes actual case studies reported by pastors; then the methods and the techniques are analyzed and evaluated by Mr. Dicks. The cases that have been discussed are those that might occur in any parish, such as a pastor who was ministering to a woman dying of cancer, a pastor who was dealing with a family who was having trouble with a daughter, the ministry in the home of the bereaved, and a pastor who was working with a patient who was mentally ill. As yet, no professional journal has appeared that deals with this work exclusively, although it has often been mentioned and is greatly needed.

In the main, this work has been well done. These volumes
have "sold" the subject. They have provided a good introduction; now more specialized studies are needed and more
original investigation must be made by religious men, which,
in the words of Dr. Boisen, will "explore the meaning of human
nature, not just take over . . . the findings of the psychologists." [50] Studies need to be made of the unique function of
the pastor and of the contribution and therapeutic power of
religion—as thorough, exhaustive, complete as anything that
has appeared in the field of psychology or medicine.

Chapter XIV

THE CHANGING EMPHASES
IN THE "CURE OF SOULS"

The development of the psychological and social sciences and the efforts of such pastors as we have discussed thus far began to bring about a changing emphasis in the age-old task of "the cure of souls." This changing conception is quite clearly seen if one compares *The Cure of Souls*,[1] as published by Ian Maclaren in 1896, with *The Cure of Souls*,[2] as published by Charles Holman in 1932. The former, which has already been described, was a significant book, in many ways ahead of its day, yet it devotes but one chapter to "The Work of the Pastor," and gives the major portion of its contents to preaching and the other activities of the preacher.

Dr. Holman's book, which he calls a "socio-psychological approach," deals exclusively with a minister's work with individuals. He begins with an analysis of the sick soul, then discusses the case-work method, and the new light from psychiatry, as well as the particular function of religion and spiritual therapeutics. As has been emphasized, many of these men of the time of Maclaren, and earlier, had a real concern for people. They gained through their experience a very practical understanding of human nature; their work was marked with significant success, and many of the methods which they used are now validated by scientific experimentation and research. The difficulty has been that, to a large extent, their thoughts regarding human nature have been influenced by theological traditions and human nature was seen as something that was subject to sin, and its primary need was conversion and salvation. The result was that, in many cases, all people were seen in a common pattern and a common remedy was applied to all. As ministers began to develop new conceptions of the cure of souls they became equally concerned about the souls of men and equally desirous of bringing them salvation, but the term began to take on new connotations and implications for the living of this life, as well as referring so exclusively to the life to come. The minister began to see human nature in a new context and with a clearer understanding of all that is involved, as well as of the sources of its difficulties. This development made three important contributions to the work of the pastor: (1) It gave new insights for the understanding of human nature; (2) it made available new methods and techniques, and (3) it provided a new relationship between the professsions. So important were these factors that John T. McNeil, after surveying their development in 1934, wrote, "We are evidently at the opening of a new era in the history of the cure of souls. The ministry to personality will be at once scientific and religious. . . ." [3]

The minister began to see that life was a unity and must be dealt with as a whole. He saw that to deal with a person's moral or religious life separate from his physical, mental or social life was both unscientific and ineffective. He saw that a difficulty in a moral or spiritual area of life might have its origin in the physical, mental or social areas of life, and, if he was to minister effectively, he must have some knowledge of life as a whole. Of even greater significance was the realization, due to the discoveries of psychoanalysts and others, that life was much more than was seen on the surface. Personality was seen as something very intricate and complex and much of the driving force and motivation came from below the level of consciousness. While the terms "subconscious" and "unconscious" were used quite loosely in the early days of psychological awareness, yet it did mean that men were aware that many of the behavior problems that were brought to the minister had their origin in deep-rooted drives and impulses that came from far below the level of sight. The importance of childhood experiences was frequently stressed and it was evident that many who were troubled with fear, anxiety, timidity or guilt were suffering from experiences they could not even remember and from difficulties of which they were not even aware.

The minister had always been aware of different natures among his people and when Jung presented his "extravert" and "introvert" classification, they were at once seized upon as an explanation of certain groups which were found in every congregation. Paradoxical as it may seem, there was also the realization that there were no types, but each individual was unique and must be dealt with as such. There was a new interest in the relationship of the normal to the abnormal, first popularized by William James who felt that much could be learned from the abnormal. The new interest in the findings of abnormal psychology had an influence on the thought of those concerned with pastoral work. It was recognized that the abnormal in many cases was but an extreme expression of that which was normal. Moods, depression, melancholy, fears, anxieties, suspicion, immaturity, anti-social behavior were seen not as confined to people in an institution but as a part of every congregation in one form or another. One of the most significant aspects was a recognition of certain native drives, impulses and emotions and of the part they play in the formation of personality and character. They were seen as a normal, natural part of life, something which must be understood and directed, not repressed and condemned.

As the findings of the phychologists became available, it was seen that the minister could not accept a person's own diagnosis of his difficulties. Neither could he judge by the outward conduct or behavior. Formerly it had been the practice to consider the immediate problem and then offer advice or suggestions as to what should be done. Now it was becoming increasingly evident that most behavior was but a symptom of the real problem and the more essential and far more difficult problem was to discover the basic cause. Instead of being concerned with what had happened, the major consideration was changed to a consideration of why it had happened.

These changes in viewpoint naturally led to changes in method and technique. In order to meet the problems with which they were confronted, the psychiatrists, psychologists and social case workers experimented in the development of practical methods and techniques, such as hypnosis, dream analysis, relaxation, word association, the case history and various mental and personality tests. There were some pastors who attempted to utilize and take over these procedures. Worcester and Weatherhead used hypnosis and deep relaxation; Simpson advocated the use of word association tests by the pastor and Schindler felt that the minister could use information from dreams as a source of understanding human nature if it was used with "discretion." While some of these men had notable success, in the main they were the exceptions, and the general emphasis was that such methods were for the use of the specialist and not the pastor.

Most of the methods and techniques suggested were simpler in nature and better adapted for use by the average pastor, such as, for example, the simple method of listening. It is true that great pastors, such as Phillips Brooks, had used this method, but now it was seen as a definite technique. The "talking out" method was used by many psychiatrists and it was stressed by them that something happened to the individual when he verbalized the problem, drained off the emotion and got it out in the open. It was not mere passive listening that was stressed, but listening that was alert, active and creative. In many cases this was directly counter to the methods that had been used by the average pastor who had been accustomed to do the speaking himself—to moralize, to give advice. The emphasis was shifted from the giving of advice, which had been the minister's traditional procedure, to the giving of counsel—

the attempt to evaluate and interpret so that the individual
could gain insight into his own problem. The minister was
coming to see that his purpose was not to solve the problem but
to help the individual to solve his own problem. To do this he
would question and interpret, evaluate and suggest, more than
he would moralize or advise.

Other methods were devised to enable the minister to understand the problem clearly and completely. Dr. Holman, of the
University of Chicago, in his classes developed a "diagnostic
guide" which was especially prepared for the use of the pastor.[4]
It was divided into four main divisions: I. The Individual's
Problem, II. Heredity and Social Background; III. Personal
History and IV. Diagnostic Summary and Proposed Treatment. Other such guides were developed, but this was perhaps
the most complete. It came to be recognized that the minister
must keep records of his counseling and sick visitation as much
as the doctor or the case worker. It was pointed out that only
by adequate records can he do his work effectively, guard
against forgetting and, most significant of all, study his own
procedures with a view to their effectiveness and improvement.

Many suggestions were made as to the carrying out of the
interview. It should take place in a quiet place, free from any
distractions or interruptions. The minister should never argue
and never condemn and never appear shocked or surprised.
One factor that all the guides emphasized was that all confidences received should be held inviolate, should never be repeated or used as veiled illustrations from the pulpit. Another
emphasis that was stressed by all was that more important than
the methods and techniques used was the personality of the
pastor himself. The new knowledge of inter-personal relationships made it quite clear that more important than the method
used was the man who used it, and that the first essential of
one who would counsel others was a mastery of his own tensions and frustrations.

A recent emphasis that has been receiving considerable attention is what is known as "non-directional" counseling, as advocated by Carl Rogers. His book, *Counseling and Psychotherapy*, has been widely accepted by industrial counselors and has also been studied closely by many interested in pastoral counseling. It is especially adapted to the non-professional counselor and does not require the extensive skill and training necessary in other types of counseling. The purpose also is in close harmony with that of the religious worker, which as stated by Rogers is "to assist the individual to grow" so that he can handle not only the present problem but any future problems as well.[5] Rogers distinguishes between the older types of counseling which he calls "the counselor-centered approach" and the new type which he calls "client-centered." In the older type much depended on the counselor's skill and training, his ability to make tests to diagnose the situation, to interpret and make suggestions as the case might require. In the new type of counseling Rogers feels that the significant things are the activities of the client, and the function of the counselor is to make it easier for the client to guide himself. In a pamphlet published by the Federal Council of Churches, "A Counseling Viewpoint," [6] published during the war, with chaplains, ministers and U.S.O. workers in mind, he said that this type of counseling was built on two basic assumptions. First, it is assumed that the integrity and personal autonomy of the individual should be respected. Each person has the right and the responsibility to make his own decisions. The second assumption is that the individual has an enormous capacity and strength within himself for adaptation and readjustment. It is this strength within the individual that is relied upon to find a solution to the situation and on which the attention and activities of the counselor are focused. This demands certain attitudes on the part of the counselor. He must accept the client as a person with a right to be different and, together with this acceptance, there must be a willingness to understand. He must also be permissive, that is, he must create a relationship in which every attitude is permitted but none is demanded. Finally, it is based on the conviction that the person is capable of managing his own life in a manner that will bring reasonable satisfaction. It is contended by those who accept this position that it is in no sense inferior to other types of counseling, and in some situations is much more effective, less likely to cause harm and can be utilized by, and taught to, a much larger group of counselors.

A method known as "group therapy," in which a group of people are dealt with at one time, has been increasingly used by psychiatrists of recent years. This was found to be of special value in the armed forces during the recent war, when staff shortages and unusual conditions forced the use of such methods. It was also found to be of real help in industrial communities, such as Oak Ridge, Tennessee, a community created for the development of the atomic bomb, where an individual approach to all the personal problems and emotional disturbances was impractical, if not impossible, and group therapy was found to be very useful, not only in supplementing individual contacts, but as an effective agency in its own right.[7] Many clinics and individual psychiatrists have been giving group therapy increased attention. In many cases they have found it to have certain advantages over individual counseling. The Menninger Clinic, of Topeka, Kansas, devoted an entire issue of its bulletin to a study of group therapy as it has been utilized in England.[8]

The church has long dealt with groups. In fact, some churches, such as Emmanuel Church in Boston, had sponsored classes in mental health and related subjects. A few churches recently have been experimenting with this newer emphasis of group therapy. One of the most noteworthy and successful of such programs has been that developed at the First Community Church of Columbus, Ohio, under the direction of Dr. Roy Burkhart. The church members have organized the entire parish on the principle of counseling, interpreted not only as freeing the person who has become blocked but also of keeping the person free so that he does not develop difficulty. They utilize both the group procedure and individual method, emphasizing both prevention and cure. They attempt to cover the entire life of the individual with a program that meets the needs of all ages. Believing that what happens to a child during his first year, in fact before he is born, is as vital as anything that comes later, they conduct classes for parents both before and after the child is born. They attempt to utilize all the regular resources of the church, such as worship, religious education and fellowship and have pioneered in the use of such programs as psycho-dramatic activities. They conduct a day nursery and kindergarten with professional leadership. They have a minister to children and a minister to youth on the staff and have also done significant work in training laymen to understand and use counseling principles. Through it all they keep in close touch with psychiatrists and physicians. Such a church is obviously an exception but an exception that indicates possibilities that can be followed to some extent and principles that could be utilized by other churches. Some churches, such as Hennepin Avenue Methodist in Minneapolis, under the guidance of Carroll Wise who is now serving as minister in charge of counseling service, Riverside Church in New York, and the First Congregational Church of Los Angeles, are also incorporating these methods and principles into the parish program.

Another factor which grew out of the development in these other fields was the realization by the minister that he was not alone in dealing with the problems of people. He was but one of many counselors. Religion was but one field that was affected by this new interest in the problems and understanding of human nature; medicine, education, social work, criminology, law, industry—all groups that dealt with people were readjusting to utilize new insights and techniques. We have already discussed the developments in medicine and social work but other areas, as well, were influenced. The concept of education was being changed from the giving of context to the guiding of growing life, and schools began to include psychologists and guidance experts to handle maladjusted children and aid in vocational guidance and personality problems and, in some places, visiting teachers were being used with real effectiveness. Colleges added deans and advisers who had specialized in emotional and psychiatric problems; some of the larger schools, such as Yale, added a department of Mental Hygiene. Psychiatrists and case workers were added to the staffs of juvenile courts and the personnel departments of business concerns gave increasing attention to the counseling function. In fact, some of the most significant recent contributions to counseling have come from the field of industrial counseling. Clinics and guidance centers were developed and sponsored by a hospital or a school or perhaps made possible by the community chest of some city. The two major areas of specialization have been child guidance and the family. The minister thus found himself to be but one of many counselors, working in the midst of a group of specialists who were giving their full time to the personal problems of people. Many of them were more thoroughly trained than he was in understanding the intricacies of human nature and in the application of scientific principles to the problems of life. It was quite different from the days of Baxter or Oberlin when the pastor was the one man in the community who could meet their needs and when, in these two cases, he had to fill the position of the physician as well—or even from the days of Gladden or Bushnell or Brooks when it was the doctor and the minister who served as the confidants and advisers of the people. Now doctors, psychiatrists, psychologists, psychoanalysts, social workers, lawyers, teachers—and all too often some sentimental or superficial adviser in the newspaper or on the radio—were dealing intimately with the problems of the people.

An organization that grew up outside the church but that

was basically religious in many ways and that utilized both individual and group techniques was "Alcoholics Anonymous." The A.A., as they are commonly called, came into existence in 1934, when a New York stock broker came to the conclusion that neither physicians, nor psychiatrists, nor his own resolutions could make him stop drinking and that he had nothing to lose in seeking help from a higher power. He found that by putting himself unreservedly into the hands of God he could stay sober. He shared his discovery with other alcoholics; the idea spread and in the first ten years they developed an organization that numbered over 15,000 members and included over 235 cities. Alcoholism has long been recognized as one of the major problems of both public health and morals and one of the most perplexing of all problems to the counselor, be he physician, psychiatrist or clergyman. Thus far Alcoholics Anonymous claim very remarkable success. It is believed that two-thirds have already laid the foundation for permanent recovery and more than half have had no relapse. Although the group embraces all faiths and religious expressions and is not religious in any formal or creedal sense, the underlying principles on which the organization is founded are basically religious. First of all, the addict must want to be cured and take the initial step himself. He must admit his own powerlessness and believe that a Power greater than himself can help him. He must be willing to turn over his will to the care of God as he understands Him and to continue to try to find that will. He must be willing to make a searching moral inventory of his own life, be willing to have God remove the defects of character that are there, to make amends to all he has harmed when that is possible. Above all, he must be willing to go to help others who are in need of help. The members of this organization feel that an ex-alcoholic can best make the contact and help the individual who wants to be helped, bring him into this new fellowship and lead him to new interests and experiences.[9]

One of the general principles that became increasingly clear as the new pastoral-counseling approach continued to develop was that it must utilize all agencies and resources available and must work in coöperation with these other professions. It was seen that the minister could not and should not attempt to do the things that others could do better. Nor could he do his job well without the assistance and help of these other groups. It was also stressed that these groups could not replace the pastor and his contribution—a new relationship must be developed. Unfortunately there was often a feeling of antagonism and misunderstanding among these groups. This is not strange, however, when one considers that the physician and the psychiatrist often misunderstood and mistrusted each other when both were working in the same profession. There were those in both groups, however, who saw the possibilities and pioneered for a better understanding and a closer relationship —such men as Osler and Cabot in medicine, and Worcester, Fosdick and Dicks in the ministry.

Charles Reynolds Brown made a statement in 1900 that need not be basically changed. "The most friendly relations and the highest form of coöperation between the doctor of medicine and the minister of religion can best be secured where both realize that each one has an entirely distinct function to perform for the service of humanity and where both realize that each can best aid the other by attending strictly to his own specialty. The spiritual ministry, which quiets the mind, steadies the nerves and fortifies the will, is of greater value to the doctor of medicine in his fight against disease. And, conversely, the removal of pain and the strengthening of the body opens the way for a more complete realization in that individual life of those high ideals held aloft by the minister of religion." [10] We might add that when the pain may not be removed and when former health and normal functions may not be restored, then is needed something that no medicine can provide. A survey of the physician-clergy relationship, made in

1942, would indicate that where such attitudes existed the coöperation of the pastor was welcomed by the physician. In the main, it must be said, however, that even yet in the average community, except in certain isolated cases, the two groups are working quite independently of each other. G. Canby Robinson, in a study of 174 patients at the Johns Hopkins Hospital, made a special effort to discover if "the church, the pastor, the priest, or religious conviction or sentiments could be utilized in coöperation with medical care." Out of the total number he found only seven with whom such coöperation could be carried out. Of these seven, five received definite benefit as a result. He did not blame either the physician or the clergyman but felt that the patient did not have the background by which such coöperation could be effective. Speaking of the pastors and their willingness to coöperate, he said, "It was not their fault that religion was of relatively little value to these patients, but it was the general indifference of the patients toward religion which created a barrier between them and the spiritual and social service which the churches could give." [11]

It was seen that there was a further service that the minister could perform that was a great help to the doctor, of inestimable value to the patient, and of real service in itself, and that was to help the family of the one who was sick. Oftentimes the patient is worried more about them than about himself; many times they are the ones who need courage; if the minister does nothing but "stand by," he has performed a great service. This further relieves the doctor of many problems that are but interruptions in his main task, yet they are very real to the people themselves and present the minister with a great opportunity. [12]

The work of the minister, in many ways, is more closely allied to that of the psychologist and psychiatrist than to any other group. Almost every minister is confronted with problems that are bordering on the abnormal—usually a few that have reached that stage and many that show marked tendencies that may result in a mental disturbance. The same general problems of hostility, worry, fear, guilt, anxiety, inadequacy, infantilism, and others that are the specialty of the psychiatrist are the problems that the minister faces over and over, to a greater or less degree. As the ministers began to take an increased interest in the problems of the people, the psychiatrists took varying attitudes—a few welcomed the action; some ridiculed it; the majority were indifferent and a few were violently opposed. In all fairness it should be said that much of the criticism was justified. There were some pastors who gained a smattering of psychology, spoke in scientific terms and attempted to become pseudo-psychotherapists. Such practices were condemned from the first by the clergymen who were pioneering in the field quite as much as by the psychiatrists. There were others who saw that there was a very close relationship both in the problems they face and in the purposes they desire. Dr. Kirkpatrick, in an article in "Mental Hygiene," in which he was speaking of the minister and the psychiatrist, said, "I am convinced that often we are talking about the same thing when we discuss the individual and his adjustment. We both want for him the best of which he is capable." [13] He then continues to stress the attitudes and approaches that a minister can take so that the two professions can work together more effectively. These men stressed the fact that the minister should be sufficiently familiar with the field of the psychiatrist so that he recognizes his own limitations and can avoid the danger of attempting to handle cases that are beyond his training and ability. He should be sufficiently familiar with mental abnormalities to be able to detect borderline and incipient cases and refer them to those who can be of real help. In extreme cases, he should turn them over to the psychiatrist; in minor cases he can consult with a psychiatrist to gain new insights and check his own judgments and procedure. The minister can perform a further function in interpreting the work of the psychologist or the psychiatrist to the patient, his family and, in fact, to the entire community. Here, as with all professions, coöperation was seen as the best solution. Some psychiatrists have recognized the therapeutic value of religion, such as Hadfield and Jung, but they have often felt that the minister is not utilizing it to the full. Jung, after he made the sweeping statement, so often quoted, that all of his patients over thirty-five years of age had fallen ill because they had lost that which a vital religion has always provided and that none of them had been healed who did not regain a religious outlook, added this statement, "Here, then, the clergyman stands before a vast horizon. But it would seem as if no one had noticed it. It also looks as though the Protestant clergyman of today was insufficiently equipped to cope with the urgent psychic needs of our age. It is indeed high time for the clergyman and the psychotherapist to join forces to meet this great spiritual task." [14] Dr. Alexander Reid Martin, in an article, "Recent Trends in Psychology of Particular Significance for Religion," stresses the fact that the church by its tradition, its appreciation of the significance of everyday human relationships, its influence on the family, the position of the pastor, and many other reasons, is in a natural position to be of real help to the psychiatrist by working with him and interpreting his work to the community.[15] Dr. Fritz Kunkel said, "The psychologist, the minister and the physician need each other. . . . These three men's skill and wisdom must fuse into one united effort to help mankind." [16]

What was true in the realm of medicine and psychiatry was equally true in other areas such as social work and education. It was seen that a great opportunity existed for teamwork between the pastor and the social worker. Their methods and purposes in view have much in common. Dr. Buttrick suggested that social workers might well be ordained, for their task was implicitly religious.[17] It was seen that a close association with the case worker offered the minister many benefits, not only in cases of economic crisis and need, although this was very important, but also in interpreting the meaning of a family situation or a problem of delinquency. The social worker, because of her training and experience, had much to offer the minister in this area. Where the two professions were able to work together, combining their resources, it was found to have distinct advantages. The case worker could also benefit the pastor because of the fact that she was much more familiar with the community agencies and resources and the various institutions that were available and could be utilized. It was also seen that the school and its staff were all-important. The minister who was concerned about the problems of the children and youth had a great ally and could increase his effectiveness by knowing and working coöperatively with their teachers, principals and superintendents. The schools which have just recently been recognizing the significance of the emotional as well as the intellectual have, as a rule, welcomed this coöperation and have been glad to make their resources available and to work with the minister.

This in no wise exhausts the list of individuals with whom the effective pastor should maintain a working relationship. The list could be extended to include attorneys, judges, especially of courts of domestic relations or the juvenile courts, probation officers and police officials. There has been a rapid development of child guidance centers and domestic counseling agencies sponsored by schools, hospitals or the general community. Child guidance clinics, for example, combining the approach of a psychologist, psychiatrist, case worker and physician, were seen as a great resource for any minister serving in a location where one was available. It was stressed that the minister should be familiar with the personnel and functions of such groups, as well as with welfare and public health agencies and any other groups that dealt intimately with the lives of the people.

There were some in these other professions who were antagonistic and opposed any attempt to work together. The majority were indifferent, like many of the clergy, each pursuing his own program; there were a few who saw the possibilities of coöperation, urged it, and even welcomed it whenever it could be done effectively. The growing emphasis upon coöperation did not lessen the significance of the work of the pastor. If anything, it enlarged it. As the tensions and strains of life increased, it became more and more evident that the minister must be prepared to meet the vast range of everyday problems of normal people. The many problems of youth, of the home, problems of life adjustment, of tension, anxiety and fear were all seen to be within his province. In some of these areas, such as the problems of youth or problems of the home, the sick, the aged, the unemployed, or even the mentally ill, or those who were under serious emotional disturbance where the individual needed the aid of other professions but where the minister also had a definite and valuable contribution, this was very vital and necessary for the best ultimate results. Then there were certain areas, the bereaved, the religiously confused, as well as many people who were despondent, perplexed, or unhappy, situations where the minister alone could handle the problem adequately. The growth of pastoral counseling and the increasing coöperation with other professions revealed the fact that the minister had a unique contribution to make—one which no other man could make.

It is thus evident that the minister must go beyond any of the other professions. His purpose is not merely to provide health, or knowledge, economic self-sufficiency or mental integration. He is interested in all these things, for they have a great part to play in the total life of the people, which is his chief concern, but he is concerned not only with the preservation but with the enrichment of life; not merely with integration of personality but with integration on the highest levels, in terms of the loftiest ideals and the eternal and abiding values. He cannot master the techniques of the specialists who are trained to see the particular problem or an immediate frustration; but he is a specialist in life as a whole, in terms of its total context, which includes faith and hope—in other words, God. He too is a specialist in the resources of religion. In the long run, this is the most difficult of all. Charles T. Holman speaks of the minister's unique task, "There are many resources for helping hurt and troubled men, and one of the greatest of these is religion. The minister, above all men, ought to be supremely interested and competent in this field. He ought to be an expert in the function of religion in the cure of souls. He ought to know what resources are available in religion to aid men and women to effect that adjustment which is necessary when consciences are troubled, when they feel themselves overwhelmed by circumstances or temptations, when life seems to have no purpose and value, when their world has gone wrong." [18] Carl Jung expressed the same thought in *Modern Man in Search of a Soul*, "We cannot expect the doctor to have anything to say about the ultimate questions of the soul. It is from the clergyman, not from the doctor, that the sufferer should expect such help." [19]

Chapter XV

THEOLOGICAL EDUCATION
AND CLINICAL TRAINING

The rapid progress in the development of the psychological
and sociological fields and their increasing application to the
practical work of the ministry was accompanied by an increasing awareness of the inadequacy of the traditional ministerial training and preparation. It was in 1873 that Henry
Drummond read his paper "Spiritual Diagnosis" before the
Theological Society, New College, in Edinburgh. His first
sentence was, "The study of the soul in health and disease
ought to be as much an object of scientific study and training
as the health and diseases of the body." [1] Henry Ward Beecher
said that the one thing in which the theological seminary failed
in his day was that it did not teach enough about men.[2] Charles
Jefferson, in 1912, criticized the curriculum of the average
theological seminary and said, "Spiritual therapeutics, casuistry
or cases of conscience, the cure of souls . . . the application
of Christian principles to specific ailments of the individual
heart, surely these are studies which have received less than
their deserts." [3] George B. Cutten, the same year, wrote,
"What does the ordinary seminary graduate know of the
histology, anatomy, physiology, or surgery of the soul? Absolutely nothing. He must stumble along through years of trying experience and look back over countless mistakes before he
understands these things even in a general way." [4]

John G. Mackenzie told of his own experience in which he
entered theological school with great expectations, hoping he
would find definite practical help that would prepare him to

give guidance and counsel. He mentioned various courses, and recognized their value, but he still did not find the one thing he needed the most. He said his last hope was in a course in pastoral theology, which was to come the last year, but all he could remember from that course was, "Don't forget to send to your host or hostess of the week-end a letter of thanks." So he stated, "My work was to bring home a Gospel able to regenerate human nature, and here I was with no systematic knowledge of human nature, indeed had been taught to suspect it." [5] Professor William Adams Brown who was associated with theological training all his life said, "Some years ago it was my privilege to take part in a study of theological education, and one of the questions we asked the graduates of our seminaries was, 'What were the subjects in which you believe your seminary training was most conspicuously deficient?' There was general agreement that among these the training given for the pastoral office was most disappointing. Again and again we met the complaint that when the graduates of our seminaries met their parishioners in the daily work of the parish, they were faced by problems with which their seminary training had not fitted them to cope." Then he added, "As a seminary teacher for many years, I must confess that the criticism is justified." [6]

To meet this deficiency there were men who attempted to study and train themselves. Beecher and Brooks, interested in the practical effectiveness of their ministry, made a definite study of the people to whom they wished it to apply. It was said of Beecher, "The study of men began to grow with Mr. Beecher into a habit which was continued throughout his life." [7] And of Brooks at a busy time in his ministry, "He might not have time to read books any longer, but he was reading more closely than ever the book of life." [8] Such study and such an outlook bore much fruit. There were others who began to think in terms of definite procedures and methods. Elwood Worcester said, "To deal with problems submitted to me I had to work out a technique of my own." [9] Dr. Fosdick sought the help of Dr. Salmon, the mental hygienist, and Dr. Weatherhead gave himself to five years "hobby-study" before beginning his psychological work. As the literature increased there were others who began to specialize in the study; they observed their own work very carefully and some of them returned to school to do graduate work in the psychological and related fields. Professors of practical theology included more and more psychological material in their courses. Following the lead of the Chicago Theological Seminary which was the first to open its curriculum to this field, such men as Charles Holman, Karl Ruf Stolz, Harrison S. Elliott and Oren H. Baker offered full courses in counseling at Chicago, Hartford, Union and Colgate-Rochester. These men had had practical experience in the pastorate and had had thorough training psychologically.

That some progress has been made in this field may be shown by comparing the training that Phillips Brooks received with the catalogue of a modern seminary. When Brooks was in seminary his courses consisted of reading the Old Testament in Hebrew, the New Testament in Greek, Ecclesiastical History and Systematic Theology. This was quite characteristic of many schools until comparatively recent times. However, due to the influence of such men as those mentioned, a study of catalogues of several schools about 1942 revealed such courses as Pastoral Counseling, Personal Religious Guidance, Ministry to Individuals, Pastoral Case Work, Work with Individuals, Pastoral Psychology, The Theory and Practice of Personal Counseling, and Case Studies in Personal Counseling.[10] There were also many closely related courses. One catalogue offered two courses in Religion and Mental Hygiene and another in Clinical Theology. Several had courses dealing with the home and family, the descriptions of which usually contained an emphasis on pre-marital and family problems. Practically all of those studied offered a course or courses in the Psychology of

Religion and courses in the department of Religious Education with considerable emphasis on such things as Character and Personality Development, the Religious and Psychological Development of the Child, the Adolescent, his experiences and his problems. A few schools offered courses listed as straight Psychology, Mental Hygiene, Abnormal Psychology and Social Psychology. Such courses as some of these mentioned soon found their way into the curriculum of the smaller schools and Bible colleges, although it was usually necessary to have them taught by one who shared his responsibility with teaching in some other field as well.

In order to determine the extent of such courses being offered, Seward Hiltner made a survey of eighty-nine schools. Sixty-nine of the eighty-nine offered a general "omnibus" course in Pastoral Theology. In twenty-eight of the schools this was the only such course offered, while in thirty-nine there were additional courses. He carried the study further by listing the titles of those who taught the courses which he admitted was at times misleading but nevertheless did give an indication of major emphases. He discovered that there were one hundred and twenty-six individuals in the eighty-nine schools who were teaching in the field of Pastoral Theology. Thirty-seven of the one hundred and twenty-six had titles where the major emphasis was pastoral such as Pastoral Psychology, Pastoral Care, Pastoral Duties, Pastoral Counseling and so forth. Twenty-four had the term Pastoral but included other subjects such as Pastoral Theology and Church History, Pastoral Theology and Christian Education, Pastoral Theology and Christian Psychology. Fourteen had titles where Psychology was the dominant feature such as Psychology of Religion, Psychology and Philosophy of Religion, Psychology and Religious Education and others. Twenty had titles featuring Religious Education and three had the term "applied" such as Applied Theology, Applied Christianity, while twenty-five had no particular relationship.[11]

Carroll Wise made a similar survey of thirty-five schools, asking them to state in terms of courses and hours the training that was offered in mental hygiene. His replies indicated that six schools gave no such training, six gave one hour, six gave two hours, five gave three hours, three gave four hours, three eight hours, one ten hours and three twelve hours. Ten of these schools reported that these courses were taught by psychologists or psychiatrists, six were taught by ministers who had had training in mental hospitals and nineteen were by ministers who had had pastoral experience and academic training but no particular clinical training.[12]

Clara Bassett, speaking as a student of mental hygiene after making a similar study of theological seminary catalogues, commended them on the courses that were offered but criticised them on the basis that they were very seldom required of all the students and, in some cases, although the courses were available, a student could graduate with as few as two semester hours credit in courses that considered personality and social problems.[13] She further criticised the seminaries on the proportion of the volumes in their libraries that dealt with the scientific study and understanding of human personality and social problems. She felt they were over-weighted with material of ancient and medieval church history and theology to the neglect of psychology, sociology, social work, physical, mental and social hygiene. Checking the libraries of two schools in 1930 against a book list containing forty-one periodicals and three hundred and forty-eight books relating to psychiatry, child psychology, child guidance, and mental hygiene, she found that one school had but twenty of these volumes and another only three and neither one subscribed to any of the periodicals. She recognized that this was a new trend and that many of the schools were building up this portion of their libraries.

All of this would indicate that definite progress has been made. While a new emphasis has been evident and certain im-

provements have been made, there are many who are still urging that more needs to be done. In 1941 Carroll Wise wrote,
"Students emerging from the average theological school today
may be experts in Biblical criticism, in philosophical and theological arguments, in certain literary devices for sermonizing,
in text book knowledge of psychology and sociology, and in
other matters of more or less value. But they are not trained
to deal with the fundamental material of the ministry—the
human personality. Their thinking and work becomes book
centered, idea-centered, or program centered, whereas it should
be centered in personality." [14] In 1942, Dr. Holman referred
to the additions in the curriculum that had been made but he
said they were mainly "patch-work" when what was needed
was a "new garment." He said that what was needed was to
re-think completely the curriculum of the theological school
in the light of the best knowledge we have regarding the actual
development and functioning of personality and in terms of
the actual task of the working minister.[15] In 1943 Russell Dicks
made the sweeping statement in the pages of a widely read
religious journal, "It is a recognized fact among clinically
trained ministers who have received their training in hospitals
and prisons after graduating from theological seminary that
there is not a single theological seminary which is today training its graduates adequately for the pastoral task of work with
individuals." [16]

One of the most significant attempts to meet these needs
has been the development of what has been termed "clinical
training" for ministers. Other professions have been utilizing
this method also. Medicine pioneered with its internship, the
educational college has used "practice teaching," law uses the
case-study, and social work uses supervised field work. If it
seems that theology has been slow to take up this approach, it
should be remembered that all these developments are somewhat recent and even yet there are psychologists who do not
have any clinical training, a fact that is causing considerable

concern among some of their leaders. In 1913, W. P. Ladd made the statement before the General Convention of the Protestant Episcopal Church that the theological courses in the seminaries needed to be supplemented by some kind of practical training.[17] Dr. Richard C. Cabot, in the early twenties, advocated a year of clinical training in theology. He said at that time, "We need a year of clinical theology, not of apprenticeship in social work, in recreational work, in nursing or in psychiatry, but of theology brought to the bedside, to the bereaved, to the dying, to the invalid, to the aged, and to the delinquent. Students need practice in bringing the strength, the purifying influence, the courage and the comfort of the Christian life to those who suffer." [18] Even earlier than this R. H. Edwards who was then with the Y.M.C.A. placed theological students in a settlement house in New York during the summer and mention has been made of a form of clinical training carried on by Graham Taylor in Chicago Commons.

It is true that most seminaries or Bible schools maintained a form of field work in which the students did gain practical first-hand experience. This was usually done by placing the student in a small, usually rural church where he conducted services on week ends or in a larger church where he worked under the supervision of the pastor. The financial aid which this could supply the student was one of the main considerations of such a program, and, while it was usually supervised to a certain extent, it was not guided nor did it make the emphasis on personality study that is implied in the term, clinical training. What emphasis was made was more in terms of preaching and the administration of a church than on the meaning and nature of personality.

One of the first steps in this direction was taken in 1922 when Dr. William S. Keller arranged with Dean Samuel A. B. Mercer of Bexley Hall, a small Episcopalian seminary, to provide students with clinical training in Cincinnati. Dr. Keller was a physician, a layman in the church and a leader in community service. He had a very deep conviction of the necessity of religion if life was to be successful, and he also felt if the ministry was to make this real they had much to learn from the fields of social work, medicine and community organizations. Thus he began his plan which at first was carried out only in the summer. The students met in his own home, having their seminars in the evening with him as the only instructor. Then the students went out in the day-time to study and help in some institution or agency, either a mental hospital, a human relations court, a public welfare program or a social hygiene society. In 1923, he had four students, in 1924 six and in 1925 they began to come from other Episcopal seminaries also. It was then named the Cincinnati Summer School in Social Work for Theological Students and Junior Clergy. It operated on this basis until 1935 when the name was changed to The Graduate School of Applied Religion. A full-time dean, Rev. Joseph Fletcher, was added, and the program was expanded to operate on a year-round basis of four quarters, with the summer still reserved for theological students but the winter quarters to provide graduate training for those who had finished seminary. Although it still maintained its connections with the Episcopalian Church by now it was non-sectarian, with representatives from many communions and many seminaries. In 1935, a building was secured for teaching and dormitory use and in 1941 a second was added.

The bulletin of the school for 1940 described its function as "Social Training for the Pastoral Ministry, an internship in the practice of religion." Among the coöperating agencies that it listed were a child guidance clinic, the Cincinnati Bureau of Social Service, the Social Hygiene Society, the Cincinnati Work House, the Court of Common Pleas, the Court of Domestic Relations, Family Consultation Services, Good Will Settlement House, Juvenile Court, Longview Psychopathic Hospital, Maternal Health Clinic, Ohio Humane Society, Public Relief Department, St. Barnabas City Mission, St. Simons

Mission and Co-operative, Transient Service Bureau, and a Children's Home. Among the lecturers who were to appear before the students were an attorney, director of a workers' education center, a physician, a professor of religious education of a Jewish College, director of probation, judge from the court of human pleas, a case-work supervisor from a family consultation service, a psychologist, a psychiatrist, a neurologist, a professor of philosophy and many others. The curriculum contained three main headings, (1) Social Adjustments, (2) Pastoral Care, (3) Parish Administration. Under the first were listed such things as case-work method, domestic and family problems, emphasizing mental hygiene and psychiatry, sex education, family disruption and divorce; industrial relations and welfare institutions. Under pastoral care were listed personal ministrations, such as parish calling, sick visitation and counseling, and religious education. The Graduate School of Applied Religion no longer operates as a separate school, having united with the Episcopal Theological School of Cambridge, where Mr. Fletcher serves on the faculty.

Contemporary with the Graduate School of Applied Religion was another pioneer effort made by Anton T. Boisen at the State Hospital at Worcester. One practical outgrowth of Boisen's experience as a patient in a mental hospital was the development of the idea of practical training or internship, for theological students. In his own words, "I had . . . watched with interest the medical internes who came to the hospital to work under guidance as part of their medical training. I had seen how real, how vital, such instruction became as they and their teachers dealt together with the actual raw material of life, and I had become convinced that the theological student might well spend less time with his books and more with the human documents found in a mental hospital. I had become convinced that clinical experience should be just as important to the man who is to be charged with the cure of souls as it is to the man who is to care for the bodies of men." [19]

He began his experiment in 1925, when he took four theological students with him into the mental hospital to serve as attendants. Boisen felt that this had a double value. From his own experience, he was convinced that no one affected the welfare of the patient more than did the attendants, and prior to 1925 they were often incompetent, with no interest in the patients. Furthermore, this method gave the student an opportunity to come in close contact with various types of cases and to observe their actions, attitudes, developments and failures. At first, they worked ten hours a day on the wards, but it was found that this did not leave sufficient time to study case records, or to attend staff meetings or the special conferences that were arranged.[20]

For five years after Boisen first took his students into the wards of the mental hospital they continued to experiment, each year bringing more students, representing more theological schools and institutions, as new methods and improvements were made in the quality of the training. In 1930, the Council for the Clinical Training of Theological Students was formed, with Dr. Cabot as Chairman of the Board, Dr. H. Flanders Dunbar as Director, and Professor Guiles as Field Secretary. The board of governors had representatives of the fields of medicine and psychiatry as well as the ministry. In 1928 there was but one training center, in 1930 there were four, in 1932 a program was begun in general hospitals, in 1936 penal and correctional institutions were added, and in 1940 institutions of juvenile delinquency.

The work of the Council of Clinical Training continued to grow and, during the year 1940, gave training to seventy-eight students, representing a wide variety of theological schools of various denominations; they had established twenty training centers in mental and general hospitals, prisons and correctional institutions, and child guidance clinics. Each training center was established in an institution which could meet certain necessary requirements. It must have on its staff an expert, called an institutional supervisor, who could give the point of view of the institution and had time to teach and assist in the direction of the work of the students. Also, there must be on the staff a trained chaplain or a theological supervisor. A theological supervisor must be an ordained minister, a graduate of a theological seminary, and he must have had at least three months training in each of the three main types of institutions. He was in charge of the curriculum and guided the religious aspects of the work. The institution shared in the maintenance of the students.

The training itself consisted of "directed case study and research into the social resources of the community; actual work with patients in the hospitals and clinics and with inmates of correctional institutions; participation in the medical ward rounds and conferences with regard to these patients and inmates; and, finally, seminars in which general physician, psychiatrist, psychologist, social worker, and theological supervisor discuss together with the students the patients and inmates with whom they are working. Thus students and pastors in training under the Council find themselves learning about human problems, not from textbooks, but from life. In their work in the wards and in their family case work they obtain a perspective with regard to their relationship to the psychologist, to the social worker, to the general physician, and to the psychiatrist, not only theoretically but also by working with them." [21] As the project developed, it became possible for the student to study rather thoroughly one or more patients, by studying their case records and by spending much time with them, talking, as a friend. It is Boisen's experience that the results have never been negative and have often been of real value to the patient as well as to the student.

Edmonds describes the nature of the work at the training center at the Rochester State Hospital, Rochester, New York, in the summer of 1940, where he was theological supervisor. The first week was devoted to orientation, consisting of introductory seminars—discussing the aims and methods of the program of the summer, the general classification of mental diseases, the student's relationship and approach to the patients, and the functioning of the hospital as a whole—together with a complete tour of the institution to prepare the students, "emotionally and otherwise," for their own work. The next eight weeks were given over to the study of cases, each one to study intensively five cases of functional disorder, stressing the history of the patient up to the time of his illness, a picture of the illness itself, and an attempt to discover what an understanding minister might have done to prevent it. Each student presented one of his cases for group discussion. A member of the medical staff was always present at these discussions. Supplementing this, nine hours a week were spent in case seminars and in attendance at all staff conferences, held twice a week, giving the opportunity to observe the doctors at work. Other seminars were held with members of the staff on subjects of mental illness, the work of the various specialists, and Dunbar's book, *Emotions and Bodily Changes*. Finally seminars were held concerning the implications of this experience for religion and the function of the minister. In addition to all of the above duties, the students had individual conferences with the theological supervisor once a week.

The chief purpose of this clinical training was to supplement the academic training of the seminary, to provide the student with understanding and techniques to prepare him more adequately for the work of the pastorate. The purpose was centered in three key words: understanding, method and cooperation. The first word expresses the aim to provide a better understanding of people, how they develop and grow, what happens when growth is thwarted, their problems and infirmities, their emotional and spiritual conflicts, their weaknesses and their strength. The second refers to the desire to develop adequate working methods for the clergyman to aid in working with "all sorts and conditions of men" and the third is to enable him to work in coöperation with all the professions for the prevention and alleviation of the sufferings of men and toward the solution of individual and social problems.[22] The Council definitely opposed making pseudo-psychiatrists or social workers of ministers, and did not encourage the use of psychiatric or psycho-analytic technique by ministers. Such training, it was hoped, would save the minister from making mistakes in dealing with people, would better enable him to coöperate with other specialists and agencies, and, perhaps most significant of all, would enable the student to understand himself in a manner he never had before, although the latter must come as a by-product for it is not the purpose of the Council to serve as a therapeutic agency. The annual catalogue of 1937 contained the information that over seven hundred students had received the training, representing nearly sixty schools and more than twenty denominations. A study made the same year, covering those who had had the training, revealed "that after graduating from theological school, about seventy-five percent of the men had entered the pastorate; six percent were teaching in theological schools and colleges; two percent were in foreign missionary work; six percent were theological supervisors with the Council or chaplains in hospitals or penal institutions; two percent had entered Y.M.C.A. work, three percent social work, and a little more than one percent were to be found in medicine. A few entered sociological and editorial work. The remaining were deceased or unknown." [23]

There has been criticism of the work of the Council on the basis that institutions where its centers are established deal with extreme cases whereas the minister deals with the everyday normal problems of people; also that some have suffered from emotional shocks from which it was difficult to recover.[24] A survey was made of those who had received the training for the purpose of discovering whether or not it had been of value. According to these replies the desired purposes of the Council were being met. A great number mentioned the increased understanding it gave them of human nature and its problems, of the ability to serve more effectively as pastors and preachers and to work in coöperation with other professions. Also about one half of the replies referred to the increased insight into their own problems and about thirty percent commented on the new appreciation of religion and the new insights they had received into the relation of theology and life.

In 1922, Professor Guiles, then Field Secretary of the Council, withdrew and enlisted the support of the Earhart Foundation for similar work in the New England area. They worked in collaboration with Andover-Newton Theological School, Harvard Divinity School and the Episcopal Theological School of Cambridge and were frequently referred to as the New England Group. They have had two major activities, the teaching of class-room courses to the students of the above mentioned schools, and part-time clinical work through the year and a full-time program for graduate students and parish ministers in the summer. Since 1936 they have confined their centers to general hospitals because they felt that the patients in a general hospital most nearly represent the kind of people to be found in the average parish and because one branch of medicine does not overshadow the others. The ideal institution, they felt, was one that included medicine, surgery, psychiatry and social service. Four basic standards governed their work, (1) the work shall be of a pastoral nature, (2) it shall be done under supervision, (3) it shall be recorded, (4) these notes shall be submitted for criticism.[25] This group have made a special emphasis upon the technique of listening, on note-writing and on the keeping and studying of records. It is through the studying of these records of actual experience that they feel real understanding comes. After such practice, then, they contend, reading in the field takes on a new meaning. As with all such groups there are many seminars included.

The first school to make such training obligatory was the

Philadelphia Divinity School, which now requires of all of its students three periods of supervised clinical training before graduation. The plan began in 1937, with a complete reorganization, in terms of what was called the "New Plan of Theological Education." Their first plan was to introduce ten weeks of clinical training annually for each student. In order to do this, they had to extend the academic year from eight months to ten. The year was divided into quarters, and the training was given to a complete class at a time, the periods being staggered. The seniors were given their training the first quarter of the year and then returned to classes; the middlers the second quarter, and the freshmen the third quarter. The freshmen were trained in the Pennsylvania Hospital, the middlers in the Morristown State Hospital and the seniors in a parish under the joint supervision of the school and of the parish. This was continued for four years and then changed, because it was felt that ten weeks were not sufficient to secure adequate training; the interruption of academic work made continuity difficult and it was discovered that students approached their classroom work with much more interest and maturity after having had the practical experience. Consequently, the plan was changed and the curriculum was reorganized in the fall of 1942, so that all of the classes had a twelve-week training period at the same time and at the beginning of the year, then returned for two terms of academic work of fifteen weeks each. The plan of using a general hospital, a mental hospital and a parish was continued. This was felt to be much more satisfactory and was noted to be continued indefinitely.

Other schools have followed similar plans. An article in "Mental Hygiene" [26] describes a program carried on by the Pittsburgh-Xenia Theological Seminary in conjunction with the Western State Psychiatric Institute and Clinic since 1942. This consisted primarily in a series of seminars using the full facilities of the hospital, the purpose being to provide understanding of such subjects as the minister and the mental hospital, religious trends in the mentally ill, special problems in the community, such as alcoholism, delinquency and the psychoneurotic; the religious cults and mental instability; the minister and the general hospital, and general adjustment problems and areas, such as adolescence, marriage and senescence. Also, a program of directed and guided reading was included. The work was extra-curricular and optional but the attendance has been good. Some schools, such as Colgate-Rochester Divinity School, Chicago Theological Seminary and General Theological School have maintained training centers near them where such training is available if the students wish it. Others, like Bangor and Andover-Newton and Episcopal Theological Seminary, have required clinical training on a part-time basis. Others, such as Bonebrake, Boston University, the University of Southern California School of Religion, Southern Baptist Theological Seminary, and General Theological Seminary and Virginia Theological Seminary, have made it available if the student wishes it. The Candler School of Theology has arranged to have a group of selected students receive training each quarter, and Emory has made full-time training available during various quarters of the year.[27]

In 1944, a national Conference on Clinical Training in Theological Education was held at Western Theological Seminary in Pittsburgh. All of the groups mentioned above and many others were represented. All of their various programs were presented, standards for clinical training in the light of their various experiences were discussed, and certain minimum standards were agreed upon. They considered such matters as the vocational aspects of clinical training in the preparation for such fields as the institutional chaplain, the classroom teacher and the parish pastor. They discussed the place of clinical training in the theological curriculum and in relation to other education for pastoral work. In an address before this conference, Russell Dicks referred to the advances that had been made in medicine since the introduction of the medical internship for the young doctor. He continued, "in our training of theological students we are at the place medical instruction was at the time of the introduction of the internship." [28]

Meanwhile both these schools and others schools not using clinical training were continuing the practice of using field work in city churches or small churches earlier mentioned. There has been an increasing attempt to make this practical work more effective by more definite supervision and evaluation of what is done. Since 1926 several of the Lutheran schools have been following the practice of giving a full-year "apprenticeship" training between the years of the academic training, in a local parish supervised by the pastor.

Many programs have been devised to aid the pastor in the field. As has already been mentioned some schools have made clinical training available in the summer. Others have included summer courses designed for this purpose: Union Theological Seminary devotes one week in its summer series of pastors' institutes exclusively to this subject and has secured some of the most experienced men available. The religious journals have been giving more and more attention to it. As yet no journal has been devoted to the field exclusively although it has frequently been referred to as a necessity and a possibility. Many bibliographies have been prepared. Various ministerial associations have made an effort to face this problem by the securing of speakers and the reading of papers. So far as is known, with the exception of the Cabot Club of Boston, none have made any extensive use of the case-study approach.

Two factors that have been stressed as needing particular attention are research and the qualifications of those entering the ministry. Carroll Wise urged the carrying on of research in institutions and churches, research of a painstaking nature that would provide factual material by which the techniques of the minister could be developed to meet the modern needs.[29] Dr. Leslie Weatherhead said, "The misery of thousands cries out for research and investigation." [30]

Regarding the matter of securing students fitted for this type of work there has been some difference of opinion. Clara Bassett criticizes the seminaries because "little effort is made to study or evaluate the personality make-up of the student, his past and present emotional reactions, his underlying motivations and his behavior as indications of mental health and stability of personality integration and of probable success in the role of 'shepherd' of stumbling and lost 'sheep.' It is highly possible that some type of personality study supplemented by a psychiatric interview would greatly aid in the elimination of those students whose mental and emotional balance is so precarious that success in the ministry is highly improbable." [31] Others, recognizing and stressing the commonly accepted fact that one who does not understand and who has not solved his own problems cannot successfully deal with the personality difficulties of others, have felt that there should be some place in the course of seminary training for the correction of personality defects and disorders.[32] Rollo May speaks of the value of a counselor being analyzed by a psycho-therapist, not to be "taken apart piece by piece" but in order to gain assistance in understanding himself. Then he continues, "We can predict that this constructive form of psychological analysis will be considered a requisite part of the training of teachers, ministers, and social workers in future generations." [33]

There were others, such as Ernest Groves, who objected to this demand and warned that there was a disagreement as to whether anyone could completely objectify himself. He contended that if it was demanded that the minister could not serve as a counselor until he was freed from every subjective influence, then only those who were most thoroughly at the mercy of subconscious motivation would feel equal to it, while the more sensitive and self-understanding, who were actually better equipped, would not feel capable. What was needed, he felt, was that the minister should understand the need of being objective and the danger of letting his personal experiences color his counseling work. Others would agree that this was sufficient to do effective work.[34]

The field of theological education has undergone some significant changes both in content and in method and the indications would seem to be that more will come in the future.

Chapter XVI

THE MENTAL HYGIENE MOVEMENT
AND THE
COMMISSION ON RELIGION AND HEALTH

The mental hygiene movement began in a most dramatic way. It began outside the church and yet, in terms of its indirect influence and the promise of future developments, it is one of the most significant developments of recent years. In one sense all that we have been discussing is mental hygiene, and the church has always been engaged in some form of mental hygiene. Also to include the complete history of mental hygiene and its backgrounds we would have to include all the thoughts and contributions of Dorothea Dix, Benjamin Rush, Pinel and many others but, for our purpose, we will begin with the unusual and outstanding career of Clifford Beers, the man who founded and to a large extent created the mental hygiene movement as we know it today.

Beers' own story is told in his now famous autobiography, *A Mind That Found Itself*, a book which he said he wrote because he felt it was his duty to do so.[1] He called his book the history of a mental civil war, for in it he described the experiences of a severe mental illness from which he suffered from his twenty-fourth year to his twenty-sixth year. His brother who previously had enjoyed perfect health was suddenly stricken with epilepsy. The whole nerve-wracking experience came as a surprise, and a shock. Beers, who was in college at the time, spent much time with his brother and became possessed with the thought that he might be similarly afflicted. He became convinced that his own breakdown was imminent. This started a time of fear, anxiety and dread, which lasted some six years. The actual break came while in a classroom at Yale where he was a student. He continued his classroom studies and completed the requirements for graduation although he was never able to make a recitation. This began a long period of misery which he describes in some detail in his book and which finally culminated in an attempt at suicide. Following graduation he entered business but the fear of epilepsy which had been growing in his mind for six years now completely overcame him. One day, when it all seemed more than he could stand, he rushed to an upstairs window, with the thought of dashing his brains out on the pavement, but in the very act of leaping from the window he turned his body, caught the sill with his hand and fell feet first instead. The result was that his feet were broken and his back painfully injured but no further damage resulted.

He was taken to a hospital where he noticed bars on the windows. When he fell, the moment that he struck the ground the fear of epilepsy left him but in its place his tormented mind was subject to a series of delusions alternating from persecution to grandeur. He left that he was under legal restraint for many crimes he must have committed, that his attendants were detectives and even that his brother was a detective in disguise as his brother, all of which, of course was absurd but "in the lurid lexicon of Unreason there is no such word as absurd." He said he lived in a world "created by my own mind from the chaos that reigned within it." [2] He describes the visions and delusions which haunted him, when the most trifling occurrences assumed vast significance.

Beers returned home for about a month but when his mental condition did not improve he was taken to a private sanitorium where he began the unusual, often tragic, experience that turned out to be a career. Here, in what he described as "this little settlement of woe," he experienced sufferings that were intense. Here he was subject to the neglect and abuse of incompetent attendants, some of whom received but eighteen dollars a month. Here he observed patients beaten, cursed, spit upon by perverted and sadistic attendants for slight offenses or harmless eccentricities for which they were not responsible. Here he was placed in a "muff" at night to reduce the expense of another attendant. On one occasion, for refusing to answer some questions, a doctor jerked him from his bed although his broken bones were not yet knitted. Later he urged all friends and relatives of the mentally ill to remember that the Golden Rule had never been suspended in regard to the insane.

He was transferred to a second institution—this time a private non-profit-making one—but the same experiences continued. The important thing, however, was the use he made of these experiences. Naturally liberty-loving and strong-willed, his sense of justice and fair play was offended by such actions. He not only rebelled against them but resolved, while still a victim of extreme delusions, that he would do something about them. Through an ingenious method by which he convinced himself of his brother's identity he was freed from his delusions and his reason began to return. At first, this change was marked by a transition from depression to elation. He was still mentally disordered but he was happy. He determined to conduct a thorough investigation of the institution. He welcomed a chance to be put in the violent ward, in fact planned his activities so that he would be. He frankly told the authorities of his plan to reform the institution and warned some of the attendants and doctors that they would suffer as a result. He once feigned suicide to get their attention and then told them what his purpose was and what he thought of them in no uncertain terms. As a result of such activities he received further abuse. For attempting to help a patient who was being mistreated he was beaten and choked. For twenty-one days he was placed in a strait-jacket.

Finally he was placed in a third institution, this time a state hospital. Similar experiences continued, although this institution was above average. He held to his plan of instituting a worldwide reform movement. Here also he wanted to be placed in the violent ward to see what methods were used. He soon found out. At one time he was imprisoned in a cold cell without any clothes but his undergarments. Once he was beaten brutally, kicked, kneed and choked. All of these things were written down. In fact, he developed a passion for writing, filling not only ordinary pieces of paper but long strips of wrapping paper with accounts of his experiences and plans for reform. He wrote for hours at a time, scarcely taking time for rest or sleep. He wrote letters to the heads of the institutions which were, of course, ignored. Then he conceived the plan of writing to the governor himself. This letter was thirty-two pages in length, so large it could not be placed in the slot of a letter-box. Since he could not trust an attendant or doctor to mail it, he smuggled it out himself, on one of the visits to town that were permitted, placed it in a magazine on a newsstand, with instructions on the envelope that it should be mailed. The letter did reach the governor and attracted his attention, as well it might, for Beers referred to him as the "head Devil" over these Hells—the institutions. In great detail he described situations as they existed. The governor did take action against one of the attendants named, but he did not instigate a general investigation. This convinced Beers that to carry on his program of reform he must get outside.

Upon regaining his freedom he resolved to write a book. *Les Miserables* had had a great influence upon him, as had *Uncle Tom's Cabin*. The latter book had a great influence on slavery and he felt that another book should be written that would free the slaves of countless asylums and sanitariums of the unnecessary abuse and neglect which were theirs. "Without malice toward those who had me in charge, I yet looked with abhorrence upon the system by which I had been treated." [3] William A. White, the great psychiatrist, said that it was his ability to see meaning where others had found only resentment that to a large extent accounted for his unusual success.[4] He frequently referred to the compensations he had received from his sufferings which, he said, "makes me feel that my suffering was worth while." [5] And again he said, "I am further compensated by the belief that I have a distinct mission in life—a chance for usefulness that might never have been mine had I enjoyed unbroken health and uninterrupted liberty." [6]

Carried forward by this compulsion, he began to record his story. When he was conscious of a recurrence of his difficulty, in the form of a mild elation, he returned voluntarily to the hospital, taking with him a sufficient supply of notebooks so that he might record his thoughts and feelings. When, after a month, he was released from the hospital, completely recovered, he finished his manuscript and presented it to several people for their opinions—among them William James. James received him kindly, but pointed to a pile of unread manuscripts on his desk and would not promise to take any time for Beers' manuscript very soon. When he did read it, however, he was very much interested, wrote a most encouraging letter and promised his support. This was a great encouragement. It not only bolstered Beers' morale, but the approval of such a personality as James soon enlisted the support of others. James provided an introduction for his book, giving it further standing.

Meanwhile Beers had resumed his old job on Wall Street and was doing very well, but he could not forget his idea of an organization for the benefit of the mentally ill, so he gave up his business career, with considerable reluctance, to assume this new and unexplored field. Naturally, the first person he invited to become a member of his society was William James. Others also showed an interest, among them Dr. Adolf Meyer, to whom goes the credit for selecting the term "mental hygiene." Beers' ambition was to form a nation-wide organization, but he was persuaded that it would be more practical to try an experiment in the state of Connecticut for a year and then expand if the project proved worthy. The first meeting was held May 6, 1908, at the residence of the Rev. Anson Phelps Stokes, with fourteen present. The first sentence of the Prospectus of this society was, "After all, what the insane most need is a friend." A year later, on February 19, 1909, the National Committee was organized. The publication of his story, *A Mind that Found Itself*, had achieved nation-wide attention in both lay and professional circles and had attracted the support of many prominent people, such as Jane Addams, Julia Lathrop, Jacob Riis, Dr. Booth Tarkington, Dr. Henry van Dyke, Cardinal Gibbons and Bishop William Lawrence, as well as James and Meyer who have already been mentioned.

The movement began, as Beers stated, with plenty of moral support but very little financial support. He borrowed $10,000 in his own name to cover expenses. A gift of $1,000 from William James was an unexpected help. A few years later a gift of $50,000 from Henry Phipps came as a veritable godsend. It was accompanied by a gift of $5,000 which Beers was to use personally, not for the Committee. This gift financed the first three years of the movement. Later other contributions were received. In 1929, the Committee on Distribution of the Conrad Hubert Estate, composed of Calvin Coolidge, Alfred Smith and Julius Rosenwald, granted $250,000 to the work of the committee. Needless to say, such contributions enabled them to carry on a much more extensive work than would otherwise have been possible. Beers served from the beginning as executive secretary and personally saw it through all of the stressful years until it became worldwide. In 1918, the Canadian National Committee was organized.

In 1928 he founded the American Foundation for Mental Hygiene, a separate yet coöperating agency, whose purposes were to finance such work and to foster research to reduce and prevent nervous and mental disorders. An International Committee was founded with Adolf Meyer as president. In May of 1930, an International Congress of Mental Hygiene was held in Washington, D.C., with William A. White as president, with representatives from more than fifty countries. The number of state societies continued to increase. In 1933, there were more than thirty such organizations. In the Epilogue to his book, included in the Twenty-fifth Anniversary number, he had the pleasure of recording these and other accomplishments and to say that the happy memories of the work and the unexpected satisfactions "have more than offset, and have practically erased, memories of my unhappy and, at times, distressing years as a mental patient." [7] His book has been recognized as a modern classic; he has received honorary degrees and recognition both at home and abroad. He served as secretary of the organization until 1939, when ill health forced him to retire. He continued as honorary secretary until his death on July 9, 1943.

The society was organized when many other similar groups in different fields were being formed, and found a public that was ready for its reception. Its aims and objectives were several-fold: to promote early diagnosis and treatment, to develop adequate hospitalization, to stimulate research, to secure public support and understanding of psychiatric and mental hygiene activities, to instruct individuals and groups in the application of mental hygiene principles and to coöperate with any government or private agencies whose work touches the field of mental hygiene. Naturally, their attention at first was turned to the improving of hospitals and the training of those who cared for the mentally ill. They hoped to correct the prevailing misconceptions regarding the nature and cause of mental illness and to remove the stigma commonly attached to the word "insane." They wanted to make it clear that mental illness was no different from any other illness and, to a large extent, could be prevented and cured. Since Beers himself had been frequently told by competent psychiatrists that his own illness might well have been avoided by guidance at the proper time, much of the work was preventive in nature. They desired to carry out an extensive program that was educational in nature, hoping to reach not only the medical profession, but also teachers, social workers, the courts, and the public at large, informing them of the nature of mental illness, enabling them to detect early symptoms and to recognize the significance of instinctive and emotional factors in delinquency, conduct disorders and child training.

The success in achieving these aims has been due not only to the ingenuity and perseverance of Beers but to many who worked with him. The names of Meyer and Salmon should especially be mentioned. Meyer was a great help in the early years and Salmon, who served as the first medical director of the National Committee, deserves much credit for putting it on a sound scientific basis. In the early days they carried on a variety of activities. They conducted surveys and investigations of many mental and penal institutions all over the country, with recommendations for their improvement. They followed up their investigations with proposed legislation to put the suggestions into effect. They carried on an extensive educational program. In 1917, they began the publication of the quarterly, "Mental Hygiene," which continues as the standard publication in the field. They have produced voluminous literature and have made available pamphlets and leaflets for a very nominal price on almost any subject related to mental hygiene. From the very beginning they have been active in the sponsoring of psychiatric and mental hygiene clinics, most notable of which have been the child guidance clinics. They launched a campaign in 1922 for the establishment of these clinics and, since 1922, more than three hundred mental hygiene clinics for children have come into existence. During World War I, the government turned to the National Committee to organize its department of neurology and psychology under the Surgeon General's office. Similar, and very extensive, coöperation was given in World War II.

Some idea of their later activities may be gained by considering the items listed in the annual report of 1942.[8] First it listed the seven-point war program that included exclusion of the mentally unstable from the armed forces, early detection and treatment of neuro-psychiatric cases in the armed forces, rehabilitation of the mentally disabled, both civilians and veterans, continuation of civilian services, maintenance of public morale, mental health guidance for civilians transferred to new environments and occupations, and the need of strengthening mental hygiene services to meet post-war demands. Then it listed the activities under nine major divisions. The division of child guidance, the division of extension and field work, the division of school studies, of psychiatric education, of psychiatric personnel, of mental hospitals, of psychiatric research, publication activities and building mental health. Perhaps the most significant work of the mental hygiene movement cannot be listed. It has had a very profound influence on the work of other groups due, in part, to the above-mentioned activities and to the fact that representatives of these groups have been active in the development and carrying forward of its program. It would be impossible to trace the changes and the improvements that have taken place in social and community welfare agencies, in social case work, in education, in medicine, in juvenile courts and correctional agencies, in penal institutions, in mental and general hospitals, and in the community at large. As has been said, there are few people in America who have not been benefited by the mental hygiene movement in some of these ways although they may not realize it or even be aware that such an organization as the National Committee for Mental Hygiene exists.

The mental hygiene movement, as such, has been separate from the church, although there have been ministers who were interested and active in its program from the very beginning. As yet, however, there has been no extensive study of the resources of religion and no attempt to utilize the agencies of the church to any great extent. There has, however, been a growing awareness of the significance of the function of the minister and of the resources of religion in relation to mental hygiene. Clara Bassett in *Mental Hygiene in the Community* included a chapter in which she stressed very strongly the unique and important part which the church, of necessity, plays in the total picture of mental hygiene. Groves and Blanchard in their *Introduction to Mental Hygiene* state that the strategic points of attack for mental hygiene are the ministry and the medical profession. Such ideas have been becoming more common. Several articles were published in the quarterly, "Mental Hygiene," dealing with the questions of religion and mental hygiene. Dr. Kirkpatrick contributed one such article in which he emphasized the idea that the minister was in the field of mental hygiene whether he wanted to be or not, the chief question was what kind of a mental hygienist he would be.[9]

Dr. Fosdick spoke before the eighteenth annual meeting of the National Committee in 1927 on the subject, "A Clergyman's View of Mental Hygiene," and he stressed the need of coöperation between the professions and also the idea that there are some cases that cannot be solved without religion. The address was reprinted in their pamphlet series. Such expressions as these have been very frequent and, although the clergy have not played a large part in the development of the movement, they have had a part. While the attention given to religion has been relatively small but steadily increasing, so the interest of the clergy in mental hygiene has been relatively small but likewise steadily increasing. The church and the ministry have benefited from the movement in a variety of ways. As well as benefiting from specific activities, such as clinics and various publications, the ministry has benefited from the changed points of view regarding the nature of mental illness, the possibility of prevention and cure, the new attitudes towards mental institutions such as hospitals, the significance of childhood and the home, and improved methods of counseling. Indirectly the movement has influenced the approach to pastoral counseling, religious education and church social work to a very great degree. In short, those who have been concerned with the application of scientific principles and findings to more efficient religious work have found here a great resource and a helpful ally. The tendency has been for both groups—physicians and ministers—to see the need of closer harmony, coöperation and understanding. As was said in the conclusion of a little booklet, *The Mental Hygiene Movement*,[10] "When . . . the co-ordinated efforts of those who heal the mind, of those who heal the body, and of those who heal the soul are brought to bear upon our world problems, shall we not see the beginnings of a brighter day—the rise of a finer and more stable civilization?"

THE FEDERAL COUNCIL'S COMMISSION
ON RELIGION AND HEALTH

Of real significance in the realm of ecumenical interchurch coöperation has been the gradual development of what is now the Commission on Religion and Health of the Federal Council of Churches of Christ in America.[11] This commission was organized in 1937 and is now the most competent unifying agency and clearing house for all new developments in the field of religion and health. However, its origin must be traced back to an informal meeting in 1923 when a group of physicians and clergymen met to discuss the possibilities of closer coöperation between the two professions. After several such conferences Dr. James Alexander Miller presented their findings to the New York Academy of Medicine. The result was a meeting of representatives of the Academy and of the Federal Council of Churches. A Joint Committee on Religion and Medicine was organized as a branch of the Public Health Relations Committee of the Academy in 1925.

The basis on which this joint committee, representing the fields of medicine and the church, began its work was that coöperation between the clergyman and the physician in ministering to the sick in body or mind was desirable and could be very helpful but, recognizing the many problems that confronted them, they were a bit uncertain as to how they should proceed. In order to be sure of themselves, to make adequate study and avoid premature publicity, they moved very slowly and cautiously. Fortunately a single contributor, whose name remains anonymous, proved a great benefactor, enabling the committee to maintain itself during this period of infancy. It was felt that the common ground on which the clergy and the physicians could meet and do their best work was the emotional field. The joint committee continued to study this field; meetings were held, papers were read and discussed. Dr. Helen Flanders Dunbar was recommended as one fitted to make a special study of the field of psychosomatic relations and in 1929 she was secured to make a year's study in Europe. In 1931 she was appointed Director of the Joint Committee. Many projects presented themselves as possibilities but her activities were confined at first to the study of the emotional field—which resulted in the now standard volume *Emotions and Bodily Changes* [12] by Dr. Dunbar—and to the guidance of the Council for Clinical Training. It is significant that the Federal Council of Churches had such an instrumental part in the development of this standard psychiatric volume.

It soon became apparent that the Joint Committee of the Federal Council of Churches and the Academy of Medicine was no longer practical, so the committee was dissolved; it then became a committee on Religion and Health of the Federal Council and later a Commission. In 1936 Dr. Dunbar resigned to give her time completely to private practice and research, and in 1938 the Rev. Seward Hiltner was appointed Executive Secretary of the Commission. He has served it most competently ever since. Four of the doctors who had served on the original committee remained on the new commission. Later two nurses were added so that their profession might also be represented and so that there might be a better understanding among them of the relationship of religion and health and of their particular opportunities. At the present time the personnel of the commission consists of ministers, professors in theological seminaries, physicians, psychiatrists, nurses, social workers, health educators, lawyers and public health workers.

The work of the Commission is primarily educational. It sponsored a large conference on Religion and Health at Greenwich, Connecticut, which was attended by representatives of the fields of religion, medicine and psychology, from all parts of the country. Since then they have sponsored many such institutes and conferences all over the United States. Many of them were held on a rather large scale, meeting at such centers as Union Theological Seminary, the University of Chicago and the University of Southern California. Others have been smaller ones, concerned primarily in bringing about closer coöperation and understanding of the problems of religion and health in local communities. In 1944, the Department sponsored a National Conference on Clinical Training in Theological Education which was widely attended and very significant in result. Collaborating in the conference were the Council for Clinical Training, the Graduate School of Applied Religion and the Institute of Pastoral Care and the representatives of the major schools who are carrying on this type of work.[13] The most recent effort of the Commission has been to act as co-sponsor with the Y.M.C.A. and the U.S.O. of numerous seminars and institutes for army and navy chaplains, ministers, Y.M.C.A. workers and U.S.O. workers during the recent war.

As much as possible the Commission has attempted to meet the needs of those agencies and organizations that have turned to it for help. This has involved considerable correspondence and is resulting in the Commission's becoming somewhat of a clearing-house for such problems and questions. It also has assisted hospitals in securing chaplains and, at the suggestion of the Greater New York Federation of Churches, it has made a study of Protestant chaplaincies in all city-owned hospitals. Later, at the request of the American Protestant Hospital Association, Mr. Hiltner and Rev. Harold Schultz, of St. Louis, made a study of religious work in 432 Protestant hospitals in the United States. As a result of such studies, many useful suggestions were made and the need was revealed for a better understanding between the various professions which so often work entirely separately, and especially the need for a more adequate religious ministry in the interest of better physical and mental health.

The function of the Commission that shows very great promise for the future is the promotion of publications. Already it has been responsible for the appearance of several volumes of real value, but, even more significant in some ways, is a series of pamphlets which have been made available at a very minimum expense. Some of these are "Religion and Health in the Local Community," "The Ministry of Counseling," by Rollo May, and "The Ministry of Listening," by Russell Dicks. Reprints are also provided of articles from such journals as "Mental Hygiene," "Religious Education," "The Pastor," "The Quarterly Journal of Studies in Alcohol," and others which are of particular value to the ministers.[14] This last is of real service to the average minister who does not have the time or facilities to locate material which is of such definite value if he is to do a thorough and scientific piece of work and keep abreast of the latest developments.

The aims of the commission as adopted in 1939 are—

To show that health of body, mind and spirit is an essential concern of religion.

To discover and demonstrate the distinctive function of religion in the maintenance, restoration and improvement of health and emotional balance.

To aid in revitalizing the pastor's ministry to individuals in special need and difficulty.

To promote practical coöperation between physicians and

clergymen, and between other leaders of religious and health work.

To improve the ministry of the churches to those in hospitals and other institutions and to those suffering from chronic illness.[15]

The secretary's report for 1945 included such general fields as "Education in Personal Counseling," "Religious Ministry in Hospitals," "Returning Service Men and Women," "Alcohol Studies," "Pastoral Aid Publications," and "Other Activities." It made mention of a proposed professional journal and a study of ministry to older people as well as of the activities of various Commission members and of the secretary.

NOTE: Since the completion of this manuscript, the Federal Council has announced, through its Bulletin of January, 1947, that plans have been approved for the formation of a new Department of Pastoral Services. This new and enlarged department will combine the Commission on Religion and Health and the Commission on Prison Chaplains, and will also create a new Commission on Ministry to Institutions. This will make possible many activities not otherwise provided for in the Federal Council program; in fact, in recent years the Commission on Religion and Health has had to assume many projects that were of a wider scope than was indicated in its title. This is a definite advancement and should lead to significant developments in the future. Rev. Seward Hiltner will serve as the Executive Secretary of the new department.

Chapter XVII

LIFE-SITUATION PREACHING, THE CHURCH'S PROGRAM AND THE CONCLUSION

The growth of the psychological and social sciences and the corresponding emphases on pastoral counseling have had a marked influence on the total work of the ministry. It is not only his work with individuals that has been affected, but, to a certain degree, all of the activities of the minister. Even preaching, the oldest and, as many would say, the most basic of all his responsibilities, has felt the influence of these developments. Preaching has become less doctrinal and more psychological. It has created what has been termed "life-situation preaching," or sometimes, problem preaching, pastoral preaching or psychological preaching. Of course, there have always been men who have done life-situation preaching. A study of the sermons of Bushnell, Beecher, Gladden and Brooks, all reveal much that would be termed problem or life-situation preaching. Emerson sensed the need of such preaching as is revealed in a statement found in his journal, "At church today I felt how unequal is the match of words against things. Cease, O thou unauthorized talker, to prate of consolation, resignation, and spiritual joys in neat and balanced sentences. For I know these men who sit below. Hush quickly, for care and calamity are things to them. There is the shopkeeper whose daughter is gone mad, and he is looking up through his spectacles to see what you have for him. Here is my friend whose scholars are leaving him and he knows not where to turn his hand next. Here is the stage driver, who has jaundice and cannot get well. Here is B, who failed last year and is looking up anxiously. Speak, thing, or hold thy peace." [1]

The power of the spoken word is something that has long been recognized and is only recently being re-discovered. This power can be used for either good or ill. Unfortunately the church's record is not altogether clean in this regard. There were, of course, individuals, and at times whole periods, when the emphasis necessary to provide guidance, insight and power, such as Emerson requested, were lacking. There were others who so overemphasized the emotional appeal, as in some revival preaching, or whose intellectual content was of such a nature that they produced "sick souls" rather than helped them; they increased tension, caused unnecessary anxiety and fear, with the total result being unwholesome and unfortunate. These situations, however, can be more than counterbalanced by the positive and wholesome results that have come from preaching to personal needs and problems. There are innumerable illustrations that could be cited of people who have testified to the faith, the courage, and the strength for the facing of life's tasks that they have received from the preaching of such men as Phillips Brooks or Horace Bushnell, when they were facing some crisis or passing through some period of sorrow or sadness in their own lives.

The students of pastoral counseling have recognized that there is a close relationship between the two functions of preaching and counseling. They have pointed out that one can weaken or strengthen the other. They have emphasized the fact that the pastor has a unique position shared by no other type of counselor in the fact that he appears before his people every week and speaks to them on the issues of life. It was seen that good preaching, preaching that had an insight and appreciation of the meaning of life and could point to the possibilities and means of solution, would both strengthen and support what was done in the interview and would also lead to further counseling. In fact Dr. Fosdick said that the test of a good sermon was the number of people who came to talk further with the minister alone. It was also seen that a good counseling program was necessary for effective preaching. Many stressed the fact that only through the facing of individual problems could a man know life well enough to speak to them in a group. It was further stressed that very often a person was so confused by some problem, so "tied-up" with anxiety, guilt or fear that only by counseling could he be freed to appreciate and utilize preaching. If such a person was helped, however, then he would listen with a new understanding and receptiveness to the one who spoke on Sunday. The primary emphasis that was made was the fact that preaching must deal with the actual problems of people. Mackenzie stressed the idea that some of the best sermons fail, not because they are not good but because they are irrelevant to the conflicts and tensions which are so real to the people who hear them.[2] Dr. Fosdick expressed his own theory in a popular magazine, "Every sermon should have for its main business the solving of some problem—a vital, important problem, puzzling minds, burdening consciences, distracting lives." [3]

Dr. Fosdick has himself been the greatest exponent of this type of preaching. A list of some sermon subjects that he has used are worthy of inclusion. "Handling Life's Second Bests," "The High Uses of Trouble," "The Cure of Disillusionment," "The Mastery of Fear," "Handicapped Lives," "When Life Goes All to Pieces," "How to Stand Up and Take It," and "Mastering Depression," are typical.[4] Into these sermons he poured the insights of study, Scripture, biography, and experience, until each one was a masterpiece. Preached from the pulpit of Riverside Church and over a national network, they have been a source of courage and strength to literally thousands and have been known to save more than one from suicide. Fosdick's influence in setting the pattern for this type of preaching has been extremely widespread. There are many others who have made this a major emphasis if not a specialty in their preaching, such as Gilkey, Peale, Day, Sockman and Weatherhead. A study of three hundred typical sermons, published in the "Christian Century Pulpit" since 1937, revealed that seventy were definitely personal and psychological in emphasis. That is, almost twenty-five percent were what would be called life-situation preaching. There were many others where this was predominant in the sermon although not the only or the major emphasis. The above seventy were only those where it was evident in the title and comprised the major body of the sermon.

Harold Ruopp, a strong advocate of this type of preaching, when serving as professor of preaching in Boston University School of Theology and Andover-Newton Theological School, made a survey with the students of these two schools in order to determine just what the problems and difficulties were that were the most real to people and how they could be met by preaching. The survey covered a seven-year period from 1931–1938. About four thousand people from over two hundred different churches responded with the information desired. The replies were studied and classified and divided into four major problem areas: (1) The Individual and the Inner Self which contained 48.7 percent of the replies, (2) The Individual in His Relationship to the Family, 21.2 percent, (3) The Individual in His Relationship to Larger Social Groups and Society, 16.7 percent, and (4) The Individual in His Relationship to God and the Universe, 13.4 percent.[5] The first section was divided into several divisions such as personality problems and difficulties, life decisions, moral problems, misfortune, thwarted ambitions and desires, the meaning of life, personal feelings of sin and guilt and others. Dr. Ruopp did not contend that as a result of these findings only 13 percent of a minister's sermons should deal with the fourth section on the person's relationship to God and the universe, and he also pointed out the further fact that if this relationship with God were more real there would be less problems listed in the first section. It does, however, indicate the problems that people felt were real.

These problems do not leave the people when they enter the

sanctuary, as Emerson so clearly saw. More recently Ernest Fremont Tittle said, "On any given Sunday morning, there is probably no single congregation assembled anywhere in this world in which there are not at least a few persons who are in truly desperate need of personal help." [6] The psychological and counseling emphasis which has made the ministry more aware of these problems also insists that the pulpit can and must aid in their solution. It is the strongest preventive agency that there is in the community. This does not mean that its function is merely one of warning, although this may be included. It does mean that the pulpit, by instruction, suggestion, inspiration, can present ideals, create a philosophy of life, stimulate growth, deepen faith and make available spiritual resources by which men can live. Karl Ruf Stolz spoke of the "therapeutic function of preaching." [7] Albert Palmer said preaching was a kind of pastoral counseling done impersonally. [8] Rollo May wrote, "Ideally, the members of the congregation should have in the church service much the same experience as the individual has in the counseling interview; they should go out from the church having experienced a psychological and spiritual catharsis, and feeling enlightened, encouraged, and strengthened by their new understanding of reality." [9] Thus the pulpit can put meaning into life, aid men in the making of adjustments and the facing of its problems, enable them to live maturely, courageously and abundantly.

THE CHURCH'S PROGRAM

The whole program of the church has been affected. Closely related to preaching has been the emphasis that has been made on the power and value of worship. For centuries this has been one of the chief functions of the church. Now it is seen to have real therapeutic values. "The beaten paths of hymn, anthem, Scripture, prayer and sermon was, after all, a path along which generations of Christians had traveled to mental and spiritual health." [10] The value of private worship and prayer was seen to have tremendous power in the life of an individual, and some of the most enthusiastic statements of recent years, concerning the value of prayer and devotion, have come from the scientists, rather than from the clergy. Religious education was seen as particularly important because of its emotional content and because of its influence on childhood and youth. The leaders of the religious education movement have been receptive to and well acquainted with the findings of the psychologists, sociologists and the students of mental hygiene. These principles were incorporated into the writings of such men as George A. Coe, William C. Bower, Theodore Soares, Paul A. Vieth, Harrison S. Elliott and others. While some churches have developed especially fine programs, there is still much to be done before they find expression in the average church and Sunday school. Evangelism received a new interest and attention. It was emphasized that evangelism must be based upon our growing knowledge of human nature; it must present a summons to men to come to terms with their ultimate loyalties until, in William James' well-known phrase, a self hitherto divided and unhappy becomes unified, strong and happy because of its hold of religious realities. Pastoral calling was no longer seen as a mere "ringing of door bells" but was seen as a real service in itself and one that often led to further and deeper contacts. The unique privilege of knowing people in their own homes was an opportunity presented to the pastor which was shared by no other counselor. The fellowship of the church, when it is genuine and sincere, and the enlisting of people in a task and uniting them with a great cause were seen to have a vital significance for the enrichment and meaning of life that could be found in no other way. The statement, "He that would save his life must lose it," has been found to be psychologically true.

Thus another of the implications of the development of pastoral counseling and mental hygiene has been to increase the significance of the total church program. Many have come to feel that no other institution has greater opportunity to aid in the development of mental health than the church. They have all stressed the fact that this does not mean the church should attempt the work of a psychiatric clinic or that the minister should attempt things for which he is not trained or prepared. The minister should always remember that he is a minister and the church is a church, a religious institution. The church and the minister, if they maintain what has been termed "person mindedness," have their greatest resources in their regular activities. The contributions of the program of the church are primarily two—they are preventive and reënforcing. Through the various functions of its regular program the church can give information and insight and can develop those purposes, habits, ideals and attitudes which are the greatest preventive powers in the world. Dr. Fosdick, in a published sermon, said, "I wish the psychiatrists no harm, but if great religion could get hold of some people first, the psychiatrists would have less to do." [11] The church's task is not only the "cure of souls" when they become sick; it is equally important to prevent such diseases of the mind and soul. Similarly, the church should provide reënforcement. Through its preaching and general program it should develop those inner resources of the spirit, those profound and tested powers of the Christian gospel, so that when the inevitable tests of life do come they will be met with courage, confidence and faith. In Jesus' words, it is to develop such character as can be compared to a house with a firm foundation, on which "the rain descended, and the floods came, and the winds blew, and beat upon that house; and it fell not; for it was founded upon a rock."

CONCLUSION

In conclusion, we would repeat the thought expressed in the Introduction and found frequently throughout the pages of this book—there is nothing that a minister does that is of greater significance than to help individuals meet the needs and problems of life. This is not to minimize the importance of any other phase of the minister's task, but is rather to stress the fact that in these days and in the days that lie ahead no more sacred responsibility will fall upon the minister than those occasions when he is confronted with the problem of some particular personality or some individual soul. Certainly no more vital, permanent or effective task can be conceived, for when an individual confronts his pastor with some actual life situation, some question or problem, some tension, anxiety or fear, at that moment destiny is in the pastor's hands. Then, if ever, he is treading on holy ground. It is not something separate from preaching, religious education and other phases of the church program; all must be done effectively, for all are part and parcel of the same thing—the attempt to meet the spiritual needs of people, but none of these can take the place of pastoral counseling and pastoral care. Beautiful buildings, an efficient organization, even scholarly and well-prepared sermons are not enough—only the faithful, sincere, devoted, well-prepared pastor can meet the needs of his people at such moments.

After following the story of the men and women who have given themselves in such service, one gains a fresh awareness of the significance of the tradition of the Christian ministry and the Christian church and of the spirit of compassion and service that is found there. It is the greatest tradition in the world. To be a part of it, to take one's place in this great movement and to stand with those of all generations who would minister to the needs of men is as great a privilege as one could ask. These men reveal in their own lives the possibilities of human nature, the possibilities that exist within the human soul. Many of them faced very real and intense personal problems, conflicts and sorrows; some could honestly have been called "tortured souls," but they adjusted to their situations, rose above them until they became "more than conquerors," an inspiration to all who knew their stories. They used their own experiences until they themselves became more useful, more understanding, more helpful than they had ever been before, or than they ever would have been without these experiences. They belong to that company who "pass through tribulation to become benefactors of the race." Furthermore, they revealed what actually could be done—they did minister unto people; they did help them in a very real and vital way. Their theories and their methods were often very different, but when their efforts were sincere, patient and faithful, they did guide and strengthen countless numbers, people who were facing confusing, discouraging, painful, often tragic situations. The "cure of souls" is no new venture. It has been demonstrated over and over what a faithful pastor can do.

Looking from the past to the present and on into the future reveals the greatest need for such ministry that the church or the world has ever faced. The recent war has greatly intensified it and has revealed to us in many ways the vast range and extent of the problem. Every newspaper is an indication of how widespread the situation is. The extent of crime and delinquency, the rising divorce rate, the rapid increase of mental illness, are all but straws in the wind that point to the tension, fear and insecurity that exist on every hand and indicate the needs of the hour. Every parish, no matter how large or small, or where it may be located, is full of such situations for those who have eyes to see. Sick, tired, discouraged, frustrated, perplexed, confused, unhappy people are in every minister's congregation and community. There are young people puzzled about their vocations, their homes and life itself. There are elderly people who are lonesome and unhappy. There are people who are hounded by a sense of guilt, haunted by fear. There are innumerable normal people who are perplexed by life's problems, burdened by life's hardships, overcome by life's sorrows. None must be neglected. The minister in these days and in the days ahead must not do less pastoral work; he must do more.

Certain definite things must be done. Our attitudes must be such that first and foremost will be the needs of the people. No one need neglect his preaching or slight his organization—all must be seen from the viewpoint of the needs of people. Every minister must prepare himself for this task. He must study and inform himself of what others have done and what others have to say regarding the most effective methods and procedures. Even more important, he must study, analyze and evaluate his own methods, his successes and failures. He must coöperate with all other agencies and professions. Groups must band themselves together for mutual study and enrichment. Some must specialize—train themselves not only to carry on this task but to teach others to do so. Some must prepare themselves to work in certain areas, such as with adolescents, with problems of the home, with the sick or with the mentally ill, or with the criminal and delinquent. Research must be carried on—as thorough, exhaustive and complete as is done in any other branch of science or religion. New books must be written, good books, books that grow out of actual experience, books that deal with both the theory and the technique, books that explore deeply the meaning of human nature and the resources of religion. Every effort must be made to keep abreast of what other fields have to offer. The best of scientific study of human nature must be utilized. To do less would be unfair to our people. With all this we must remember always that the ministry also is a specialty and has a unique contribution to make, and that religion has a value for which no amount of scientific knowledge is a substitute. Seminaries and theological schools must continue to experiment and pioneer. Advances have been made but they only indicate the way; continued progress must be made until we go far beyond what we have at present in the way of preparing men for this most sacred of all tasks.

If we do strive to do these things, then the future, with all its needs and problems, has much of promise and is challenging in its possibilities. Recent years have seen many advances in our scientific knowledge of human nature, and in the development of more effective methods and techniques. However, it is all still in its infancy—there will be much more that will be done. If we can combine our scientific knowledge with the spirit of compassion of the Christian tradition, if we can learn to utilize new methods and techniques in understanding and helping people, together with the traditional spirit of service and the resources and power of a deep and genuine Christian faith, then there is no limit to the possibilities that lie in the future.

Finally, we would say that he who strives to the best of his ability to fulfill this task has the inner assurance that comes from the knowledge that in no other way can one follow more closely the One Who "came not to be ministered unto, but to minister," Who always had time and took care to minister to each individual, whoever it might be, in whatever manner the need was greatest; the One Who said, "inasmuch as ye have done it unto one of the least of these my brethren ye have done it unto me."

NOTES

Chapter I

THE NEW TESTAMENT PERIOD

OLD TESTAMENT BACKGROUND

[1] See McNeil and Gomer, *Medieval Handbook of Penance*, Columbia, 1938, and McNeil, *Historical Types of Methods in the Cure of Souls*, "Crozer Quarterly," 1943, p. 324

[2] Exodus 18:13

[3] Exodus 18:13–27; Hastings, *Dictionary of the Bible*, Article, "Judge, Judging"

[4] See Exodus 22:18; Leviticus 19:26, 31; 20:27

[5] I Samuel 28:3–25

[6] See Knudson, *Beacon Lights of Prophecy*, Methodist Book Concern, 1914, p. 166 and Johnson, *Psychology of Religion*, Abingdon-Cokesbury, 1945, p. 18

[7] See Fleming James, *Personalities of the Old Testament*, Scribner, 1939, pp. 501–3

[8] Proverbs 12:15; 11:14

JESUS' MINISTRY TO INDIVIDUALS

[9] John 2:25, Revised Standard Version

[10] Mark 6:33ff, Moffatt

[11] Luke 4:18ff, Moffatt

[12] Matt. 25:45

[13] Mark 1:32, 45

[14] Kunkel, *In Search of Maturity*, Scribner, 1943, p. 12

[15] Stolz, *Church and Psychotherapy*, Abingdon-Cokesbury, 1943, p. 60

[16] Hadfield and Browne, *Psychology and the Church*, Macmillan, 1925, p. 190

[17] Klausner, *Jesus of Nazareth*, Macmillan, 1925, p. 266

[18] Mark 1:29ff, Moffatt

[19] Mackinnon, *The Historic Jesus*, Longmans Green, 1931, p. 351

[20] *Ibid.*, p. 359

[21] Cf. Eddy, *The Portrait of Jesus*, Harper, 1943, p. 37

[22] Stolz, *ibid.*, pp. 29–30

[23] Mark 5:19ff

[24] Luke 4:40

[25] Bassett, *Mental Hygiene in the Community*, Macmillan, 1936, p. 275

[26] Burnham, *Great Teachers and Mental Hygiene*, D. Appleton, 1926, p. 37

[27] Mark 7:20, Moffatt

[28] Luke 6:45

[29] Mark 12:14
[30] Hadfield and Browne, *ibid.*, p. 173
[31] Lyman, *Jesus*, Association Press, 1930, p. 38

THE PASTORAL MINISTRY OF PAUL

[32] See Riddle, *Paul, Man of Conflict*, Cokesbury, 1940
[33] Romans 7:15, 18, 19, 24, Revised Standard Version
[34] Philippians 4:6, 7, 13
[35] See Dibelius, *A Fresh Approach to the New Testament and Early Christian Literature*, Scribner, 1936, chap. 1, and Goodspeed, *Christianity Goes to Press*, Macmillan, 1940, chap. 1
[36] Craig, *The Study of the New Testament*, Abingdon-Cokesbury, 1939, p. 76
[37] Galatians 5:1; Philippians 4:2, Philemon
[38] See Goodspeed, *Christianity Goes to Press*, pp. 17ff
[39] See Romans 1:28ff and II Corinthians 12:20ff
[40] Cf. Lyman, *The Christian Epic*, Scribner, 1936, p. 47
[41] I Corinthians 13:11; Ephesians 4:13
[42] Romans 13:8; I Corinthians 13
[43] Philippians 4:8

THE EARLY CHURCH

[44] Angus, *Environment of Early Christianity*, Scribner, 1928
[45] James 1:27
[46] See Article in "Outline of Christianity," Vol. I, by Burton S. Easton, pp. 344-5, Dodd Mead & Co., 1926, also Hastings *Dictionary of the Bible*, Vol. I, article "Deacons"
[47] Case, *Social Triumph of the Ancient Church*, Harper, 1933, p. 80
[48] See *Outline of Christianity*, Vol. II, pp. 65-6
[49] Dargan, *History of Preaching*, Hodder & Stoughton, 1906, Vol. I, pp. 99ff

Chapter II

THE MEDIEVAL PERIOD

[1] See Conway, *The Question Box*, Paulist Press, 1929, pp. 280ff, also Geddes, *The Catholic Church and the Confessional*, Macmillan, 1928
[2] See Geddes, pp. 56ff
[3] Cf. Slater, *Short History of Moral Theology*, Benziger Brothers, 1909
[4] Geddes, *ibid.*, pp. 68-9
[5] See McNeil and Gomer, *Medieval Handbooks of Penance*, Columbia University Press, 1938, pp. 9ff

[6] Conway, *ibid.*, p. 286
[7] Conway, *ibid.*, pp. 284ff
[8] See McNeil and Gomer, *ibid.*, also Slater, *ibid.*
[9] McNeil, *ibid.*, p. 99
[10] *Ibid.*, pp. 148ff
[11] *Ibid.*, pp. 221ff
[12] *Ibid.*, pp. 251ff
[13] *Ibid.*, pp. 30ff
[14] *Ibid.*, pp. 45-6ff
[15] See Schaff-Herzog, *Encyclopedia of Religious Knowledge*, Funk and Wagnalls, 1891, p. 530
[16] Cf. McNeil, pp. 413-4
[17] Cf. Conway, p. 282
[18] Cf. Geddes, p. 46
[19] Conway, *ibid.*, pp. 289-90
[20] Heidbreder, *Seven Psychologies*, D. Appleton Century, 1933, p. 34
[21] Walker, *A Manual of Church History*, American Baptist Publication Society, 1933, p. 362
[22] See *Confessions of St. Augustine*, Collier and Son, 1909, pp. 16, 139
[23] *Confessions*, p. 142
[24] *Confessions*, p. 138
[25] Kershner, *Pioneers of Christian Thought*, Bobbs Merrill, 1930, p. 161
[26] Boggs, *Christian Sage*, Vol. I, Macmillan, 1931, p. 242
[27] See Pillsbury, *History of Psychology*, George Wahr, 1923, pp. 45-7, also Zilboorg, *History of Medical Psychology*, Norton, 1941, p. 112
[28] See Howard, *Princes of the Pulpit and Pastorate*, Cokesbury, 1929, p. 211
[29] See Walsh, *The Catholic Church and Healing*, Macmillan, 1928, p. 49
[30] See Cunningham, *Cure of Souls*, Cambridge University Press, 1908, pp. 38-9 quotes Bede, *Histo. Eccl. III*, p. 26
[31] See Steere, *On Beginning From Within*, Harper, 1943, p. 51
[32] See Gladden, *Christian Pastor*, Scribner, 1898, pp. 293ff

Chapter III

THE PERIOD OF THE REFORMATION AND THE PROTESTANT PASTOR

[1] See McNeil article, "Historical Types of Method in the Cure of Souls," "Crozer Quarterly," July, 1934
[2] James 5:16
[3] See McNeil, *Medieval Handbook of Penance*, Columbia University Press, 1938, p. 415
[4] Nebe, *Luther as Spiritual Adviser*, Lutheran Publication Society, 1894
[5] *Ibid.*, p. 106
[6] *Ibid.*, p. 140
[7] *Ibid.*, p. 40

[8] *Ibid.*, p. 32

[9] *Ibid.*, p. 177

[10] *Ibid.*, p. 212

[11] Dargan, *History of Preaching*, Vol. I, Hodder & Stoughton, 1905, p. 402

[12] *Ibid.*, pp. 499–500

[13] Pattison, *History of Christian Preaching*, American Baptist Publication Society, 1909, p. 262

[14] *Ibid.*, p. 191

[15] Baxter, *The Reformed Pastor*, American Tract Society, 1909, p. 262

[16] *Ibid.*, p. 80

[17] Quoted in Howard, *Princes of the Christian Pulpit and Pastorate*, Vol. II, Cokesbury, 1928, p. 77

[18] *Reformed Pastor*, p. 80

[19] *Ibid.*, p. 81

[20] *Autobiography of Richard Baxter*, Everyman's Library, 1931, p. 78

[21] *Ibid.*, p. 115

[22] *Ibid.*, p. 265

[23] Brown, *Since Calvary*, Macmillan, 1931, p. 392

[24] See Davenport, *Primitive Traits in Religious Revivals*, pp. 159–161

[25] Quoted in Northridge, *Health for Mind and Spirit*, Abingdon, 1938, p. 176

[26] See Beard, *The Story of John Frederick Oberlin*, Pilgrim Press, 1909, p. 138

[27] John Frederick Oberlin Bicentennial Address, given in Finney Chapel, Sept. 18, 1940, p. 5

[28] See Atkins, *Great Sermons of the 19th Century*, Willett Clark, 1940, chapter I

[29] Wilberforce, *Practical View of Christianity*

[30] See Howard, *Princes of Christian Pulpit and Pastorate*, Cokesbury, 1928, pp. 127–8

[31] Pattison, *History of Christian Preaching*, p. 292

[32] Quoted in Smith, *Lyric Religion*, D. Appleton Century, 1931, p. 145

[33] See Howard, *Princes of Christian Pulpit and Pastorate*, Vol. 1, p. 232

[34] Nicoll, *Ian Maclaren, The Life of the Reverend John Watson*, Dodd, Mead & Co., 1908

[35] Smith, George Adam; *Life of Henry Drummond*, Hodder & Stoughton, 1898, p. 145

[36] Above quotations from Drummond, *The New Evangelism*, Dodd, Mead & Co., 1899, paper, "Spiritual Diagnosis," pp. 257ff

[37] Simpson, *Henry Drummond*, Scribner, 1901, p. 44

[38] Smith, *Life of Henry Drummond*

[39] *Ibid.*, p. 105

[40] Drummond, *Natural Law in the Spiritual World*

[41] See Lennox, *The Practical Life Work of Henry Drummond*, James Patt & Co., 1901, pp. 56ff

[42] Quoted in Lennox, *ibid.*, p. 227

[43] Smith, *ibid.*, p. 77

[44] From Paper, "Spiritual Diagnosis"

[45] Smith, *ibid.*, p. 115

[46] Smith, *ibid.*, p. 6

Chapter IV

THE PROTESTANT PASTOR IN AMERICA

[1] Quoted in *Horace Bushnell* by Warren Seymour Archibald, Edwin Valentine Mitchell, 1930, p. 89

[2] Mary Bushnell Cheney, *Life and Letters of Horace Bushnell*, Scribner, 1903, p. 518

[3] *Ibid.*, p. 229

[4] *Ibid.*, p. 290

[5] *Ibid.*, p. 291

[6] *Ibid.*, pp. 466–7

[7] *Ibid.*, p. 518

[8] Bushnell, *Christian Nurture*, Scribner, 1916

[9] See Northridge, *Health for Mind and Spirit*, Abingdon, 1938, p. 130

[10] Bushnell, *ibid.*, pp. 211–2

[11] *Ibid.*, p. 205

[12] *Ibid.*, p. 287

[13] Bushnell, *Moral Use of Dark Things*, Scribner, 1905

[14] *Ibid.*, p. 103

[15] *Ibid.*, p. 267

[16] *Ibid.*, p. 424

[17] Chadwick, *Theodore Parker, Preacher and Reformer*, Houghton Mifflin, 1900, p. 293

[18] Abbott, *Henry Ward Beecher*, Houghton Mifflin, 1903, pp. 67–70

[19] Crocker, *Henry Ward Beecher's Speaking Art*, Fleming H. Revell, 1937, p. 124

[20] Allen, *Life and Letters of Phillips Brooks*, E. P. Dutton, 1901, Vol. II, p. 190

[21] *Ibid.*, Vol. I, p. 455

[22] *Ibid.*, Vol. II, p. 807

[23] *Ibid.*, Vol. II, p. 776

[24] Lawrence, *Life of Phillips Brooks*, Harper, 1937, p. 47

[25] Allen, *ibid.*, Vol. II, p. 673

[26] Lawrence, *ibid.*, p. 113

[27] Allen, *ibid.*, Vol. II, p. 592

[28] Allen, *ibid.*, Vol. II, p. 807

[29] Allen, *ibid.*, Vol. II, p. 798

[30] Allen, *ibid.*, Vol. II, p. 673

[31] Allen, *ibid.*, Vol. II, p. 674

[32] Allen, *ibid.*, Vol. II, p. 788

[33] Allen, *ibid.*, Vol. II, p. 571

[34] Allen, *ibid.*, Vol. II, p. 809

[35] See *Sermons* by Phillips Brooks, E. P. Dutton, 1876

[36] Allen, *ibid.*, Vol. II, p. 192

[37] Allen, *ibid.*, Vol. II, p. 497

[38] Allen, *ibid.*, Vol. II, p. 853

Chapter V

THE NEW PSYCHOLOGY

[1] White, *The Warfare of Science with Theology*, Appleton

[2] Elliott, *The Bearing of Psychology upon Religion*, Association Press, 1927, p. 7

[3] See Pillsbury, *History of Psychology*, Norton, 1929; also Boring, *History of Experimental Psychology*, Appleton Century, 1929

[4] See Boring, *ibid.*, p. 385

[5] James, *Principles of Psychology*, Henry Holt, 1890

[6] Boring, *ibid.*, p. 624

[7] James, *Briefer Course*, Henry Holt, 1892

[8] James, *Talks to Teachers on Psychology*, Henry Holt, 1899

[9] See Worcester and McComb, *Body, Mind and Spirit*, chapter, "The Energies of Men"

[10] James: *The Man and the Thinker*, Centenary Addresses, University of Wisconsin Press, 1942, p. 38

[11] *Ibid.*, p. 59

[12] *Ibid.*, p. 59

[13] See G. Stanley Hall, *Life and Confessions of a Psychologist*, Appleton, 1923, p. 178

[14] James, *Adolescence: Its Psychology and Its Relation to Physiology, Anthropology, Sociology, Sex, Crime, Religion and Education*, Appleton, 1904

[15] Pruette, *G. Stanley Hall*, Appleton, 1926, p. 221

[16] *Ibid.*, p. 258

[17] Hall, *Senescence*, Appleton, 1922

[18] See Garrett, *Great Experiments in Psychology*, Appleton Century, 1941, p. 177

[19] *Ibid.*, pp. 124ff

[20] Angell, *Psychology*, Henry Holt, 1904; Dewey, *Human Nature and Conduct*, Henry Holt, 1922

[21] See Watson, *Behaviorism*, W. W. Norton, 1925, or Heideneder, *Seven Psychologies*, chapter VII, or Woodworth, *Contemporary Schools of Psychology*, chapter III

[22] Zilboorg, *A History of Medical Psychology*, Norton, 1941

[23] See Deutsch, *The Mentally Ill in America*, Doubleday Doran, 1938, pp. 72ff

[24] Zilboorg, *ibid.*, 323–324

[25] See Zilboorg, *ibid.*, p. 359

[26] Woodworth, *Contemporary Schools of Psychology*, Ronald Press, 1931, p. 141

[27] See Orgler, *Alfred Adler: The Man and His Work*, C. W. Daniel Co., 1939; Phyllis Bottome, *Alfed Adler*, G. P. Putnam, 1939

[28] Orgler, *ibid.*, p. 14

[29] Bottome, *ibid.*, p. 37

[30] Bottome, *ibid.*, p. 161

[31] For a brief summary of the psychology of Jung, see Jacobi, *The Psychology of Jung*, Yale University Press, 1943. (Accepted by Jung himself)

[32] Jung, *Modern Man in Search of a Soul*, Harcourt Brace, 1939, pp. 264–5

Chapter VI

PASTORAL THEOLOGY
AND THE PSYCHOLOGY OF RELIGION

[1] Baxter, *The Reformed Pastor*, American Tract Society, 1656

[2] See *Autobiography of Richard Baxter*, p. 97, Dutton, 1931

[3] *Ibid.*, pp. 149–152

[4] *Ibid.*, p. 139

[5] *Ibid.*, pp. 178–9

[6] Introduction to *Reformed Pastor*, p. 50

[7] *Ibid.*, p. 19

[8] Schaff-Herzog *Encyclopedia of Religious Knowledge*, Funk & Wagnalls, 1883

[9] *Ibid.*, p. 1759

[10] *Ibid.*, p. 1760

[11] Maclaren, *The Cure of Souls*, Dodd, Mead & Co., 1896

[12] *Ibid.*, p. 225

[13] *Ibid.*, pp. 240–1

[14] Gladden, *The Christian Pastor*, Scribner, 1899

[15] *Ibid.*, p. 174

[16] *Ibid.*, p. 177

[17] *Ibid.*, p. 186

[18] Quayle, *The Pastor-Preacher*, Jennings & Graham, 1910

[19] *Ibid.*, p. 142

[20] *Ibid.*, p. 155

[21] Jefferson, *The Minister as Shepherd*, Thomas Y. Crowell, 1912

[22] *Ibid.*, pp. 61–3

[23] Erdman, *The Work of the Pastor*, Westminster Press, 1924

[24] *Ibid.*, p. 67

[25] Adams, *The Pastoral Ministry*, Cokesbury, 1932

[26] Palmer, *The Minister's Job*, Willett Clark, 1937

[27] Blackwood, *Pastoral Work*, Westminster, 1945

[28] For a more complete list of these early articles, see G. A. Coe, *Psychology of Religion*, p. 1

[29] Starbuck, *The Psychology of Religion*, Scribner, 1900

[30] Coe, *The Spiritual Life*, Eaton & Mains, 1900

[31] *Ibid.*, p. 21

[32] James, *Varieties of Religious Experience*, p. 189; Longmans, 1902

[33] Davenport, *Primitive Traits in Religious Revivals*, Macmillan, 1905

[34] Wundt, *Folk Psychology*

[35] Pratt, *Psychology of Religious Belief*, Macmillan, 1907

[36] Cutten, *The Psychological Phenomena of Christianity*, Scribner, 1912

[37] Ames, *Psychology of Religious Experience*, Houghton Mifflin, 1910
[38] Leuba, *Psychological Study of Religion*, Macmillan, 1912
[39] Coe, *Psychology of Religion*, University of Chicago Press, 1916
[40] Hall, *Jesus the Christ, in the Light of Psychology*, Appleton Century, 1917
[41] Pratt, *Religious Consciousness*, Macmillan, 1920
[42] Thouless, *An Introduction to the Psychology of Religion*, Macmillan, 1923
[43] Josey, *The Psychology of Religion*, Macmillan, 1927
[44] Conklin, *The Psychology of Religious Adjustment*, Macmillan, 1929
[45] Horton, *A Psychological Approach to Theology*, Harper, 1931
[46] Boisen, *The Exploration of the Inner World*, Willett Clark, 1936
[47] Wieman and Wieman, *A Normative Psychology of Religion*, Crowell, 1935
[48] Stolz, *The Psychology of Religious Living*, Abingdon-Cokesbury, 1937
[49] Ligon, *Psychology of Christian Personality*, Macmillan, 1940
[50] McKenzie, *Psychology, Psychotherapy and Evangelicalism*, Macmillan, 1940
[51] Johnson, *Psychology of Religion*, Abingdon-Cokesbury, 1945

Chapter VII

MORE GREAT PASTORS

[1] Quoted in Howard, *Princes of the Christian Pulpit and Pastorate*, Vol. I, p. 360, Cokesbury, 1927
[2] Quoted in Iddleman, *Peter Ainslee*, Willett Clark, 1941, pp. 46–7
[3] *Ibid.*, p. 54
[4] *Ibid.*, p. 94
[5] Weigle, *Pageant of America*, Yale University Press, 1928, p. 215
[6] Gladden *Recollections*, Houghton Mifflin, 1909, p. 11
[7] *Ibid.*, p. 61
[8] *Ibid.*, p. 59
[9] *Ibid.*, p. 36
[10] *Ibid.*, p. 38
[11] *Ibid.*, p. 39
[12] Gladden, *Christian Pastor*, Scribner, 1898, p. 51
[13] *Ibid.*, pp. 177–8
[14] *Recollections*, pp. 325–6
[15] *Ibid.*, p. 258
[16] *Christian Pastor*, p. 73
[17] See Worcester, *Life's Adventures*, pp. 275ff
[18] *Ibid.*, p. 279
[19] *Ibid.*, p. 285
[20] Worcester, McComb & Coriat, *Religion and Medicine*, Moffatt, Yard & Co., 1908, p. 2
[21] Worcester, *Life's Adventures*, p. 290
[22] *Religion and Medicine*, p. 5

[23] Worcester, McComb and Coriat, *Religion and Medicine*
Worcester and McComb, *Body, Mind and Spirit*, Marshall Jones & Co., 1931
[24] *Ibid.*
[25] *Ibid.*, p. 195
[26] Lichliter, *The Healing of Souls*, Abingdon, 1931, p. 23
[27] See C. R. Brown, *Faith and Health*, Thomas Y. Crowell, 1910, Chapter, "Emmanuel Movement"
[28] Jefferson, *Minister As Shepherd*, Crowell, 1912, pp. 94-5
[29] *Ibid.*, p. 102
[30] *Ibid.*, p. 187
[31] P. W. James, *George W. Truett*, Macmillan, 1939, pp. 95-6
[32] Newton, *Living Masters of the Pulpit*, George H. Doran, 1923, p. 227
[33] James, *ibid.*, p. 89
[34] *Ibid.*, pp. 290-91
[35] *Ibid.*, pp. 135, 141
[36] *Ibid.*, p. 263
[37] *Charles S. Medbury*, Christian Board of Publication, 1932, pp. 33-4
[38] *Ibid.*, pp. 35-6
[39] Used by permission of Mrs. Charles S. Medbury

Chapter VIII

REVIVALISM AND MISSIONS

REVIVALISM

[1] Davenport, *Primitive Traits in Religious Revivals*, Macmillan, 1926, p. 31
[2] *Ibid.*, pp. 85-86
[3] Groves & Blanchard, *Introduction to Mental Hygiene*, Henry Holt, 1936, p. 317
[4] Bates, *American Faith*, Norton, 1940, p. 211
[5] McGiffert, *Jonathan Edwards*, Harper, 1932, pp. 11-12
[6] *Ibid.*, pp. 56 and 68
[7] Davenport—*ibid.*, p. 76
[8] See Sweet, *Revivalism in America*, Scribner, 1945, p. 127
[9] Garrison, *March of Faith*, Harper, 1933, p. 74
[10] See Sweet, *ibid.*, pp. 170ff, also Ellis, *Billy Sunday, the Man and His Message*, L. T. Myers, 1914
[11] *Ibid.*, pp. 132-4

MISSIONS

[12] Hiltner, *Religion and Health*, Macmillan, 1943, p. 46
[13] Latourette, *Advance through the Storm*, Harper, p. 362
[14] Quoted in Hocking, *Re-Thinking Missions*, Harper, 1932, p. 66
[15] *Ibid.*, p. 201
[16] *Ibid.*, p. 205
[17] *The World Mission of the Church*, Findings and Recommendations of

the International Missionary Council, Tambaram, Madras, India, 1939, p. 81
[18] See Schweitzer, *Out of My Life and Thought*, Henry Holt, 1933, pp. 102–5
[19] Jones, *Is the Kingdom of God Realism*, Abingdon-Cokesbury, 1940
[19] Abingdon-Cokesbury, 1940
[20] *Ibid.*, p. 99
[21] Jones, *Abundant Living*, Abingdon-Cokesbury

Chapter IX

HUMANITARIANISM AND THE SOCIAL GOSPEL

[1] Macmillan, 1934, p. 291
[2] Baxter, *Autobiography*, J. M. Dent & Sons, 1931, pp. 195–6
[3] See Johnson, *Psychology of Religion*, Abingdon-Cokesbury, 1945, pp. 239–40
[4] See Walsh, *The Catholic Church and Healing*, Macmillan, 1928, p. 26
[5] From the Dedicatory Address of Rev. Paul R. Zwilling, as reported in the Bulletin of the American Protestant Hospital Association, December, 1942, p. 3
[6] See Albert Deutsch, *The Mentally Ill in America*, Doubleday Doran, 1938, pp. 58ff
[7] For a complete story of Dorothea Lynde Dix, see *Dorothea Dix: Forgotten Samaritan*, by Helen E. Marshall, University of North Carolina Press, 1937; for a brief account see chapter IX, "Dorothea Lynde Dix, Militant Crusader," in Deutsch, *Mentally Ill in America*.
[8] Gates, *Heroes of the Faith*, Bible Study Publishing Co., p. 59
[9] Quoted in Gates, *Heroes of the Faith*, Bible Study Publishing Co., p. 53
[10] Whitney, *Elizabeth Fry: Quaker Heroine*, Little, Brown, 1937, p. 209
[11] Raelton, *General William Booth*, Hodder and Stoughton, pp. 195–6
[12] Fleming H. Revell, 1909
[13] See Lester, *It Occurred to Me*, Harper, 1937

THE SOCIAL GOSPEL

[14] Strong, *The Rise of the Social Gospel in American Protestantism*, Yale, 1940, p. 3
[15] Gladden, *Recollections*, p. 294
[16] See Sharpe, *Walter Rauschenbusch*, Macmillan, 1942, pp. 61–2
[17] *Ibid.*, p. xii
[18] *Ibid.*, p. 274
[19] *Ibid.*, p. 79
[20] *Ibid.*, p. 160
[21] *Ibid.*, p. 447
[22] Eastman, *Men of Power*, Vol. IV, Cokesbury, 1939, p. 193
[23] *Ibid.*, p. 207
[24] See Weatherhead, *In Quest of a Kingdom*, Abingdon-Cokesbury, 1945, p. 32

Chapter X

FAITH HEALING, CHRISTIAN SCIENCE
AND THE CULTS

[1] Cutten, *Three Thousand Years of Mental Healing*, Scribner, 1911

[2] Cutten, *Psychological Phenomena of Christianity*, Scribner, 1906, p. 202

[3] Cutten, *Three Thousand Years of Mental Healing*, pp. 75ff

[4] Cutten, *ibid.*, p. 209

[5] See Boring, *History of Experimental Psychology*, Appleton Century, 1929, pp. 49ff

[6] See Crocker, *Henry Ward Beecher's Speaking Art*, Revell, 1937, chapter "Phrenology, How to Make a Preaching Hit"

[7] Atkins, *Modern Religious Cults and Movements*, Revell, 1923, p. 116

[8] There are a great many books and biographies that tell the story of Mary Baker Eddy and the early years of the Christian Science Movement. Of course many of these are quite contradictory in nature. No attempt will be made to list them all but a few that should be mentioned are—*The Life of Mary Baker Eddy* by Sibyl Wilbur, the Christian Science Publication Society. This is the authorized biography. *Retrospection and Introspection* by Mrs. Eddy, 1891, The Christian Science Publication Society, is an autobiographical account of her early life and the steps leading to the discovery and founding of Christian Science. *Mrs. Eddy; the Biography of a Virginal Mind*, by Edwin Dakin, 1929, Blue Ribbon Books, is perhaps the most thorough of all volumes that attempt to evaluate her life. It contains an abundance of references from her own writing and a complete bibliography. There are also many briefer accounts given in general books, one of the best being in Atkins, *Modern Religious Cults and Movements*, Revell, 1923.

[9] Atkins, *ibid.*, p. 190

[10] Atkins, *ibid.*, see whole chapter on Christian Science as a Theology

[11] Cutten, *Three Thousand Years of Mental Healing*, pp. 290ff

[12] Atkins, *ibid.*, pp. 228ff

[13] *Health is Catching*, published by Unity School of Christianity

[14] See article, "Healing and Health in American Churches," Federal Council Bulletin, May 1944

[15] Brooks and Charles, *Christianity and Autosuggestion*, Dodd, Mead and Co., 1923, p. 158

[16] Brooks and Charles, *ibid.*, p. 75

[17] See Fosdick, *As I See Religion*, Harper, 1923, p. 17

[18] See Kunkel, *In Search of Maturity*, Scribner, 1943, p. 20

Chapter XI

ADVANCES IN PSYCHOLOGY, CASE WORK
AND PSYCHOSOMATIC MEDICINE

[1] Seabury, *How Jesus Heals Our Minds Today*, Little Brown, 1940, p. 18

[2] Horney, *The Neurotic Personality of Our Time*, Norton, 1937, p. 270

SOCIAL CASE WORK

3 See Jarns, *The Quakers as Pioneers in Social Work*, Macmillan, 1931

4 Strode, *Introduction to Social Case Work*, Harper, 1940, chapter 4

5 Richmond, *Social Diagnosis*, Russell Sage Foundation, 1917

6 Richmond, *What Is Social Case Work?* Russell Sage Foundation, 1922

7 Robinson, *A Changing Pschology in Social Case Work*, University of North Carolina Press, 1930

8 Young, *Interviewing in Social Work*, McGraw Hill, 1935

Garrett, *Interviewing, Its Principles and Methods*, Family Welfare Association, 1942

9 de Schweinitz, *The Art of Helping People Out of Trouble*, Houghton Mifflin, 1924, p. 207

10 See "Christian Century," news report, August 25, 1943

PSYCHOSOMATIC MEDICINE

11 Quoted in Cutten, *Three Thousand Years of Mental Healing*, Scribner, 1911

12 Quoted in Dunbar, *Emotions and Bodily Changes*, Columbia, 1946

13 Mitchell, *Doctor and Patient*, J. B. Lippincott, 1887

14 Cabot, *What Men Live By*, Houghton Mifflin, 1914

15 See Lewis, *Psychiatric Advancement*, Norton, 1941, pp. 182ff

16 Cannon, *Bodily Changes in Pain, Hunger, Fear and Rage*, D. Appleton, 1929

17 See note 12 above

18 Dunbar, *ibid.*, p. xl

19 Robinson, *The Patient as a Person*, Commonwealth Fund, 1939

20 *Ibid.*, p. 4

21 Quoted in Gray, *Advancing Front of Medicine*, Whittlesey House, 1941, pp. 212-3

22 *Ibid.*, p. 216

23 Dunbar, p. 410

24 Gray, *ibid.*

25 *Ibid.*, p. 229

26 Carrell, *Man the Unknown*, quoted in "Clear Horizons," June, 1941

27 *The Spirit*, edited by Canon Streeter, Macmillan, p. 114

28 Kunkel, *In Search of Maturity*, Scribner, 1943, p. 10

Chapter XII

SOME MODERN PASTORS AND PASTORAL SPECIALISTS

1 Lotz, *Creative Personalities*, Association Press, 1940, Vol. I, p. 142

2 Fosdick, *On Being a Real Person*, Harper, 1943, Introduction

3 *Ibid.*, p. viii

[4] Fosdick, *Living Under Tension*, Harper, 1941, p. 187

[5] Quoted in Holman, *Religion of a Healthy Mind*, Round Table, 1939, p. 109

[6] From sermon, "Finding Unfailing Resources," "Church Monthly," December, 1941

[7] Fosdick, *On Being a Real Person*, Harper, 1943, p. 210

[8] *Ibid.*, p. ix

[9] Weatherhead, *Psychology in Service of the Soul*, Epworth Press, 1929, p. xx

[10] *Ibid.*, p. 20

[11] Case told in Weatherhead, *Psychology and Life*, Abingdon-Cokesbury, 1935, pp. 225ff

[12] *Ibid.*, p. 20

[13] Cameron, *Clinic of a Cleric*, Long & Smith, 1931

[14] See Bonnell, *Pastoral Psychology*, chapters 1 and 2, "My Father" and "An Apprenticeship to the Ministry," Harper, 1938

[15] Groves & Blanchard, *Introduction to Mental Hygiene*, Henry Holt, 1931, pp. 335–6

[16] Holman, *Church at Work in the Modern World*, Edited by W. C. Bower, University of Chicago Press, 1935

[17] Boisen, *Exploration of the Inner World*, Willett Clark, 1936, p. 2

[18] *Ibid.*, p. 7

[19] "Mental Hygiene," October, 1942, "Improving Protestant Worship in Mental Hospitals," Seward Hiltner, p. 606

[20] Boisen, *ibid.*, p. 259

[21] See "Protestant Religious Work in Mental Hospitals," published by American Protestant Hospital Association, 1944

[22] Cabot and Dicks, *The Art of Ministering to the Sick*, Macmillan, 1938, p. 285

[23] Dicks, *Who Is My Patient?* Macmillan, 1941, p. 146

[24] Dicks, *And Ye Visited Me*, Harper, 1939, pp. 6–7

[25] Dicks, *Pastoral Work and Personal Counseling*, Macmillan, 1944, p. 6

[26] See "Coronet," article, "Clergymen in White," by Edith M. Stern, September, 1942

[27] "Study of Religious Work in Protestant Hospitals," published by American Hospital Association, 1941, also reported in Hiltner, *Religion and Health*, p. 255

[28] "Devotional Literature in Protestant Hospitals," by Seward Hiltner, reported in Bulletin of American Protestant Hospital Association, December, 1942

[29] "Report on the Clergy-Physician Relationship in Protestant Hospitals," published by American Protestant Hospital Association, 1942

[30] "Standards for the Work of the Chaplain in the General Hospital," by Russell Dicks, in "Hospital," November, 1940

[31] See Rowe, *History of Religion in United States*, Macmillan, 1924, p. 95

[32] Sutherland, *Principles of Criminology*, J. B. Lippincott, 1934, p. 452

[33] *Ibid.*, p. 453

[34] Article in "Mental Hygiene," "Mental Hygiene in Corrective Institutions," October, 1942, p. 583

[35] Colgate-Rochester Divinity School Bulletin, February, 1941, p. 86

36 These illustrations, in fact most of the material in this section is taken from an unpublished manuscript, presented for a Master's thesis and found in the library of Drake University, "The Program of the Church for Later Adolescence," by Charles F. Kemp

37 See Beaven, *Putting the Church on a Full-Time Basis*, chapter VIII, Harper; *Fireside Sermons*, Harper, 1928; also *The Fine Art of Living Together*, Harper

38 Burkhart, *Thinking About Marriage*, Association Press, 1934; *From Friendship to Marriage*, Harper, 1937; *A Guide for a Man and Woman Looking Toward Marriage*, Hearthside Press; *Marriages Not Made With Hands*, Community Books Inc.

39 Groves, *Christianity and the Family*, Macmillan, 1942

40 Wood, *Family Life—A Bibliography*, Federal Council of Churches, 1941

Chapter XIII

A NEW FIELD OF RELIGIOUS LITERATURE

1 Worcester, McComb and Coriat, *Religion and Medicine*, Moffatt, Yard & Co., 1908

2 Brown, *Religion and Health*, Crowell, 1910

3 Hocking, *Human Nature and Its Remaking*, Yale University Press, 1918

4 Miller, *The New Psychology and the Preacher*, Boni, 1924

5 Mackenzie, *Souls in the Making*, Macmillan, 1929

6 *Ibid.*, p. 6

7 Weatherhead, *Psychology in Service of the Soul*, Epworth Press, 1929

8 Halliday, *Psychology and Religious Experience*, Richard R. Smith, 1930

9 Lichliter, *The Healing of Souls*, Abingdon, 1931

10 Cameron, *The Clinic of a Cleric*, Long and Smith, 1931

11 Holman, *The Cure of Souls*, University of Chicago, 1932

12 Oliver, *Psychiatry and Mental Health*, Scribner, 1932

13 Worcester and McComb, *Body, Mind and Spirit*, Marshall Jones, 1932

14 Stolz, *Pastoral Psychology*, Abingdon-Cokesbury, Revised, 1940

15 Weatherhead, *Psychology and Life*, Abingdon, 1935

16 Burkhart, *Guiding Individual Growth*, Abingdon, 1935

17 Cabot and Dicks, *The Art of Ministering to the Sick*, Macmillan, 1936

18 Dicks, *Meditations for the Sick*, Willett Clark, 1937

19 Dicks, *When You Call on the Sick*, Harper, 1938

20 Dicks, *And Ye Visited Me*, Harper, 1939

21 Dicks, *Who Is My Patient?* Macmillan, 1941

22 Dicks, *Yourself and Health*, Harper, 1939

23 Dicks, *Thy Health Shall Spring Forth*, Macmillan, 1945

24 Dicks, *Pastoral Work and Personal Counseling*, Macmillan, 1944

25 Elliott and Elliott, *Solving Personal Problems*, Henry Holt, 1936

26 Bonnell, *Pastoral Psychiatry*, Harper, 1938

27 Hollington, *Psychology Serving Religion*, Abingdon, 1938

28 Northridge, *Health for Mind and Spirit*, Abingdon, 1938

29 Zahniser, *The Soul Doctor*, Round Table Press, 1938
30 May, *Art of Counseling*, Abingdon-Cokesbury, 1939
31 May, *Springs of Creative Living*, Abingdon-Cokesbury, 1940
32 Holman, *Getting Down to Cases*, Macmillan, 1942
33 Wise, *Religion in Illness and Health*, Harper, 1942
34 Schindler, *The Pastor as Personal Counselor*, Muhlenberg, 1942
35 Stolz, *The Church and Psycho-Therapy*, Abingdon-Cokesbury, 1943
36 Hiltner, *Religion and Health*, Macmillan, 1943
37 Simpson, *Pastoral Care of Nervous People*, Morehouse Gorham, 1945
38 Groves, *Christianity and the Family*, Macmillan, 1942
39 Weatherhead, *The Mastery of Sex Through Psychology and Religion*, Macmillan, 1932
40 Stolz, *Making the Most of the Rest of Life*, Abingdon-Cokesbury, 1941
41 Day, *Jesus and Human Personality*, Abingdon, 1934
42 Buttrick, *Prayer*, Abingdon-Cokesbury, 1942
43 Calkins, *How Jesus Dealt with Men*, Abingdon-Cokesbury, 1942
44 Holman, *Religion of a Healthy Mind*, Round Table, 1939
45 Werner, *And We Are Whole Again*, Abingdon-Cokesbury, 1945
46 Miller, *Take a Look at Yourself*, Abingdon-Cokesbury, 1944
47 Blanton and Peale, *Faith Is the Answer*, Abingdon-Cokesbury, 1940
48 Fosdick, *On Being a Real Person*, Harper, 1943
49 From a book review in the Federal Council Bulletin, by Seward Hiltner, May, 1943, p. 17
50 Boisen, *ibid.*, p. 235

Chapter XIV

THE CHANGING EMPHASES IN THE "CURE OF SOULS"

1 Maclaren, *The Cure of Souls*, Dodd, Mead & Co., 1896
2 Holman, *The Cure of Souls*, University of Chicago Press, 1932
3 "Crozer Quarterly," July, 1934, article by McNeil, "Some Historical Aspects of the Cure of Souls"
4 See Holman, *Cure of Souls*, pp. 115ff, or *Getting Down to Cases*, pp. 176ff
5 See Rogers, *Counseling and Psychotherapy*, Houghton Mifflin, 1942, p. 28
6 Rogers, *A Counseling Viewpoint*, Federal Council of Churches, 1945
7 See Article, "Industrial Psychiatry in the Community of Oak Ridge," "Industrial Medicine," April, 1946
8 See Bulletin of the Menninger Clinic, May, 1946
9 See *Alcoholics Anonymous*
   See also Information Service of the Federal Council of Churches, April, 1942, article by Hiltner, "Alcohol Addiction, A Problem of the Church"
10 Brown, *Faith and Health*, Crowell, 1910, p. 166
11 Robinson, *The Patient as a Person*, The Commonwealth Fund, 1939, p. 39
12 See article, "Ministering to the Families of Those Who Are Sick," by Charles F. Kemp, "Church Management," February, 1945

[13] Mental Hygiene, July, 1940, article, "Mental Hygiene and Religion"
[14] Jung, *Modern Man in Search of a Soul*, Harcourt Brace, 1939, pp. 264-5
[15] Published by the Federal Council of Churches, 1945
[16] Kunkel, *In Search of Maturity*, Scribner, 1934, p. 10
[17] See Buttrick, *Prayer*, Abingdon-Cokesbury, 1941, p. 278
[18] Holman, *The Cure of Souls*, University of Chicago Press, p. 219
[19] Jung, *Modern Man in Search of a Soul*, p. 262

Chapter XV

THEOLOGICAL EDUCATION AND CLINICAL TRAINING

[1] Drummond, *The New Evangelism*, Dodd, Mead & Co., 1894, p. 251
[2] See Crocker, *Henry Ward Beecher's Speaking Art*, Revell, 1937, p. 94
[3] Jefferson, *Minister as Shepherd*, Crowell, 1912, p. 29
[4] Cutten, *Psychological Phenomena of Christianity*, Scribner, 1912, p. 7
[5] Mackenzie, *Souls in the Making*, Macmillan, 1929, pp. 16-8
[6] Brown, *The Minister, His World and His Work*, Cokesbury, 1937, p. 194
[7] Abbott, *Henry Ward Beecher*, Houghton Mifflin, 1903, p. 61
[8] Allen, *Life of Phillips Brooks*, Vol. II, p. 675
[9] Worcester, *Life's Adventure*, pp. 80-1
[10] The catalogues studied were those of Andover-Newton, Colgate-Rochester, Union Theological Seminary, Chicago Theological Seminary, University of Chicago, Yale, Drake Bible College
[11] See *Clinical Pastoral Training*, edited by Seward Hiltner, 1945, Commission on Religion and Health
[12] See Wise, "The Role of the Clergy in Relation to the Mentally Ill," Publication No. 9, American Association for the Advancement of Science
[13] Bassett, *Mental Hygiene and the Community*, Macmillan, 1934, pp. 285-6
[14] Wise, *Religion in Illness and Health*, Harper, 1941, p. 263
[15] Holman, *Getting Down to Cases*, Macmillan, 1942, p. 194
[16] From an article on "The Pastor," February, 1943, also in Federal Council Reprint "Seminaries With Army Chaplains," p. 3
[17] Quoted by Hiltner, *Clinical Pastoral Training*, p. 137
[18] Quoted by E. C. Herrick in *Clinical Pastoral Training*, p. 81
[19] Boisen, *Exploration of the Inner World*, Willett Clark, 1938
[20] *Ibid.*, pp. 9-10, 253-4
[21] Colgate-Rochester Divinity School Bulletin, February, 1941, p. 87
[22] See Federal Council Information Service, May 21, 1938
[23] Colgate-Rochester Bulletin, *ibid.*, p. 87
[24] See Wieman and Wieman, *Normative Psychology of Religion*, p. 417, and Hollington, *Psychology Serving Religion*, p. 148
[25] *Clinical Pastoral Training*, p. 83
[26] "Mental Hygiene," January, 1946, article, "A Seminar in Psychiatry for Theological Students" by Clark and Baldinger
[27] See article, "Clinical Education and Mental Hygiene," by Seward Hilt-

ner in "Religious Education," May–June, 1943, reprinted for Commission of Religion and Health

[28] *Ibid.*, p. 50

[29] From an address "Mental Hygiene and the Clergy," delivered at the Michigan Society for Mental Hygiene, April 21, 1939

[30] Weatherhead, *Psychology and Life*, Abingdon-Cokesbury, 1935, p. 15

[31] Bassett, *ibid.*, p. 289

[32] See Halliday, *Psychology and Religious Experience*, p. 29, and Elliott and Elliott, *Solving Personal Problems*, p. 281

[33] May, *The Art of Counseling*, Abingdon-Cokesbury, 1939, p. 167

[34] See Groves, *Christianity and the Family*, Macmillan, 1942, p. 167

Chapter XVI

THE MENTAL HYGIENE MOVEMENT AND THE COMMISSION ON RELIGION AND HEALTH

[1] Beers, *A Mind that Found Itself*, Doubleday Doran, 25th Anniversary edition, 1944. Most of this material is taken from this volume. For briefer sketches of his career see *The Mental Hygiene Movement and Its Founder*, published by the National Committee for Mental Hygiene, or the chapter, "The Mental Hygiene Movement and Its Founder" in *The Mentally Ill in America* by Albert Deutsch.

[2] Beers, *ibid.*, p. 28

[3] *Ibid.*, p. 212

[4] *Ibid.*, p. 388

[5] *Ibid.*, p. 87

[6] *Ibid.*, p. 204

[7] *Ibid.*, p. 297

[8] *Mental Hygiene Yesterday, Today and Tomorrow*, published by the National Committee for Mental Hygiene

[9] Article, "Mental Hygiene and Religion," "Mental Hygiene," July, 1940

[10] *The Mental Hygiene Movement from the Philanthropic Standpoint*, National Committee

[11] This material is taken mainly from two pamphlets, "Five Years of Accomplishment," the Chairman's report on the Commission on Religion and Health for 1943, and "Religion and Health, Origin and Five Years of Progress" by Ethel P. S. Hoyt. Both are published by the Federal Council of Churches of Christ in America.

[12] Dunbar, *Emotions and Bodily Changes*, Columbia University Press, third edition, 1946

[13] For a report on the conference see, "Clinical Pastoral Training," edited by Seward Hiltner, published by the Commission on Religion and Health

[14] These and many other such pamphlets may be secured from the Commission on Religion and Health of the Federal Council of Churches of Christ in America, 297 Fourth Ave., New York City

[15] Frontpiece of Chairman's Report, 1943

Chapter XVII

LIFE-SITUATION PREACHING, THE CHURCH'S PROGRAM AND THE CONCLUSION

[1] Quoted by Luccock, *Christianity and the Individual in a World of Crowds*, Cokesbury, 1937, pp. 135–6

[2] Mackenzie, *Souls in the Making*, Macmillan, 1929, p. 115

[3] "Harpers," July, 1928

[4] See Fosdick, *Hope of the World*, Harper, 1933; *Secret of Victorious Living*, Harper, 1934; *Power to See It Through*, Harper, 1935; *Successful Christian Living*, Harper, 1937; *Living Under Tension*, Harper, 1941; *A Great Time to Be Alive*, Harper, 1944

[5] See the "Christian Century Pulpit," June, 1941, article, "Life Situation Preaching" by Harold Ruopp

[6] Tittle, *The Foolishness of Preaching*, Henry Holt, 1930, p. 6

[7] See Stolz, *The Church and Psychotherapy*, Abingdon-Cokesbury, 1943, chapter IX

[8] Palmer, *The Minister's Job*, Willett Clark, p. 26

[9] May, *The Art of Counseling*, Abingdon-Cokesbury, 1939, p. 124

[10] Lichliter, *The Healing of Souls*, Abingdon, 1931, p. 23

[11] Fosdick, sermon, "Roots of Dependable Character," published in "Church Monthly," June, 1938

INDEX

Abnormal, guide to normal, 228
Absolution, 31, 32
Adams, Hampton, 99
Addams, Jane, 150, 267
Adler, Alfred, 85 ff., 221
Adolescence, 100 ff., 209 ff.
Ainslee, Peter, 109 ff.
Albertus Magnus, 34
Alcoholics Anonymous, 234 ff.
Ambrose of Milan, 25, 27, 33
American Foundation for Mental
 Hygiene, 267
American Journal of Insanity, 81
American Journal of Psychology,
 74
American Protestant Hospital
 Ass'n., 141, 203
American Psychological Ass'n., 74
Ames, Edward Scribner, 103
Amulets, 157
Andover-Newton Theological
 School, 197, 256, 258, 280
Angell, James Rowland, 77
Anglo-Catholic, 39
Applied Religion, Graduate
 School of, 250
Aquinas, 34 ff.
Aristotle, 35, 70
Asclepiades, 79
Atkins, G. G., 162, 165
Augustine, 27, 32 ff.
Auto-suggestion, 170 ff.
Awakening, The Great, 128

Baker, Judge, Foundation, 209
Baker, Oren H., 245
Banay, Ralph S., 205

Barnabas, 22
Barton, Clara, 145, 146 ff.
Basil, 24, 27, 141
Bassett, Clara, 140, 247, 260, 271
Baxter, Richard, 42 ff., 91 ff., 140
Baylor, Courtenay, 117
Beaupré, St. Anne de, 158
Beaven, Albert W., 211
Beecher, Henry Ward, 60, 73,
 159, 243, 247
Beers, Clifford, 262 ff.
Begbie, Harold, 150
Behaviorism, 77
Behavior, a symptom, 228 ff.
Berkley, 70
Bernheim, 81
Bicêtre, Asylum of, 81
Binet, Alfred, 78
Biographical study, 102
Black Friars, 36
Blackwood, Andrew, 100
Blanton, Dr. Smiley, 195, 223
Blumhardt, Pastor, 167
Boisen, Anton T., 105, 196 ff.,
 225, 251 ff.
Bonnell, John Sutherland, 193,
 219
Booth, William, 149
Boston Psychopathic Hospital,
 179, 198
Boston, University of, 208, 258,
 280
Bower, William C., 282
Bradford, John, 42
Brahman Codes, 3
Braid, 82, 160
Breuer, 82, 83, 84